Anscombe on Wittgenstein

Anscombe on Wittgenstein

Reminiscences of a Philosophical Friendship

Edited by
JOHN BERKMAN AND ROGER TEICHMANN

OXFORD
UNIVERSITY PRESS

OXFORD
UNIVERSITY PRESS

Oxford University Press is a department of the University of Oxford.
It furthers the University's objective of excellence in research, scholarship,
and education by publishing worldwide. Oxford is a registered trade mark of
Oxford University Press in the UK and in certain other countries.

Published in the United States of America by Oxford University Press
198 Madison Avenue, New York, NY 10016, United States of America.

CIP data is on file at the Library of Congress

ISBN 9780197648957

DOI: 10.1093/9780197648988.001.0001

Printed by Integrated Books International, United States of America

The manufacturer's authorized representative in the EU for product safety is
Oxford University Press España S.A., Parque Empresarial San Fernando de Henares,
Avenida de Castilla, 2 – 28830 Madrid (www.oup.es/en or product.safety@oup.com).
OUP España S.A. also acts as importer into Spain of products made by the manufacturer.

Contents

Preface

Ludwig Wittgenstein was one of the greatest philosophers of the modern era, while his pupil and friend Elizabeth Anscombe is increasingly being recognized as one of the most important philosophers of the twentieth century. Anscombe's reminiscences of Wittgenstein therefore constitute a uniquely valuable document, one that throws light on the intellectual and personal characters of both philosophers as well as touching on a wide range of topics, cultural, historical, and psychological. She wrote them over a period of time in a series of notebooks which she headed 'Anecdotes about Wittgenstein'. The slightly self-deprecating 'anecdotes' may reflect Anscombe's awareness that what she was writing was not a structured memoir, but 'Reminiscences' seems preferable as a title: the reader will encounter much more than the stuff of amusing dinner conversation (something suggested by the term 'anecdotes'). A three-dimensional and subtly drawn portrait of Wittgenstein the man emerges from these pages, one that can be positioned alongside those other portraits we already have from Norman Malcolm, Con Drury, and other people who knew him, and like those other portraits reflecting and expressing the character of its author.

The original manuscript is divided into paragraphs or sections of varying lengths. The transcription first made by Luke Gormally as far as possible retained these sectional divisions, and the numbers in square brackets which have been placed after each section in the present publication correspond to the original ordering in Luke's transcription. The sections have been reordered along thematic lines; as is explained more fully in Roger Teichmann's essay (chapter 2), this approach was thought best as enabling the reader to perceive more vividly the contours of Anscombe's subject, rather than jumping from one theme to another. Anscombe's daughter and literary executor, Mary Geach, has approved this reordering and this edition of her mother's reminiscences. An Appendix to the *Reminiscences* (chapter 6) contains biographical material relating to the more significant of the characters mentioned therein; biographical details of more minor characters will be found in the footnotes of the *Reminiscences*.

In addition to the *Reminiscences*, the present volume contains two other documents by Anscombe relating to Wittgenstein the originals of which are to be found among her papers. The first of these (chapter 4) comprises notes which Anscombe wrote up of meetings between her, Wittgenstein, and Wasfi Hijab that took place in late 1946 and early 1947. The second is an as yet unpublished essay by Anscombe, 'Cardhouses: the "metaphysical"' (chapter 5).

As to the former, Anscombe evidently went home after each meeting and wrote the conversations up while they were still fresh in her mind, rather than writing them as they were going on. The 'voices' of the three participants are indicated by their initials (as in a play), and it is clear that even if not strictly verbatim the notes give us a pretty close record of what was said. The two characters who speak most, unsurprisingly, are 'W' and 'EA'. Hijab is a more reticent presence. Topics covered include rule-following, necessity, and the notion of the 'indefinite'—all topics at the heart of Wittgenstein's later philosophy. 'Cardhouses', meanwhile, is an example of Anscombe's mature philosophy dealing with Wittgenstein's thoughts on sense and nonsense, metaphysics, grammar, and so forth. Anscombe is as always her own thinker. Towards the end of the essay we find her discussing Wittgenstein's statement 'When a sentence is called senseless it is not as it were its sense that is senseless. But a combination of words is being excluded from the language' (*Philosophical Investigations* 500); some philosophers will be surprised to find her writing, 'It would be better to say: Certain combinations of senses are excluded.' But she has laid out the thinking behind that statement in a way that any commentator will need to grapple with and address if they are to take issue with it.

Two introductory essays by the editors contextualize Anscombe's relationship with Wittgenstein. The first one (chapter 1), by Berkman, allows the reader to see the development of their relationship and to date many of the *Reminiscences*. The second one, by Teichmann (chapter 2), deals with various biographical and philosophical themes that emerge from the *Reminiscences*.

As stated above, it was Luke Gormally who first transcribed Anscombe's 'Anecdotes'. Luke was the husband of Mary Geach, Anscombe's daughter and literary executor. He passed away in April 2023 and so did not live to see the publication of this volume, but he gave invaluable advice, criticism, and encouragement concerning the project at every stage of its gestation. Gratitude is also, and especially, due to Mary Geach for allowing the publication of the *Reminiscences* as well as of the two other pieces by her mother. We would also like to thank the Collegium Institute at the University of Pennsylvania for allowing access to the relevant manuscripts in the Anscombe archive there. Finally, we owe a huge debt of gratitude to Lucy Randall and Chelsea Hogue, our editors at OUP, whose encouragement and patience over the last few years have been truly commendable.

Roger Teichmann
John Berkman

1

Anscombe's Relationship with Wittgenstein

Contextualizing the *Reminiscences*

John Berkman

1941–1942: Prelude

Life changed rather drastically for Ludwig Wittgenstein in the autumn of 1941. Externally, his life was going well, having been elected professor of philosophy at Cambridge University in 1939, which gave Wittgenstein financial security, but more importantly, a British passport, not a small thing for an Austrian Jew where the only alternative was a Nazi-government issued passport. But internally, Wittgenstein was miserable. While he had always been dubious about the value of his teaching philosophy, with the advent of war Wittgenstein was desperate to contribute to the war effort, to do something 'useful'. Wittgenstein wanted to do manual labour, in a location which would expose him to the same dangers confronting his adopted countrymen. But potential employers were not looking for employees with a German name and Austrian background.[1]

On 11 October his collaborator and ever-present friend Francis Skinner died after failing to receive prompt treatment for an attack of

---

[1] See Ray Monk, *The Duty of Genius* (New York: Free Press, 1990), 425.

John Berkman, *Anscombe's Relationship with Wittgenstein* In: *Anscombe on Wittgenstein*. Edited by: John Berkman and Roger Teichmann, Oxford University Press. © Oxford University Press 2025. DOI: 10.1093/9780197648988.003.0001

polio.[2] Struck by both grief and guilt, Wittgenstein underwent a
nervous breakdown of sorts. While Skinner was deeply and un-
ambiguously attached to Wittgenstein, in the waning years of their
relationship Wittgenstein had felt ambivalence towards Skinner.
After Skinner's death, Wittgenstein resolved to honour their friendship by finally finding war work, something both Skinner and he
had wanted. First, he packed up the manuscripts the two of them
had been working on for a number of years and sent them to
Reuben Goodstein, a mathematician and mutual friend then living
in Birmingham.[3] Second, Wittgenstein sent a letter of resignation to the vice chancellor of Cambridge University, and met with
Dr. John Ryle, who managed to find him a job at Guy's Hospital in
London.[4] Despite his wishes, Cambridge University refused to accept Wittgenstein's resignation, but granted him leave to work on
behalf of the war effort.

Less than a month after Skinner's death, Wittgenstein started
work as a dispensary porter, thus fulfilling his posthumous vow to
Francis. For the next eighteen months he worked in the centre of
London and was certainly exposing himself to danger.[5] The Blitz
had begun two months earlier and London was being bombed by
the Luftwaffe almost every night. Lasting more than nine months,
the Blitz would kill close to 20,000 Londoners, and damage or de-
stroy close to a million homes. Despite this, Wittgenstein did not

[2] Approximately a week prior to the night that Wittgenstein took Skinner to hospital,
there had been two nights of bombing of an air force base not far from Cambridge, and
the hospital in Cambridge was inundated with wounded military personnel. Apparently
not realizing the seriousness of Skinner's condition, the hospital did not attend to him
for many hours, and by the time that they did, Skinner was already dying.

[3] These manuscripts have been recently edited and published. See Arthur Gibson
and Niamh O'Mahony, eds., *Ludwig Wittgenstein: Dictating Philosophy* (New York:
Springer, 2020).

[4] John Ryle was former professor of Physic (i.e. medicine) at Cambridge University
and doing research on behalf of the war effort. John Ryle was also the brother of the
Oxford philosopher Gilbert Ryle, who likely facilitated Wittgenstein's meeting with
John Ryle.

[5] For an account of Francis Skinner's death and Wittgenstein's move to London, see
Gibson and O'Mahony, 5–11.

entirely abandon his academic work. During the Cambridge terms Wittgenstein travelled up every second weekend to give classes. It was at these weekend lectures, starting in October 1942, that Elizabeth Anscombe first met Wittgenstein.

Elizabeth Anscombe was an undergraduate at the University of Oxford from 1937 to 1941. During those years, she engaged with Wittgenstein's philosophy, reading his *Tractatus Logico-Philosophicus*, which sufficiently impressed her that she had her fiancé Peter Geach read it as well.[6] In her final term as an undergraduate, while preparing to write her final exams, Anscombe chose to respond to a paper by Friedrich Waismann, an Austrian Jewish refugee who was teaching in Oxford.[7] At that time, Waismann's reputation was built largely on his association with Wittgenstein and the Vienna Circle, and whose publications acknowledged the influence of Wittgenstein's more recent, unpublished work. This was the start of Anscombe's working with Waismann, which continued for the next three years. What she did not know at the time was

---

[6] 'I cannot remember when I first read the Tractatus. Elizabeth read it before I did, browsing in Blackwells, and bought a copy; I am sure I had read it before our marriage.' Geach, 'A Philosophical Autobiography' at https://triablogue.blogspot.com/2019/08/a-philosophical-autobiography.html.

[7] Seeking to escape the deteriorating political situation in Austria, and as a Jew lacking academic employment, Waismann had originally come to Cambridge in the fall of 1937. After the Anschluss, it was impossible for him to return to Austria, so he stayed in England as a refugee. In 1938–1939, Waismann's stay was underwritten in part by the University of Cambridge's Moral Science Board. Friends then advised him that his academic opportunities would be greater in Oxford. When early in 1940 Magdalen College and All Souls College offered him grants, he and his wife and son moved to Oxford. That summer the three of them were classified as 'enemy aliens' and placed in an internment camp for ten weeks. Once the internment was over, Waismann's small allowance from two societies supporting refugee scholars was supplemented by anonymous gifts and funds. This allowed him to get by until the end of the war. It was only in 1945 that Oxford would create a proper post for him, as University Lecturer in the philosophy of mathematics. For further details, see Gordon Baker, ed., *The Voices of Wittgenstein* (London: Routledge, 2003), xx–xxii.

Thus, when Anscombe was assigned to work under Waismann for her DPhil he had very little status in the University, but with most of the philosophy faculty dispersed for war service, presumably he was deemed the most suitable supervisor for Anscombe, given her interest in logic.

that Wittgenstein considered Waismann not to have merely been influenced by him, but to have taken his ideas and examples and published them—in various places verbatim—as his own work.

Anscombe received a First in her final examinations in Trinity term of 1941. Only about 10 percent of students received a First, and this made her eligible to do post-graduate studies in philosophy. Of equal importance was Anscombe's being awarded the Gilchrist scholarship, which provided the funds necessary for her to remain in Oxford and begin studying for a DPhil degree. She was assigned Waismann as her DPhil supervisor, and within weeks of beginning her studies obtained approval for a very long dissertation title, namely:

> An enquiry into space, extension, and numerical identity and difference together with subst–al change; with an examination of some solutions proposed to these problems by the Aristotelian philosophical tradition, in the light of modern logical and epistemological methods.[8]

However, within a month or two of getting this title approved Anscombe applied to change it to the much simpler title 'The Identity of Bodies'. The form requested the reasons for changing the title of the dissertation, so Anscombe explained as follows:

> a) the original title is long and nasty b) it suggests that the enquiry into space and extension and change is co-ordinate with that into numerical identity and difference. I always knew that the questions about space and extension were subordinate to the question about numerical identity and difference; so this part was bad construction of the original title. In the course of my work I have found the enquiry into change also to fall under

---

[8] Anscombe file, St. Hugh's College archives.

the enquiry into numerical identity and difference. The subject matter of the thesis has remained unchanged.

This dissertation would occupy most of Anscombe's labours for the next three years.

During her first term of graduate studies (Michaelmas 1941), Anscombe was extremely productive. This was not particularly surprising. As an undergraduate she had been known for doing philosophy almost non-stop, and spent a lot of time instructing her classmates on how to philosophize.[9] In the autumn of 1941, besides revising her dissertation title, Anscombe was president of the Jowett (philosophical) Society and read papers at two of the meetings.[10] Curiously, she also delivered a paper to the Cambridge Moral Science (i.e. philosophy) Club (CMSC), whose chairman was Wittgenstein. Why she was invited to give this paper is a mystery, since Anscombe had no contact or relationship with the CMSC, and it was rare if not unheard of for an Oxford undergraduate to speak at the CMSC.[11] The likely explanation is that Donald MacKinnon—the one Oxford philosopher who had spoken at the CMSC the previous term—had commended her to Wittgenstein or the CMSC secretary J. H. Hopkins.[12] MacKinnon knew Anscombe

[9] Anscombe's teaching of her classmates is recounted by Mary Midgley (see e.g. Midgley, *The Owl of Minerva* [Abington: Routledge, 2005], 115). Anscombe's ongoing influence on Philippa Foot and Iris Murdoch can be found in Lipscomb, *The Women Are Up to Something*, and Mac Cumhaill and Wiseman, *Metaphysical Animals.*

[10] On 29 October, along with her undergraduate tutor Donald MacKinnon, she presented notes on 'Possibility'. On 3 December, she presented 'Rudimentary Reflections on Numbers'. Here Anscombe was presenting some lines of argument she was developing in her DPhil dissertation and so asked Waismann to respond to her paper. (See Jowett Society Minutes, Bodleian Library, Oxford, Ms. top. oxon. d. 359/2.)

[11] While Anscombe was a graduate student starting in Michaelmas of 1941, invitations to speak were sent out the previous term, so Anscombe had been invited in May or June 1941 while she was still an undergraduate.

[12] As I shall discuss later, it was the chairman's and the secretary's job to secure the speakers for the CMSC. MacKinnon read 'The Concept of Necessity' at the CMSC on 22 May 1941. The Cambridge University Moral Science Club Minute Book, Cambridge University Library, Min., ix, 44, p. 121.

well, having tutored her as an undergraduate and advised her on a publication.[13]

So on 20 November 1941 she read 'Can We Discard Space?' to the CMSC. While Wittgenstein as chair would normally have been present, Anscombe's visit occurred two weeks after Wittgenstein started at Guy's Hospital, London. It is therefore highly unlikely Wittgenstein attended Anscombe's paper. The first meeting of Anscombe and Wittgenstein would have to wait almost another year.

Three months into her graduate studies, on 26 December 1941, she married Peter Geach, a fellow philosopher. It was apparently a very small wedding and very informal. Anscombe was wearing 'an old mackintosh'.[14] After Geach and Anscombe had been in the priest's presence for some time, the priest apparently turned to Anscombe and said, 'So you're the bride?' Neither Anscombe's nor Geach's family attended the wedding. Geach had had a tragic upbringing, and was in practice orphaned by the time he completed his undergraduate studies at Oxford in 1938. It would seem that by the time of the wedding, Anscombe was distanced from her family, and so like Geach was living without the comfort and support of a family.

Since her Gilchrist scholarship was only for one year, Anscombe applied for further funding to continue her DPhil studies. Newnham College, Cambridge, awarded Anscombe the Sarah Smithson studentship, a two-year research scholarship for the years 1942–1944. A rather unusual arrangement was then made: Since she was already engaged in a DPhil at St. Hugh's College, Oxford and because

---

[13] For more on Anscombe's relationship with MacKinnon, and their shared views on World War II, see John Berkman, 'The Function of the Church in a Time of War: The Resolute Voices of Donald MacKinnon and Elizabeth Anscombe', *Studies in Christian Ethics Special Issue: Just War or Just Peace? The Future of Catholic Thinking on Just War and Just Peace* (Summer 2024).

[14] Mary Geach, correspondence with the author, June 2023.

Cambridge did not yet award degrees to women, Newnham admitted Anscombe to the college but not to Cambridge University, thus allowing her to continue with her DPhil at Oxford.[15] A further oddity was that Anscombe did not reside in Cambridge for most of the next academic year, but remained in Oxford. She was teaching for a number of Oxford colleges, plus leading short courses in philosophy for cadets under her former teacher Donald McKinnon.[16] This arrangement acknowledges something never explicitly stated at the time. The Newnham scholarship was not sufficient to sustain someone without further support, and so Anscombe was living in poverty.

While Anscombe had grown up moderately well-off in Sydenham, a middle-class suburb of London, her family's financial situation deteriorated precipitously while she was an undergraduate. In the summer of 1939, her father Allan Anscombe, a schoolmaster at nearby Dulwich College, died of colon cancer. Further tragedy struck eighteen months later, during her final undergraduate year. The family's Sydenham home at 49 Trewsbury Road was severely damaged in the Blitz, leaving her sixty-six-year-old mother Gertrude homeless. Gertrude then lived for a while with Anscombe or her brother Thomas. However, Gertrude soon developed dementia, and at some point during the latter part of the war was institutionalized at St. Andrew's Hospital in Northampton, a charity-run mental health facility.[17]

---

[15] Details to be found in a letter from Miss Gwyer, Principal of St. Hugh's College, Oxford to Miss Curtis, Principal of Newnham College, 25 June 1942. Courtesy of St. Hugh's College archives.

[16] In Anscombe's 23 April 1946 application for a position at Bedford College, she writes that 'During the academic years 1941–3 I was employed occasionally as a tutor for Greats and Modern Greats by three Oxford Colleges, and also by the University Chest to lecture to R.A.F. cadets who were taking philosophy courses at Oxford.' (File 370, Anscombe Archives, Philadelphia.)

[17] Gertrude Anscombe would remain at St. Andrew's until her death in 1955. Anscombe was executor of Gertrude's estate. I am grateful to John Anscombe for providing me with records of Gertrude Anscombe's death and estate.

Fig 1.1 Anscombe's family home at 49 Trewsbury Rd., London, was destroyed during World War II but was similar to all the other houses on that side of the street. This is a neighbouring house, as of 2024. *Photo by John Berkman*

1942–1944: Act 1: Anscombe at
Newnham College

In the autumn of 1942 Anscombe would first meet Wittgenstein at his weekend lectures.[18] In her *Reminiscences* (sec. 149), she writes about them, noting that Wittgenstein tried to return the money he was paid to give them, since he thought that they were 'no good'. During this term and the next one, Anscombe and Wittgenstein were both commuting to these lectures—he from London and she from Oxford. Geach would have wanted to attend the lectures, but was not able to do so, since as a conscientious objector he was assigned to forestry work in southcentral England.[19]

Although it would require frequent (and expensive) travel, Anscombe was eager to take advantage of the opportunity to participate in the philosophical clubs and societies of *two* universities. During her first term commuting to Cambridge, she not only delivered two papers to the Jowett Society in Oxford and attended all its weekly meetings, but also presented to the CMSC and the Newnham Classical Society in Cambridge. When Anscombe needed to stay overnight in Cambridge, she lodged at 58 Bateman Street with two young Cambridge philosophers, Margaret Masterman and her husband Richard Braithwaite.[20]

---

[18] During Michaelmas 1942 and Lent 1943, Wittgenstein lectured on the foundations of mathematics. See Wittgenstein to Rhees, 4 November 1942, in B. McGuinness, ed., *Wittgenstein in Cambridge: Letters and Documents 1911–1951* (Oxford: Blackwell, 2008), sec. 304, p. 354.

[19] Geach's forestry work was apparently not the most onerous. For the next two years Geach managed to attend the Jowett Society and the CMSC periodically, and gave papers to both societies. With regards to Geach's decision to become a conscientious objector, it should be noted that like Anscombe, Peter Geach was not a pacifist, but held a strict 'just war' viewpoint. According to Anthony Kenny, Geach attempted (unsuccessfully) to join the Polish Army. (Anthony Kenny, 'Peter Thomas Geach 1916–2013', *Biographical Memoirs of Fellows of the British Academy*, XIV, 185–203.) John Geach surmises that Peter Geach, having very poor eyesight, flat feet, and latent tuberculosis, was unlikely to have been accepted into any branch of the military. (Conversation with John Geach, June 2023.)

[20] For Anscombe's Cambridge address in 1942, see the CMSC minutes book in the Cambridge University Archives. Masterman at the time was herself a relatively recent

It was also during Anscombe's first term in Cambridge that we get the first evidence of her so-called 'rudeness'.[21] Was this in part the classic double-standard of the time whereby a man would be commended for 'perceptive criticism', but a woman doing the same would be considered 'rude'? For example, when Anscombe read a paper at the Newnham Classical Society, she criticized one interpreter of Plato so vociferously that some of the female undergraduates who attended the meeting felt it necessary to come to the writer's defence.[22]

People who knew Anscombe as an undergraduate, and then later as a research fellow at Oxford, sometimes remarked on a change in her personality under the influence of Wittgenstein.[23] We get an interesting perspective on the influence of Wittgenstein on his students in a 1943 letter that the Oxford don (and one of Anscombe's undergraduate tutors) Martha Kneale wrote to her husband William Kneale (also an Oxford don) before Anscombe had come to know Wittgenstein. Kneale remarks on the friendship between Casimir Lewy and Anscombe. '[Casimir Lewy] spent a lot of time looking for lodgings before [Anscombe] went back [to Cambridge]. I always thought he was rather nice underneath the awful manners copied from Wittgenstein.'[24] Kneale's private

graduate of Newnham College; she had studied moral science (i.e. philosophy) in the early 1930s, when she was one of Wittgenstein's inner circle of students. In 1932 she married Richard Braithwaite, who since the early 1920s had been a philosophy tutor at King's College, Cambridge. Masterman and Braithwaite were heavily involved in various social causes. From the late 1930s onwards, they were on various committees to assist refugee academics from Nazi Germany. One of the refugees whom they assisted, and in fact welcomed into their home for an extended period prior to the war, was Anscombe's supervisor Waismann. It may be that Anscombe learned from Waismann of the possibility of staying with Masterman and Braithwaite when she was in Cambridge.

[21] For other accounts of Anscombe's 'rudeness', see Midgley, *The Owl of Minerva*, 115, and the extended discussion by Mac Cumhaill and Wiseman, *Metaphysical Animals*, 195–198.

[22] From the Newnham Classical Society records held at the Newnham College Archives.

[23] See e.g. Midgley, *The Owl of Minerva*, 115.

[24] From the letters of Martha to William Kneale, 1943. (Jane Heal email correspondence with author, 22 August 2022. Access to the letters is courtesy of Professor Jane Heal.)

remark to her husband indicates that, prior to Anscombe getting to know Wittgenstein, he already had a reputation for deleteriously influencing the manners of his students.

After Lent term of 1943, Wittgenstein moved to Newcastle with a research team from Guy's Hospital, and thus discontinued his Cambridge lectures. But during his time in Newcastle, Wittgenstein began to long to get back to his philosophy book, which was the only work—as he put it—that 'really bucks me up'.[25] In February 1944, Cambridge granted him nine months leave to finish his 'book', and he spent it in Swansea, Wales. When he began his sabbatical, Wittgenstein's 'book' consisted of sec. 1–188 of the later published version of *Philosophical Investigations* (PI). During a prolific nine months of writing, the 'book' more than doubled in length, and Wittgenstein returned to Cambridge in October 1944 with a typescript of the expanded 'book', which now corresponded to sec. 1–421 of the later published version of PI.[26] Over the next few years, Wittgenstein's 'book' would continue to expand.

On 22 April 1943, just after Wittgenstein had left for Newcastle, Anscombe gave birth to her first child Barbara at Ruskin College in Walton Street, which had been turned into a maternity hospital for the duration of the war.[27] Barbara was duly baptized at St. Aloysius Church in Oxford on 3 May, the godparents being Anscombe's best friend Ruth Daniel née Pethybridge, and Kasimierz Komierowski, the Polish consul general in Southampton whom Geach had gotten

[25] Norman Malcolm, *Ludwig Wittgenstein: A Memoir* (Oxford: Oxford University Press, 1958), 34.

[26] See Monk, *Duty of Genius*, 470. Wittgenstein left Swansea in October 1944 with a typescript of what corresponds to the final version of PI up to sec. 421. It was to this typescript that Wittgenstein wrote a preface dated January 1945, which would appear in the published version of the PI.

[27] See https://www.ruskin.ac.uk/about-us/history. That Barbara was born at Ruskin College is attested to by Mary Geach in conversation with the author, 27 August 2024.

to know while doing his wartime forestry work.[28] Not long after the baptism, Anscombe moved to Cambridge. Casimir Lewy,[29] a fellow student at Wittgenstein's lectures who had become friends with both her and Peter, found a room at 12 Trumpington Street for Anscombe and Barbara. Having just wrapped up his own doctoral dissertation, Lewy became fascinated with baby care books, and spent many evenings once Anscombe and Barbara moved to Cambridge functioning as a surrogate 'grandmother', looking after Barbara when Anscombe needed to get out for meetings or shopping.

As a graduate student, Anscombe's poverty gradually grew, despite efforts to find opportunities for tutoring. This poverty would continue for the next eight years, during which Anscombe and her family would become the object of charity of numerous individuals.[30] During her two-year studentship at Newnham, her financial saviours were two female dons. In 1942–1943, her former tutor and now friend and confidante Martha Kneale became so concerned about Anscombe living in 'absolute squalor' that she had Rachel Kydd, a fellow graduate student and friend, anonymously deliver a substantial sum of money to help her when Barbara was born.[31] The following year, her benefactor was Newnham College

[28] See Barbara Geach's baptismal record from St. Aloysius Church, Oxford, courtesy of Fr. Dominic Jacob at St. Aloysius Church, Oxford, and Jacek Jadacki, 'Piotr Tomasz Geach,' *Przegląd Filozoficzny—Nowa Seria*, R. 23: 2014, Nr 3 (91), ISSN 1230-1493. I am grateful to Piotr Szalek for bringing the article by Jadacki to my attention.

[29] Casimir Lewy had been attending Wittgenstein's lectures since he was an undergraduate in the late 1930s. He was a student of G. E. Moore and in the early 1940s managed the philosophy journal *Mind*, while Moore, who was editor, spent two years in America. Lewy would obtain his PhD from Cambridge in 1943, and in 1945 would take a post at Liverpool University. Lewy was both Polish and Jewish. Early in the war he attempted to enlist in the RAF in one of the Polish Fighter Squadrons. According to Michael Nedo, Lewy reported that when he attempted to enlist in London with the Polish Squadron within the RAF and they found out that he was Jewish, he was kicked down the stairs. (Michael Nedo correspondence with author, September 2023).

[30] Anscombe's financial situation would begin to change shortly after November 1950 when she was appointed a University Lecturer, which with its £300 stipend effectively doubled her income.

[31] The information in this paragraph is found in letters between Martha and William Kneale in the spring of 1943. (Jane Heal email correspondence with author, 22 August 2022. Access to the letters is courtesy of Professor Jane Heal.)

classics don Jocelyn Toynbee.[32] On 4 June 1944, on hearing of the liberation of Rome from the Nazis, Toynbee announced to Anscombe that she was giving her £100.[33]

The timing of Toynbee's financial generosity to Anscombe was somewhat eccentric, unless one knows something about the nature of their relationship. Toynbee was not only Newnham's classics don, but also ran Newnham College's Classics Society, which Anscombe attended and where she presented papers. Anscombe and Toynbee soon became fast friends. Besides their shared background in classics, the two women were drawn together by their fervent Catholic faith. During Anscombe's two years at Newnham, Toynbee was influencing numerous Newnham undergraduates to become Catholic—a nun in at least one case—and in doing so was provoking the outrage of some Newnham parents.[34] No doubt Anscombe was aiding Toynbee in her efforts.

Toynbee's speciality in classics at the time was ancient Roman artefacts, and so the liberation of Ancient Rome without its destruction was a great *academic* gift to her. In addition, because she was a fervent Catholic, the liberation of Catholic Rome without the destruction of the Vatican or the great Churches of Rome was a great *spiritual* gift to her. So, one can understand why Toynbee, in her joy, would wish to help out Anscombe, with whom she shared so

[32] Although one will learn very little about Jocelyn Toynbee in it, the extended Toynbee family is discussed in Polly Toynbee, *An Uneasy Inheritance: My Family and Other Radicals* (London: Atlantic Books, 2023).

[33] Mary Geach in conversation with the author. Toynbee was also the sister-in-law of another Catholic convert, the well-known Catholic apologist Rosalind Murray (Toynbee), author of works like *The Good Pagan's Failure*, a thinly veiled critique of her own parents, the virtuous and indefatigable do-gooders Sir Gilbert and Lady Mary Murray.

[34] During 1942–1943 and 1943–1944, parents of at least two Newnham undergraduates wrote letters to the head of Newnham College, Myra Curtis, begging her to somehow restrain their daughters from becoming Catholics, indicating that they thought their daughters' lives would be ruined, that they would disown their daughters, and so on. Curtis wrote sympathetic responses, but gently indicated that the evolving religious beliefs and attitudes of Newnham students were not within the purview of her role as Principal of Newnham College. From the Myra Curtis Files, courtesy of Newnham College Archives.

much. Coming at the end of Anscombe's second year at Newnham, Toynbee's timing was impeccable, for reasons discussed below.

It is worth noting that Martha Kneale and Anscombe may well have had different views on what would qualify as 'absolute squalor'. In an interview in the late 1950s, when asked how she managed to combine her career with raising five children, one of her answers was 'you just have to realize that dirt doesn't matter'.[35] Anscombe's poverty was exacerbated by the fact that she had a major addiction to cigarettes, and that she was more likely to spend her time and money on books than on keeping her flat clean and tidy. In the *Reminiscences* (sec. 221), Anscombe contrasts her habits of cleanliness with those of Wittgenstein.

In the spring of 1944, Anscombe was finishing her third year of graduate studies. At the time, it was expected that a student would write a DPhil dissertation in one to two years. At the end of her third year, she had completed a dissertation, but she was not happy with it. This was a long-standing issue for Anscombe. As a teenager, she had found inadequate an argument in a philosophy textbook that claimed to prove that 'every event must have a cause'. So she tried to fix the argument, but found a flaw in her own revised proof. She went at it again and again, but each time found the same error under a different guise.[36] Anscombe was never one to be satisfied with less than adequate arguments, and as a graduate student she was regularly writing and rewriting her thesis.[37] Eventually, Anscombe's confidence in her dissertation would be completely undermined when she showed it to Wittgenstein, whose comment on it was merely that it was 'not house-trained' (*Reminiscences*

---

[35] See John Searle, 'Oxford Philosophy in the 1950s', *Philosophy* 90, no. 2 (2015): 181.

[36] Anscombe, *Metaphysics and the Philosophy of Mind: The Collected Philosophical Papers of G. E. M. Anscombe*, Vol. 2 (Oxford: Blackwell, 1981), vii.

[37] In her application letter for the Somerville research fellowship, Anscombe notes that she had three versions of her dissertation, and enclosed two versions of it with her application.

sec. 188). Anscombe well recognized the scatalogical nature of Wittgenstein's comment, and thus deposited her dissertation in a file folder labeled 'shit on the floor'. While Anscombe remained registered as an Oxford DPhil student through 1949, there is no evidence she ever submitted the thesis.

With her two-year studentship at Newnham coming to an end, Anscombe needed to apply for further funding, and thus had to show what she had accomplished. Her dissertation 'The Identity of Bodies' consisted of eight chapters and was more than 200 pages in length.[38] On 30 April 1944, when she applied to Newnham for the Sarah Smithson fellowship, she submitted the dissertation, along with her CV and a cover letter. Whereas the Smithson studentship which Anscombe currently held was a graduate student scholarship, the Smithson fellowship for which she now applied was akin to a post-doctoral scholarship or a junior faculty research grant. For the fellowship, Anscombe proposed to continue work on the topics in the final chapter of her dissertation. In response to a request for an evaluation from the Principal of Newnham, Friedrich Waismann wrote:

Dear Miss Curtis, [...]

Mrs. G. E. M. Geach has worked under my supervision for three years. During this time she has done some very original work. This has not merely been concerned with analysis and criticism of the work of older philosophers, but has been an attempt to approach certain problems from a new direction and to work out a genuinely new position in relation to them.

At the same time she has shown considerable knowledge of the contributions which philosophers have made to problems with which she has been concerned. Her main interest, however, lies in certain modern aspects of problems which have occupied

---

[38] This claim is based on the existing copy of 'The Identity of Bodies' at the Anscombe Archives in the Kislak Centre at the University of Pennsylvania.

the mind of philosophers from Aristotle on. She approaches her work with great concentration and singleness of mind, she does not shrink from revising her work repeatedly, never being satisfied with an apparent solution of a problem so long as she has any suspicion that it may conceal unsolved difficulties.

During the time I have worked with her she has given me the impression of having an acute mind combined with a considerable faculty of insight into the minute structure of thought as it manifests itself in language. She has a lively philosophical imagination. I should like to add that I consider her very conscientious in her work.

For all these reasons I regard Mrs. Geach as highly suitable for undertaking original research work and hence I can warmly recommend her for your Research Fellowship.

Yours sincerely, (Signed) F. WAISMANN[39]

While Waismann writes very favourably about Anscombe's ability and promise as a philosopher, the Fellowship committee at Newnham College naturally wanted an outside evaluation, and requested one from G. E. Moore and C. D. Broad, who besides Wittgenstein were Cambridge's two other professors of philosophy. For various reasons Moore and Broad declined. So Newnham asked John Wisdom, a don at Trinity College. Wisdom was not an ideal evaluator, requiring assistance from Moore to read the untranslated Latin and Greek passages in her thesis.[40] Unfortunately for Anscombe, Wisdom formed a low opinion of it. In fact, his opinion was so low that he claimed that even if Newnham College received no other applications for the fellowship, Anscombe

---

[39] 'Letter from Friedrich Waismann to Miss Curtis in support of G. E. M. Anscombe's Fellowship Application', 15 May 1944. Courtesy of the Newnham College Archives, AC/5/2.

[40] See Clare Mac Cumhaill and Rachel Wiseman, *Metaphysical Animals* (London: Bloomsbury, 2022), 119.

should not be awarded it.[41] After some fairly harsh remarks about muddles and confusions in various places, Wisdom finished his evaluation by indicating that the thesis was not without merit, that it showed far more originality and independence of mind than most theses, and that Anscombe might in time produce good work.[42] But considering the rest of Wisdom's evaluation, these final comments were likely interpreted as further damning with faint praise.

With such an evaluation in hand, Newnham could hardly grant her the Smithson fellowship. For Anscombe, it must have been a terrible blow. She would henceforth have practically no status in Cambridge, never having been a member of the university, and no longer receiving a scholarship from her Cambridge college. Equally significant was that Anscombe was in dire straits financially, having only Jocelyn Toynbee's gift on which to live. However, during the summer of 1944, Anscombe was given another gift. The kindly landlady of 19 Fitzwilliam Street in Cambridge allowed poor families to rent houses from her, and then sub-let rooms to others, thus generating some income for the family.[43] With Peter away doing forestry work, Anscombe was effectively a single mother with no source of income, and thus clearly qualified in this landlady's eyes.[44]

---

[41] Considering how harshly Wisdom's own book manuscript had been evaluated seven years earlier, one might have hoped that he would have been more generous in his evaluation of a student's thesis. See Isaiah Berlin, *Flourishing: Letters 1930–1946* (London: Chatto & Windus, 2004), 651–653.

[42] John Wisdom, 'Report to the Fellowship Electors Newnham College on Mrs. Geach's (Miss Anscombe's) dissertation—1944'. Courtesy of Newnham College archives.

[43] See Benjamin Lipscomb, *The Women are Up to Something* (Oxford: Oxford University Press, 2022), 88.

[44] When Anscombe first acquired the tenancy, she only rented rooms to lodgers. After Peter arrived back from war work, Peter began to take boarders, Peter providing the board as well as the room. According to John Geach, who lived at 19 Fitzwilliam Street for the first six years of his life, his father's efforts were reminiscent of the television show 'Fawlty Towers'. Interview with John Geach, 5 June 2023.

1945–1946: Act 2: Anscombe
Gets to Know Wittgenstein

With her scholarship at Newnham now finished, it would have been reasonable for Anscombe to return to Oxford, where she had friends and a wider network of support. As of the summer of 1944 Anscombe had only been living in Cambridge for fifteen months, whereas she had lived in Oxford for the majority of the six years before that. So why did Anscombe remain in Cambridge?

Anscombe's decision to stay on in Cambridge in the summer of 1944 was not because Wittgenstein would be back at Cambridge that autumn. He had no plans to return to Cambridge, wishing to do further war-work once his sabbatical was done[45] (see *Reminiscences* sec. 140). Furthermore, at this point Wittgenstein had yet to 'notice' Anscombe; they may not as yet have had a single one-on-one conversation. Furthermore, having been rejected by Newnham, Anscombe must have harboured some concern, even if Wittgenstein did return, as to whether he would be interested in working with her. Rather, what kept her in Cambridge was her new home at 19 Fitzwilliam Street, which doubled as a source of income to pay the bills.

Regardless, shortly before Michaelmas 1944, it was announced that Wittgenstein would once more be lecturing, and so Anscombe was again off to his lectures at the top of Whewell's Court tower.[46] Late in the term, Wittgenstein first mentions Anscombe in a letter, noting the participation of 'a woman, Mrs so and so who calls herself Miss Anscombe, who certainly is intelligent'.[47] That

---

[45] Wittgenstein decided at the last minute to return to Cambridge for Michaelmas 1944. James Klagge notes that the initial publication of lectures for Michaelmas 1944 did not include any by Wittgenstein, but that one was added at the last minute. See Klagge, 'The Wittgenstein Lectures, Revisited', *Nordic Wittgenstein Review* 8, no. 1–2 (2019): 53.

[46] Whewell's Court was an annex of Trinity College, Cambridge, the entrance to it being across the street from the main gate.

[47] Wittgenstein to Rhees, 28 November 1944. Letter sec. 321 in B. McGuinness, ed., *Wittgenstein in Cambridge*, 371.

term, despite having a baby at home, she took every opportunity for further interactions with Wittgenstein, participating in discussion groups he attended, which typically went late into the evening. Anscombe attended a meeting of a literary society that J. B. S. Butler, secretary of the CMSC, had organized. Peter Stern, who had invited Wittgenstein to speak on Saturday 25 November 1944,[48] describes that meeting:

> The occasion was a bleak November evening in war-weary Cambridge. In a very small society of mainly literary undergraduates an unremarkable paper (on the scheme of virtues extolled in *The Iliad*) was followed by an emphatic but untidy discussion: did we really know what we meant by virtue, was it the same as what the Greeks meant by it? (It was the 'What-exactly-do-you-mean-by...?' era.)
>
> A stranger, whom I had noticed sitting by himself in a corner (wisely he hadn't taken off his macintosh, his cap lay on his knee, his hands rested on an ash plant), was introduced by the chairman and took up the conversation. Speaking with a voice that was foreign yet entirely unhesitant, clear yet resonant, in words which occasionally seemed old-fashioned yet never quaint, he began by describing some of the ways in which the history of a concept such as 'virtue' connects us with the past, as with a rope. None of the threads of a rope reach from end to end, its whole strength derives from the short fibres that overlap each other. And what is true of words like 'virtue' or 'courage' (he continued) is also true of what people at various times meant by 'history', 'philosophy', and words of that kind. 'And "truth?"', I asked. Was there any reason (he replied) why 'the grammar of "truth"' (the phrase struck me as odd) should be different? I could think of no reason.

[48] Stern's name and that date are found in Wittgenstein's 1944–1945 Cambridge Pocket Diary. Access to the diary is courtesy of Michael Nedo.

As the speaker moved on, to other illustrations and uses, I suddenly saw in his central metaphor an answer to some of the questions which the literary critics I was reading at the time had failed to solve. His name meant nothing to me. Yet when he spoke I became almost instantly aware of a presence perfectly possessed of the occasion, compelling attention and dominating it by the sheer force and clarity of the argument. The thing seemed—indeed it is—so obvious that I doubt whether, but for that voice and presence, I would have seen its importance, seen the perfect fittingness of the images he used, let alone the range of instances to which it could be applied.[49]

Wittgenstein only attended one meeting of the group—he was 'disgusted with what he heard' (*Reminiscences* sec. 45, 48, 49, 53)—but he invited Anscombe to participate in a smaller discussion group with Butler and Stern for the rest of the 1944–1945 academic year.[50]

It was in early 1945 that their relationship blossomed. On 5 February 1945 Anscombe read 'Appearance and Reality' at the CMSC (*Reminiscences* sec. 203). The paper impressed Wittgenstein, and his estimation of her suddenly grew significantly, as shown by a number of his actions.[51] First, he asked her to be secretary of the CMSC for the following academic year.[52] His choice was remarkable, since Anscombe probably became the first secretary of the

---

[49] J. P. Stern, *The Dear Purchase* (Cambridge: Cambridge University Press 1995), 19–20.

[50] We can date these meetings to 1944–1945 because Butler (and Stern) graduated that year, and hence would no longer have rooms at King's College. Thanks to Thomas Davies, archivist at King's College, Cambridge, for furnishing me with this and other information; email correspondence, 4 March 2021.

[51] This paper was one of only two that Wittgenstein ever told her he liked (see *Reminiscences* sec. 203).

[52] In the fall of 1944 Wittgenstein had returned to his position as chairman of the CMSC, and it was the chairman's responsibility to select a secretary for the Club for the following year. Geach says that Wittgenstein had to 'persuade' Anscombe to take on the job of CMSC secretary (Geach, *Wittgenstein's Lectures*, xii).

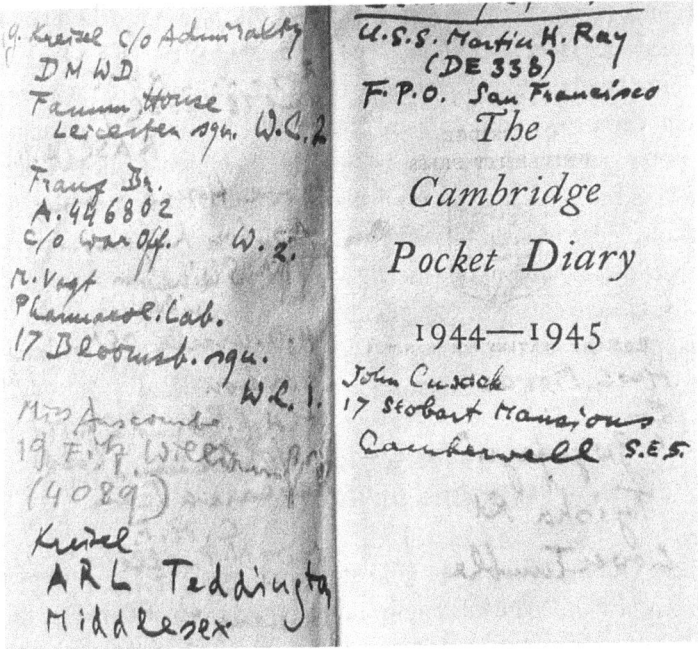

Fig 1.2 Wittgenstein's 1944–1945 pocket diary with Anscombe's address and phone number. Anscombe was a significant person in Wittgenstein's life by early 1945. *Photo by John Berkman, used by permission of Michael Nedo, who owns the pocket diary*

CMSC with no formal status at the university.[53] Second, when she reapplied for the Smithson fellowship, Wittgenstein (and Lord Russell) wrote on her behalf, but the former did more than merely write a strong reference letter. Recognizing not only her philosophical ability, but also her financial need, Wittgenstein did two highly unusual things. First, he made an appointment to speak to Newnham's principal Myra Curtis to urge her to offer the fellowship to Anscombe, and also to find her teaching opportunities.

---

[53] She was elected at the CMSC meeting on 7 June 1944 and served as secretary for the 1945–1946 academic year.

Second, he uncharacteristically donned a tie so as to make a good appearance (see *Reminiscences* sec. 189).

Shockingly, despite favourable references from two of the twentieth century's most eminent philosophers, and Wittgenstein's supererogatory efforts on her behalf, Newnham College again declined to offer her the Sarah Smithson fellowship. Refusing to acknowledge Anscombe's capacities and promise as a philosopher, the fellowship committee merely took pity on her, and so awarded 'Mrs. Geach' £50 with the 'possibility of further assistance' if she reapplied during the [following] academic year.[54]

1945–1946: Act 3: Anscombe and Wittgenstein Run the CMSC

At the end of Trinity 1944 (and at the end of the next two terms) Anscombe and Wittgenstein would meet to discuss and finalize the following term's list of speakers. Geach recalls her meeting with Wittgenstein in December 1945:

> Elizabeth did not let her pregnancy interfere with attendance at Moral Science Club meetings and at Wittgenstein's lectures. I remember his coming round a little before our son's birth to discuss the next term's programme for the Club. One slot in the card remained to be filled: 'We could invite N. N.' said Wittgenstein, naming a Cambridge colleague. 'But let's face it, old man, that's scraping the bottom of the barrel.' (N.N. accepted the invitation.)[55]

[54] Letter from Myra Curtis to Mrs. White on 6 June 1945. Courtesy of the Newnham College Archives. Anscombe would make an additional application later that year and Newnham apparently granted her another £50 during the academic year 1945–1946.

[55] From Peter Geach, *Wittgenstein's Lectures on Philosophical Psychology 1946–47* (Chicago: University of Chicago Press, 1989), xi–xii.

For Michaelmas 1945, the speakers were Professors Wittgenstein, Moore, and Dingle, Dr. Ewing, Mr. Wisdom, and Mr. Smythies, with one impromptu discussion. For Lent 1946 (the subject of the discussion referred to by Geach above), the speakers were Professors Broad, Ryle, and Adrian, Dr. Lewy, Mr. Geach, with two impromptu discussions on Descartes' 'Cogito' introduced by Hijab[56] and Anscombe. For Easter 1946 the speakers were Mr. Ayer, Mr. MacKinnon, Mr. Braithwaite, Mr. Hijab, and Miss Anscombe, with two impromptu discussions introduced by Mr. Smythies.[57]

The complete list of speakers in 1945–1946 is very revealing in terms of whom Wittgenstein and Anscombe considered worth inviting to the CMSC. Besides inviting professors and prominent philosophers from Cambridge (Wittgenstein, Moore, Broad, Ewing, Wisdom, Braithwaite, and Edgar Adrian [a Nobel Prize winner in physiology], Oxford (Ryle, Ayer, and MacKinnon) and from the University of London (Herbert Dingle, a philosopher of science), all of the other speakers that year—Yorick Smythies, Peter Geach, Casimir Lewy, Wasfi Hijab, and Anscombe herself—were personal friends of Wittgenstein and/or Anscombe.[58]

Once the war ended, Peter Geach returned full-time to Cambridge.[59] Neither Anscombe nor Geach had any regular employment. Peter would later write of them having to sell many of their most prized books that year.[60] In the *Reminiscences* she periodically makes references to her poverty (e.g. sec. 197), but she does not convey the precariousness of her financial situation throughout

---

[56] See Appendix.

[57] See Appendix.

[58] NB: only one of these five friends of Wittgenstein (Hijab) was currently a student at Cambridge.

[59] 'After the end of hostilities in Europe Peter would have been able to join her in Cambridge on a permanent basis after the end of his conscripted war work in the New Forest.' Luke Gormally, 'Elizabeth Anscombe: Some Details of Early Career and Married Life. [1941–1951]'. Notes. Unpublished manuscript shared with me by the author.

[60] Geach, *Wittgenstein's Lectures*.

the time she knew Wittgenstein. In 1945–1946 Wittgenstein became a third benefactor to Anscombe. On various occasions he bought her a raincoat (sec. 215), chairs (sec. 219), and a wastepaper basket (sec. 219), and when Anscombe was due to deliver John Richard in December 1945, Wittgenstein paid her hospital bill.[61] Wittgenstein must have arranged it in advance, since he himself spent Christmas with a family in Swansea. When John Richard was baptized shortly afterwards, his godparents were Jocelyn Toynbee and Norman Daniel.

But as Geach notes, neither her pregnancy nor the arrival of a second child interrupted Anscombe's appetite for philosophical discussions, and by that time Anscombe was establishing a set of trusted conversation partners, foremost among them being Yorick Smythies. In the autumn of 1945 Wasfi Hijab and Kanti Shah arrived and soon joined in as partners in nearly constant philosophical conversation.[62] The enigmatic Georg Kreisel was also a conversation partner, as would be Iris Murdoch once she arrived in Cambridge in 1947.

During 1945–1946, Anscombe attended Wittgenstein's lectures, while Geach remained at home looking after Barbara, and John Richard once he was born.[63] But Geach regularly heard Wittgenstein at the evening CMSC meetings. That year, Wittgenstein also started dropping by their house on Fitzwilliam Street, going for walks with whichever one of them was available. Geach writes:

Before I attended his lectures I had gone for walks with Wittgenstein. This continued to happen from time to time while he was Professor in Cambridge. The walks were very beneficial

---

[61] In his *A Philosophical Autobiography* Geach writes: 'Personally Wittgenstein was a trusty and generous friend. His practical advice was sound and often helpful; he wrote references both for me and for Elizabeth when we were looking for academic work. [...] He helped us financially when our second child was born.' See Harry A. Lewis, ed., *Peter Geach: Philosophical Encounters* (Dordrecht: Kluwer Academic Publishers, 1991), 14.

[62] See Appendix.

[63] Geach, *Wittgenstein's Lectures*, xi.

to me, but I found them a considerable strain. Wittgenstein did not go in for small talk and did not tolerate casual thoughtless remarks; there would fall silences that I dared not break. The concentration of mind he demanded was fatiguing.[64]

Geach goes on to describe how early in Wittgenstein's relationship with Anscombe 'I heard him address Elizabeth as "old man" on several occasions.'[65] Anscombe mentions this habit, but notes that Wittgenstein soon started calling her 'm'dear' (*Reminiscences* sec. 180). What neither Anscombe nor Geach seemed to realize was that 'old' was one of Wittgenstein's greatest terms of endearment and affection.[66] 'Old face', 'old heart', 'old so-and-so', and 'bl....y old' were some of the frequent appellations Wittgenstein used for his dearest friend Ben Richards in his letters to him in the late 1940s.[67]

Geach also thought of Wittgenstein as having an 'anti-woman' attitude.[68] This is a view about Wittgenstein which has come to be widely held. The source of many of the claims that Wittgenstein was anti-women can be traced to Georg Kreisel.[69] Anscombe was not the only person to regard Kreisel as an unreliable witness (see *Reminiscences* sec. 70); according to his longtime close friend Michael Nedo, Kreisel often took an extraordinarily flippant attitude even in serious matters, and it could be very hard to distinguish when what he said should be taken seriously.[70]

[64] Geach, *Wittgenstein's Lectures*, xi.

[65] Geach, *Wittgenstein's Lectures*, xii.

[66] While speculation on the author's part, Wittgenstein would not likely have called Anscombe 'old woman' since it had distinctly negative connotations.

[67] See Schmidt and Citron, eds., *Der Briefwechsel zwischen Ludwig Wittgensteins und Ben Richards 1946–1951* (Innsbruck: Haymon Verlag, 2023).

[68] Geach, *Wittgenstein's Lectures*, xii.

[69] For example, Kreisel, in a conversation with Peter Conradi, said, 'Wittgenstein famously did not think women, in any case, could do philosophy: "men are foul, but women are viler" he would remark.' See Peter Conradi, *Iris Murdoch: A Life* (New York: W. W. Norton, 2001), 266. My thanks to Prof. James Klagge for pointing me to this reference.

[70] Conversation with Michael Nedo, September 2023, and correspondence of 20 April 2024.

During his years teaching at Cambridge, Wittgenstein had a disproportionately large number of female students, many of whom were in his 'inner circle' over the years.[71] So Anscombe was no exception in this matter. Many other examples could be given. For instance, while Wittgenstein consulted many, many physicians, he praised Dr. Louise Mooney at Cornell as the best physician he had ever consulted.[72]

In the spring of 1946, Anscombe received good news. She was appointed to Somerville College, Oxford as the Mary Somerville Research Scholar, a three-year research-only appointment. However, it did not pay well, with a stipend of only some £325 a year.[73] Although the fellowship was for research and (minimal) lecturing, Anscombe was allowed to supplement her income by doing some teaching on the side.[74] With Peter and the children ensconced at 19 Fitzwilliam Street in Cambridge, generating an income as sub-landlord, Anscombe's accepting the research scholarship at Somerville meant that for the next three years she would

---

[71] As can be seen from McGuinness and Monk's biographies, Wittgenstein, especially when he was young, had a variety of problematic attitudes about 'women'. However, in terms of his students at Cambridge, it was largely female students (e.g. Alice Ambrose, Margaret Masterman, and Margaret MacDonald, along with Francis Skinner) to whom Wittgenstein dictated the Blue, Brown, and Yellow books in the 1930s.

[72] '[Wittgenstein] decided to go to a second doctor, [Dr. Louise Mooney] . . . Wittgenstein liked his doctor very much. "Wittgenstein has a very good doctor now, although he didn't at first." (Malcolm to Von Wright Sept 15, 1949). Once back in England, Wittgenstein often inquired about Dr. Mooney, and sent greetings to her, via Malcolm. . . . She also appears in the last letter Wittgenstein wrote before his death: "Remember me to Dr. Mooney. I like to think of her."' In Trevor Pinch and Richard Swedberg, 'Wittgenstein's Visit to Ithaca in 1949: On the Importance of Details', *Distinktion: Scandinavian Journal of Social Theory* 14, no. 1 (2013): 17–18.

[73] In 1949, Anscombe's stipend was increased to £350. For purposes of comparison, Anscombe's colleague Philippa Foot would have been making close to £600 annually. Newly appointed fellows in the men's colleges would generally be making considerably more, although the exact figure would depend somewhat on the wealth of the college.

[74] According to Lipscomb, 'by a special dispensation from the usual regulations governing the Mary Somerville Fellowship, Anscombe did a little teaching on the side' (Lipscomb, *The Women*, 89).

commute between Oxford and Cambridge.[75] Generally speaking, she would live in Oxford during term, returning to Cambridge for meetings, appointments, and on some weekends, and then live in Cambridge outside term.[76]

1946–1947: Act 4: Anscombe Commutes to Cambridge to Be Tutored by Wittgenstein

There is no doubt that Anscombe created a sensation among the philosophers during her first term back in Oxford. For Anscombe, philosophy had to be done in conversation. So, soon after arriving, she engaged in philosophical conversations at every opportunity. On Friday afternoons, she attended a seminar entitled 'Things', run by J. L. Austin and Isaiah Berlin. This famous seminar was set up to attack phenomenalism, the doctrine that all our knowledge of the world can be reduced to our knowledge of our personal experiences, that is, our sense-data. The topic was one that both Austin and Berlin had thought about extensively. In a small philosophical group that met between 1936 and 1939, Austin, Berlin, and A. J. Ayer had been arguing about this doctrine ad nauseam.[77] Now that the war was over, they reinitiated the discussion. David Pears had a ringside seat in the class to watch Austin and Anscombe spar with each other for the eight weeks of Michaelmas term. As Pears describes it, Austin and Anscombe

---

[75] Geach would later refer to their marriage as 'telegamy', since for most of the next thirty-two years the pair would be spending their working weeks in different and distant cities. See Anthony Kenny, 'Peter Thomas Geach 1916–2013', British Academy Obituary.

[76] Anscombe would only obtain the tenancy of 27 St John Street in the fall of 1949, after the death of Mrs. Lawson. In the summer of 1951, when Geach was shortly to begin teaching at the University of Birmingham (which was much closer to Oxford than to Cambridge), the entire family moved from Cambridge to Oxford.

[77] Berlin discusses in detail the debates in these years between Austin, Ayer. and himself in 'J. L. Austin and the Early Beginnings of Oxford Philosophy' (in Berlin 2018).

both opposed the kind of phenomenalism that Ayer was defending at the time in his lectures and they both subscribed to the vaguely formulated thesis that 'sense-data are not objects'. But they meant quite different things by it. What Austin meant was that the subtle differences marked by qualifying verbs in ordinary language were lost when the verbs were replaced by the single, levelling noun, 'sense-data'. If, as Berlin put it, 'things don't always look what they seem', the verbs should be retained and the translation into the language of sense-data should be resisted. Anscombe rejected this line of argument and attacked Ayer's theory from a different angle. When she denied the status of objects to sense data, she meant that they were not basic objects which could be described independently of any connection with the physical world. So while Austin regarded Ayer's building-blocks as a crude philosophical fabrication, Anscombe accepted them, but not their proposed function, because, according to her, they depended on the very structures that they were supposed to be used to produce. Her criticism was an application of Wittgenstein's still unpublished Private Language Argument.[78]

While Austin considered himself to be opposing Ayer, Anscombe would argue that Austin made the same type of error as Ayer, as both understood an 'object of sight' to always be a kind of thing. Her approach, challenging both of the standard approaches to the question, bore the influence of her teacher.[79]

While Anscombe was making a huge impression in Oxford, she seemed oblivious to this fact. Another attendee of the Austin-Berlin seminar, Mary Wilson (later Warnock), writes in her diary of an evening spent visiting Anscombe at her house after term was over:

---

[78] See Pears's essay 'Philosophy and the History of Philosophy', in A. and E. Margalit, eds., *Isaiah Berlin: A Celebration* (London: Hogarth Press, 1991), 31–39.

[79] According to Mac Cumhaill and Wiseman, in the 'The Intentionality of Sensation' (1965), Anscombe would publish her reply to Austin. (Mac Cumhaill and Wiseman, *Metaphysical Animals*, 225.)

An incredibly nice evening [...] Elizabeth smoking a pipe, having given up cigarettes. Talked ... a little about Oxford and the Class but not too much or scornfully. Then about Elizabeth's reputation in Oxford. She seemed genuinely surprised.[80]

Anscombe was simply trying to wrestle with philosophical problems, and she was oblivious to how different her ethos and way of philosophising was from what was beginning to prevail in Oxford. Over the next few years, exacerbated by the influence of Wittgenstein, Anscombe would develop a scathing attitude towards the prevailing intellectual ethos amongst Oxford philosophers. After a conversation with her on 25 September 1950, Bouwsma describes her view:

What interests me is her attitude towards philosophers at Oxford.... She thought I would find the atmosphere depressing. Cheap. Cheap. There aren't any problems. And these people are all above it. They have easy dispositions for all difficulties ... a certain shallowness which goes with their cleverness. It's as though they feel they have the key to all mysteries and feel now a delight in their unmasking of the emptiness of all pursuits.

Wittgenstein talks about [some] men as serious and deep. Perhaps it's just that these [clever but shallow] men strike Miss Anscombe as like magicians who with a certain trickery and sleight of hand expose the poor ninny philosophers whom they seize upon. The ninny philosophers may not have had the benefit of borrowed cleverness, but they were very earnest, they had problems to which they gave their lives and hard labor. These people have nothing to do but debunk.... It isn't then that these people are mistaken in what they say. It is that they have nothing but this show they put on. What a clever boy I am! These other

<hr />

[80] Mary Wilson (Warnock) diary, 7 January 7 1947. Used with permission of Kitty Warnock.

philosophers made mistakes, in earnest, but what now are you doing in earnest? There you are crowing over the mistakes of earnest men. So you will never make an important mistake, for nothing is important to you. Wonderful! Crow![81]

Her attitude towards the prevailing Oxford philosophy was shared by her friends Philippa Foot, Iris Murdoch, and Mary Midgley. For example, Midgley thought that Oxford philosophers were driven by a fear of being seen as either weak or judgmental. So they became narrowly focused and conventional, avoiding any kind of substantive claims, especially in the area of morality.[82] Similarly, Murdoch saw in Anscombe something she didn't find in other philosophers in Oxford. Murdoch was in awe of Anscombe's moral seriousness and her 'ruthless authenticity'.[83] When Foot and Murdoch put forward their critiques of other Oxford philosophers, they raised their objections in friendly and polite ways. But Anscombe's fearlessness in saying what she thought, and her sometimes caustic or profane outbursts, began to make her both a feared, and eventually reviled, figure among much of Oxford's philosophical establishment.

Meanwhile, for Michaelmas 1946 in Cambridge, Wittgenstein took on an extraordinarily heavy teaching schedule. His twice weekly lectures in his small sitting room in Whewell Court were jammed, with students occupying every nook and cranny.[84] He also had an 'at-home' class late on Saturday afternoons.[85] After these classes,

[81] See O. K. Bouwsma, *Wittgenstein Conversations 1949–1951*, ed. J. L. Craft and Ronald E. Hustwit (Indianapolis: Hackett, 1986). The full quotation can be found in a notebook held at the Bouwsma archives of the Ransom Center at the University of Texas.

[82] See Midgley, *The Owl of Minerva* (Abington: Routledge, 2005), 124ff., 156ff.

[83] Murdoch's journal from 1947 is held at the Iris Murdoch Archive at Kingston University. All quotations from Iris Murdoch's unpublished journals are by permission of Kingston University.

[84] Malcolm, *A Memoir*, 24.

[85] For details of these Saturday discussions see 'Wittgenstein's Saturday Discussions: 1946–1947 Notes of Gibert Harris Edwards', in *Public and Private Occasions*, ed. James Klagge and Alfred Nordmann (Lanham, MD: Rowman & Littlefield, 2003), 401–404.

Wittgenstein would be mentally exhausted, and ask someone to join him in going to a 'flick'.[86] Wittgenstein preferred to sit in the front row, having his entire field of view captured by the screen. 'He wished to become totally absorbed in the film no matter how trivial or artificial it was, in order to free his mind temporarily from the philosophical thoughts that tortured and exhausted him.'[87]

Anscombe planned to attend Wittgenstein's lectures in 1946–1947 but Wittgenstein suggested that she instead come along on Tuesday afternoons to supervisions he was giving to Wasfi Hijab, a doctoral student of Wittgenstein's writing a dissertation entitled 'Some Philosophic Problems between Science and Religion'.[88] Notes that Anscombe took in the discussions with Wittgenstein and Hijab are included in this volume. It would seem that she took rather more notes than are extant, since regarding these meetings she wrote in her report to the Mary Somerville Research Committee that:

> I have engaged in and recorded for myself detailed discussions with Prof. L. Wittgenstein on the related concepts: 'the same', 'and so on', 'following a rule', 'a principle', 'explanation', 'regularities'; and have I think got a lot of profit out of them.[89]

Notwithstanding his busy schedule, Wittgenstein took time to care for those in need. On a Saturday in early October, Wittgenstein took Malcolm with him to visit two prisoner of war (P.O.W.) camps outside of Cambridge.[90] Despite the war's having been over for a

---

[86] See *Reminiscences* sec. 205 and Malcolm, *A Memoir*, 26.

[87] Malcolm, *A Memoir*, 26.

[88] Thanks to James Klagge, email correspondence 21 August 2023, for the title of Hijab's dissertation. For more on Hijab, see James Klagge, 'Wasfi Hijab's Wittgenstein', in *Wittgenstein and Other Philosophers: His Influence on Historical and Contemporary Analytic Philosophers*, Vol. II, ed. Ali Hossein Khani and Gary Kemp (Routledge, forthcoming).

[89] Elizabeth Anscombe, Report to the Mary Somerville Research Committee Year One 1946–47. Somerville College Archives.

[90] Wittgenstein letter to Ben Richards, 6 October 1946, in Schmidt and Citron, eds., *Der Briefwechsel zwischen Ludwig Wittgensteins und Ben Richards 1946-1951*.

year and a half, the camps were still full. Having been a POW himself in World War I, Wittgenstein was determined to do something to improve the prisoners' lives. After conferring with those at the camp, Wittgenstein acquired music and instruments for them.[91] Wittgenstein's efforts to aid others were typically done anonymously. For example, at the beginning of the war, Wittgenstein had secretly directed funds via the SPSL (Society for the Protection of Learning and Science) to support fellow Austrian Jewish philosopher Rose Rand.[92]

As soon as Michaelmas term was over, Wittgenstein headed back to Swansea, his place of retreat and refuge in these years. After his holidays, but before returning to Cambridge, Wittgenstein went to the Isle of Wight, where he went on retreat to Quarr Abbey.[93] Yorick Smythies, who had arranged for Wittgenstein to make this visit, would years later tell the story that when Wittgenstein departed the Abbey, the Abbot expressed the hope that Wittgenstein had enjoyed his visit, and Wittgenstein replied that he had *not* enjoyed it.[94] Presumably Wittgenstein was not intending to insult the Abbot, but rather that Wittgenstein had not gone to the Abbey to 'enjoy' himself, but for rather different purposes. Wittgenstein's character was such that he could not allow himself to mislead the

---

[91] Malcolm, *A Memoir*, 47–48.

[92] See Ray Cooper, ed., *Refugee Scholars: Conversation with Tess Simpson* (Leeds: Moreland Books, 1992), 89–91. The SPSL eventually forbade Wittgenstein from continuing to fund her. While Simpson does not identify the Austrian female refugee philosopher that Wittgenstein was supporting, I am grateful to Michael Kremer for positively identifying this scholar as being Rose Rand (email correspondence 3 June 2024), on the basis of the S.P.S.L. file on Rose Rand found in the Bodleian Library, MS. S.P.S.L. 347/1.

[93] Wittgenstein refers to his visit to Quarr Abbey in MS 133, Wittgenstein's Nachlass, 10.1.1947. Furthermore, in his 1945–1946 Cambridge pocket diary, Wittgenstein has the addresses 'Abby, Caldy [*sic*] Island, Tenby, Pembrokeshire' and 'The Monastery, Roscrea, County Offaly, Eire', so it is likely that Wittgenstein also visited one or both of those monasteries in 1946. Information from Wittgenstein's 1945–46 pocket diary courtesy of Michael Nedo.

[94] Bouwsma, *Bouwsma's Commonplace book notes on Yorick Smythies and Related Papers, Assembled, edited and Introduced by Ronald E. Hustwit, Sr.* (unpublished) The date of the conversation between Smythies and Bouwsma is 13 November 1955.

Abbot. As Anscombe notes in the *Reminiscences*, this is a good example of why it was that so many people found Wittgenstein difficult or intolerable to be around (*Reminiscences* sec. 41).

Wittgenstein was not the only one with a demanding schedule in 1946–1947, as Anscombe's commuting schedule between Oxford and Cambridge verged on the ludicrous. For example, in Michaelmas term, she had Tuesday afternoon tutorials in Cambridge with Wittgenstein, Wednesday evening Jowett Society meetings in Oxford, Thursday evening CMSC meetings in Cambridge (of which she attended at least some), and the Friday afternoons Austin/Berlin seminar in Oxford.

When Oscar Wood was elected president of the Jowett Society in March 1947 for Trinity Term, he got Anscombe to do a favour for him that no one had previously succeeded in doing, namely getting Wittgenstein to come to a philosophical meeting in Oxford. It was not Oxford's prestigious dons-only Philosophical Society, but rather the student-led Jowett Society.[95] Wittgenstein would respond to Wood's presidential address. It was agreed that Wittgenstein would be made chairman for the meeting, and in that capacity would respond to Wood.

It was not accidental that Anscombe instructed Wood to present on Descartes' famous claim 'I think, therefore I am,' a topic of great interest to Anscombe, which she had discussed with Wittgenstein and others while working on her own paper on the subject throughout that academic year.[96] Furthermore, she had led discussions meetings at the CMSC on that topic the previous year. Stories from Wittgenstein's appearance at the Jowett Society

[95] For a discussion of the many previously failed attempts to have Wittgenstein come to give a lecture at Oxford, see Mac Cumhaill and Wiseman, *Metaphysical Animals*, 171–174.

[96] For example, with Philippa Foot: 'What sort of argument is it? Is it supposed to prove the existence of some object, and if so what is that object? Isn't it uncommunicable? Should it lead one to solipsism?' See Iris Murdoch's diary entry of 17 March 1947 for a reference to Anscombe's discussions with Foot.

at Magdalen College in Oxford on 17 May 1947 are legion.[97] Anscombe only wryly recounts how H. A. Prichard "came but didn't hear anything, obviously" (*Reminiscences* sec. 156).

That same term, the Finnish philosopher Georg Henrik von Wright, who had come to Cambridge to deliver a series of lectures, also attended Wittgenstein's classes. It was then that von Wright first met Anscombe.[98] Von Wright and Wittgenstein later corresponded, each indicating that they held Anscombe in high regard.[99] Von Wright also wrote Wittgenstein to indicate the ways in which he was influencing him. Since Wittgenstein was similarly influencing Anscombe, von Wright's reflections are worth considering.

First, von Wright addresses Wittgenstein's philosophical influence:

I learnt an enormous mass [of] philosophy.... What will be the consequences of it, is not as yet to be foreseen.... I know that a hard struggle is needed before the imported goods will become my own.... [I shall] always have to acknowledge that I learnt from you, how difficult philosophy must be.

Second, von Wright addresses Wittgenstein's influence on his character:

Still more, perhaps, did the stay in Cambridge mean to my being human.... Things which I hardly thought of before, became of vital importance, new values and ideals appeared and greatly revised my outlook on life.

---

[97] For numerous accounts of the evening, see F. A. Flowers II and Ian Ground, eds., *Portraits of Wittgenstein*, Vol. 2 (London: Bloomsbury, 2016).

[98] Von Wright and Anscombe (along with Rush Rhees) would later be appointed Wittgenstein's literary executors and collaborate extensively on the editing and publication of Wittgenstein's philosophical writings. For more on this, see Christian Erbacher, 'Wittgenstein and His Literary Executors', *Journal for the History of Analytical Philosophy* 4, no. 3 (2016).

[99] Wittgenstein to von Wright, 24 May 1947.

Third, von Wright addresses Wittgenstein's influence on his spiritual life, what must be addressed for him to truly change his life:

> nothing I consciously undertake for the sake of my soul can make me substantially different from what I am, a pharisee in minutest details, because I shall always lack courage to let myself down in the abyss of despair which I know I had to pass in order to be saved.[100]

It seems that there was something about Wittgenstein's very character that urged people like Anscombe and von Wright to question their own character, and to seek to change themselves in significant ways.

1947–1949: Act 5: Anscombe and Wittgenstein's Long-Distance Friendship

Just before the beginning of Michaelmas term 1947, Wittgenstein resigned his professorship. Anscombe wrote von Wright:

> You will ... have heard of Wittgenstein's resignation from the professorship at Cambridge.... [H]e has not done it for the reasons which he used to have ... his feeling of incongruity about his being in that job ... but because he can't get on with his book.
>
> In a few weeks he is going to live near Dublin, so I suppose none of us will see him for some time. He is in a rather depressed state at present, but is not, he tells me, having any twinges of doubt about his resignation, and I think that if when he gets away he is able to work he is going to find it a great relief.[101]

---

[100] Von Wright to Wittgenstein, 31 July 1947.
[101] Wittgenstein was in Cambridge from 10 October to 18 November 1947. Wittgenstein would not return to Cambridge until 30 September 1948. In the intervening

Having become accustomed to seeing Wittgenstein regularly during term time for three years, once he left Cambridge in mid-November, Anscombe would sadly not see him until the following August.

While Wittgenstein was preparing to leave Cambridge, Anscombe's old friend Iris Murdoch had just arrived. Both were present at the CMSC when Anscombe read an early version of her paper on Plato's *Parmenides* entitled 'The Past'.[102] Having wanted to study with Wittgenstein, Murdoch was deeply disappointed about his imminent departure, and asked Anscombe to introduce them. Anscombe initially refused, but a few days later relented. Murdoch's diary for 23 October 1947 begins 'Today I met Wittgenstein' and then simply quotes their dialogue:

> WITTGENSTEIN: It is as if I have an apple tree in my garden and everyone is carting away the apples and sending them all over the world. And you ask: may I have an apple from your tree?
>
> MURDOCH: Yes; but I'm never sure when I'm given an apple whether it really *is* from your tree.
>
> WITTGENSTEIN: True. I should say though, they are not good apples.
>
> WITTGENSTEIN: What's the use of having one philosophical discussion? It's like having one piano lesson.
>
> MURDOCH: Okey doke![103]

months, the only other time we know Anscombe saw Wittgenstein was August 1948. See Wittgenstein letter to Ben Richards, 8 August 1947, in Schmidt and Citron, eds., *Der Briefwechsel zwischen Ludwig Wittgensteins und Ben Richards 1946–1951*.

[102] At this time Anscombe received an invitation from Max Black at Cornell University to contribute to a volume on linguistic analysis, and so proposed to submit a revised version of her CMSC paper.

[103] Iris Murdoch Journal #4, 23 October 1947, KUAS 202/1/4, The Iris Murdoch Archive at Kingston University. All quotations from Iris Murdoch's unpublished journals are by permission of Kingston University.

Just before Wittgenstein left for Ireland, he gave Anscombe the best possible present, letting her continue to possess for some time a copy of 'his book', which by this time was the entire Part I of what would later be published as the PI. As Anscombe notes in the *Reminiscences* (sec. 199), the previous year she had told him she was beginning to learn German, and he had been pleased, saying that then she would be able to read his book. During the next year, they would discuss parts of his book, with him coaching her as she translated parts of it for him. Anscombe clearly had a facility for languages. In little more than a year, Anscombe's competence in reading German attained a level whereby Wittgenstein considered it worthwhile to leave one of his three typescript copies with her. By November 1947 Anscombe must have been in possession of a copy of Wittgenstein's book for some time, since at that point she had not merely one copy, but also parts of a second.[104] By the spring of 1948, Anscombe was sharing portions of her translations and the German text itself with at least two students, Mary Wilson (Warnock) and Iris Murdoch. Warnock writes:

> Elizabeth [...] fell into the habit of reading some of her translation aloud, and discussing linguistic or grammatical points or, some-times, substantial points about the text [. . .] On one occasion she lent me a few sheets of her translation to take back with me to LMH, to copy out if I liked. So it happened that before many people in Oxford had seen any of the later work of Wittgenstein, I saw some of it directly. I was deeply grateful to Elizabeth for this

---

[104] That Anscombe had parts of two copies of Wittgenstein's book in November 1947 is attested to by Wittgenstein in a letter to G. E. Moore from that month (B. McGuinness, ed., *Wittgenstein in Cambridge*, sec. 374, p. 417). That she still had them in November 1948 is attested to in a letter to Norman Malcolm: 'I should like you to have a type-script of my stuff but I don't see how I can let you have one at present. There exist only 3 copies. One I have (& I need it), Miss Anscombe has one, Moore has half, or 3/4 of one & the remaining half or 1/4 is somewhere among my things in Cambridge.' Malcolm, *A Memoir*, 113.

[. . .] [These] sheets I took back to college, copied out and more or
less committed to memory before I sat my examinations.[105]

Similarly, in June 1948 Murdoch writes, 'I have been reading (via
Elizabeth Anscombe) part of Wittgenstein's new book (in German)
and it is like nothing on sea or land.'[106] Wittgenstein was lending
out (e.g. to G. E. Moore) his three typescript copies, and each of
them would include unique comments and corrections by him. For
Wittgenstein to entrust to Anscombe a typescript of his book for
extended periods means that Wittgenstein saw a unique importance to her having a copy.

Wittgenstein departed Cambridge on 18 November 1947. After
visits to Smythies in Oxford and Richards in London, he flew from
London to Dublin on 25 November. Staying with his friend Con
Drury for two weeks while he looked for a place to live and work,
he finally found Kilpatrick House, a farmhouse with rented rooms
outside of Wicklow, on the east coast of Ireland, about 60 kilometers
south of Dublin. In the late 1940s, it was a three-hour bus trip from
Dublin to Wicklow, so Drury and Wittgenstein met rarely during
his four months in Wicklow.

On 3 February 1948, Anscombe wrote to him, primarily to
tell him about the previous evening at the Socratic Club, where
Anscombe had critiqued a chapter from C. S. Lewis's recently
published book *Miracles.* The Socratic Club, founded in 1942
with Lewis as its president, has as its mission providing intellectual defenses of various aspects of the Christian faith. The motto
of the Socratic Club was 'follow the argument where it goes'. The

---

[105] Mary Warnock, *A Memoir: People and Places* (London: Duckworth, 2000), 62–
63, 67. The fact that Warnock writes of memorizing these passages prior to her final
examinations in May–June 1948 suggests that she first read them at the latest in the
spring of 1948.

[106] Iris Murdoch Journal #5, June 1948, KUAS 202/1/5, The Iris Murdoch Archive
at Kingston University. All quotations from Iris Murdoch's unpublished journals are by
permission of Kingston University.

Club typically had two speakers, one defending a Christian view on some topic, and the other speaker coming from an alternative, typically non-Christian perspective. Anscombe, despite Wittgenstein's disapproval, was a regular attender of the Socratic Club, and no doubt was known as a defender of a Christian perspective on any manner of topic. This being the case, it is odd that Anscombe was invited to critique something written by Lewis himself.

Anscombe's 'debate' with C. S. Lewis is no doubt the most written about intellectual exchange in which Anscombe was ever involved, and likely the most written about intellectual exchange for Lewis as well. Most discussions of their exchange appear in volumes on or about Lewis. These discussions often focus on the 'aftermath' of their exchange, how Lewis reacted to being 'defeated', and so on, with dubious claims being asserted about Lewis, for instance, how it led Lewis to cease writing works in Christian apologetics. Much of this material is ill-informed or ridiculous, written from the perspective of either his staunch defenders or those who wish to mock or ridicule him.[107]

There are a few points of note regarding Anscombe's engagement with Lewis. First, Lewis was an extremely good debater, and he rarely if ever lost debates in which he was engaged. There are many accounts written at the time by students attending the Socratic Club in the 1940s, who spoke of so looking forward to hearing Lewis because he more or less always won the debate. Lewis's exchange with Anscombe on 2 February 1948 was a rare occasion in which Lewis was bested, and ironically, bested by a fellow Christian. Second, in her letter to Wittgenstein, she acknowledges that her response to Lewis would likely have been as problematic as Lewis's own rhetoric and argument, but that fortunately she showed it to Yorick Smythies who had written 'shit' while reviewing a draft of her response, and forced her to rewrite a more

---

[107] For an authoritative discussion of the meeting, see James Stockton and Benjamin Lipscomb, 'The Anscombe-Lewis Debate: New Archival Sources Considered', *Journal of Inklings Studies* 11, no. 1 (2021): 35–57.

adequate response.[108] Third, the Socratic Club showed its intellectual integrity in publishing Anscombe's critique in the next issue of *The Socratic Digest*.[109] Fourth, Lewis was evidently grateful for Anscombe's philosophical abilities. Lewis wanted Anscombe back at the Socratic Club. In a June 1950 letter, Lewis was proposing a list of potential speakers for the following term: 'I should press hard for [Miss Anscombe]. . . . The lady is quite right to refute what she thinks bad theistic arguments, but does this not almost oblige her as a Christian to find good ones in their place: having obliterated me as an Apologist, ought she not to succeed me?'[110]

Wittgenstein returned from Ireland in the summer of 1948, and went to Oxford for the first two weeks of August to have conversations with Smythies and Anscombe. Since Anscombe was only a lodger at 27 St John Street, Wittgenstein stayed a short walk away at the Smythies' flat at 22 Banbury Road, Yorick and Polly having moved back to Oxford the previous summer. On 9 August the Smythies left on vacation, and Wittgenstein continued to have daily conversations with Anscombe for another week.[111]

Polly Smythies, who was never part of the philosophical conversations, jokes about Wittgenstein, Yorick, and Anscombe having 'seances' or confabulations in their living room on Banbury Road. She says they would sit in silence, until one of them had a thought. Polly was instructed by Yorick not to interrupt their meeting by enquiring whether tea or coffee was desired, but to bring tea or coffee as a gift.[112] In this, Yorick was following one of

[108] See Stockton and Lipscomb, *Anscombe-Lewis Debate*, 47–48. The full text of Anscombe's letter to Wittgenstein can be found there.

[109] G. E. M. Anscombe, 'A Reply to Mr. C.S. Lewis's Argument that "Naturalism" Is Self-Refuting', *Socratic Digest* 4, no. 2 (1948): 7–16.

[110] C. S. Lewis, *Collected Letters*, Vol. 3, ed. Walter Hooper (London: HarperCollins, 2006), 35.

[111] Wittgenstein letter to Richards, 9 August 1948. See Schmidt and Citron, eds., *Der Briefwechsel zwischen Ludwig Wittgensteins und Ben Richards 1946–1951*.

[112] Polly Smythies interview with Peter Conradi, 1998. File KUAS1-50-1, Peter Conradi archives, Kingston University.

Wittgenstein's favorite prescriptive anecdotes, one which he also told Anscombe (*Reminiscences* sec. 38) and Malcolm. Malcolm writes that 'the lady of the house had inquired of Wittgenstein whether he would like some tea, and whether he would also like this and that other thing. Her husband called to her from another room: "Do not ask; *give!*" Wittgenstein was most favourably impressed by this exclamation.'[113]

Anscombe notes that it was hard for people (including herself and Yorick) to be natural with Wittgenstein because of 'the bright light of close attention and hard thought which he was apt to scrutinize their sayings with' (*Reminiscences* sec. 190). Polly Smythies further explains this when she notes that Yorick warned her 'against laughing or quoting from a newspaper, in case Wittgenstein took it the wrong way', and that more generally that 'people were so scared of [Wittgenstein] that they would not say a *word* in his presence.'[114] Polly's experience of Wittgenstein was that he simply took no part in the everyday kinds of conversation that lubricate ordinary social interactions. Although certainly not universal, Polly's experience of Wittgenstein was not uncommon.

During the war, Wittgenstein had been separated from his family and friends in Vienna. Once it was over, Wittgenstein would make four trips to Vienna in the last years of his life to see his sisters and family friends. After the second of these trips, Wittgenstein came to Cambridge on 30 September 1948, planning to spend two weeks there to get manuscripts typed.[115] Wittgenstein initially stayed at 19 Fitzwilliam Street. At the time five-year-old Barbara was having a hard time learning maths, and was somewhat emotionally

---

[113] Malcolm, *A Memoir*, 53.
[114] Polly Smythies interview with Peter Conradi, 1998.
[115] Wittgenstein was having typed up the revised remarks that he worked on while living in Ireland in the late spring and summer of 1948. For an account of Wittgenstein having his manuscripts typed up in October of 1948 (which is TS 232 in Wittgenstein's nachlass), (TS 232) see Gina Deutsch Arnold, 'Recollections of Wittgenstein', in F. A. Flowers II and Ian Ground, eds., *Portraits of Wittgenstein*, Vol. II (London: Bloomsbury, 2016), 755–756.

exercised about it. Wittgenstein told Anscombe to let him deal with it, and in a very kindly way, explained the concepts in a way that Barbara was able to understand, and the difficulty was happily resolved.[116]

Wittgenstein, however, did not stay at the Fitzwilliam Street house for long. Finding their boarding house too noisy, he soon rented a room in a large house overlooking the River Cam for the rest of his stay.[117] Despite the new accommodations, Wittgenstein still saw a lot of Anscombe during those two weeks, and upon departing Cambridge he again left one of the three copies of the *Philosophical Investigations* in Anscombe's possession.[118]

The academic year 1948–1949 was particularly intense and stressful for Anscombe. A month before the term began, she had written Wittgenstein indicating her stress and feeling ill.[119] Anscombe certainly had a lot of possible reasons for feeling stressed during the eight-week Michaelmas term from mid-October to early December 1948. First, Anscombe gave her inaugural set of lectures in Oxford. Entitled 'Some Ground Problems in the Theory of Knowledge', they were Anscombe's attempt at 'philosophy for beginners', using Plato's *Theaetetus* as a way in to introduce fundamental philosophical questions.[120] Although Anscombe hated lecturing, and was

---

[116] John Geach interview with the author, 5 June 2023. See also Harry Lewis, ed., *Peter Geach*, 14.

[117] Wittgenstein writes Ben Richards on 3 October 1948: 'This afternoon I moved to the above address [49 Chesterton Road, Cambridge]. I wish I could have stayed with Miss Anscombe, but the house was by far too noisy. I couldn't have stood it, not even for a few more days.' In Schmidt and Citron, eds., *Der Briefwechsel zwischen Ludwig Wittgensteins und Ben Richards 1946–1951*.

[118] Letter to Malcolm, 6 November 1948. See Malcolm, *A Memoir*.

[119] Wittgenstein refers to Anscombe's letter to him in Wittgenstein's letter to Ben Richards, 20 September 1948. In Schmidt and Citron, eds., *Der Briefwechsel zwischen Ludwig Wittgensteins und Ben Richards 1946–1951*.

[120] In Anscombe's Report to the Mary Somerville Research Committee Year Three 1948–1949 she refers to this set of lectures as being 'on Plato's Theaetetus'. Somerville College Archives. Anscombe also reports that she 'read a certain amount of empirical psychology and of psycho-analytic writing', although she put this in the context of her philosophical work on the soul rather than in connection with any personal issues.

Fig 1.3 Anscombe and Geach with Barbara and John Richard are in the backyard of 19 Fitzwilliam St., Cambridge, circa 1949–1950. Peter Geach and the children lived in Cambridge up until the summer of 1951, with Anscombe commuting between Oxford and Cambridge. *Photo by John Berkman, who took a picture of the original photo with the permission of Rebecca Morgan, G. E. M. Anscombe's literary executor*

not a natural lecturer, she had a large crowd on her Tuesday and Thursday morning lectures, about 120 students.[121]

The previous spring, Anscombe discussed this plan in a letter to von Wright:

It is a very striking point about Wittgenstein's thought that he reverts to problems of Greek philosophy. . . . In Oxford no one takes the Greek philosophers seriously, as genuine philosophy, (though it is only a symptom of the fact that no one is concerned with philosophical problems except either to shew his cleverness in shelving them as soon as possible, or, if he is more old fashioned, as material for very academical scholastic kind of analyzing. But without a doubt you will remember this.) I am probably going to lecture here next [academic] year end I am thinking of offering a lecture on epistemological problems which will in fact occupy itself with Plato's *Theaetetus*, in the hope of getting people to read it, which they do not do.[122]

While Wittgenstein famously said that he never read a word of Aristotle, he was deeply impressed with Plato and read his dialogues widely and deeply.[123] In her first set of lectures, we see

---

[121] Letter from Clerk of Schools to the Senior Proctor, 14 October 1948. From the archives of the Senior Proctor at the Bodleian Library, Oxford. The following term Anscombe would deliver sixteen more lectures, entitled 'The Problem of False Belief'. Considering that these were Anscombe's first public academic lectures and that she gave thirty-two of them—twice what a University Lecturer was expected to deliver in an academic year—in a period of five months, the whole experience would no doubt have involved a considerable level of stress.

[122] Anscombe's letter to von Wright. From early to mid-May 1948.

[123] We know that Wittgenstein was highly familiar with the *Theaetetus* and had likely commended it to Anscombe prior to this letter that Anscombe writes to von Wright. For example, in the summer of 1944, shortly before he returned to teach at Cambridge, Wittgenstein sent Drury a copy of the *Theaetetus*, recommending that Drury read it, and writing in the accompanying letter that 'Plato in this dialogue is occupied with the same problems that I am writing about', which Hayes understands to have been questions about the nature of knowledge. John Hayes, 'Drury and Wittgenstein: Kindred Souls', in *The Selected Writings of Maurice O'Connor Drury: On Wittgenstein, Philosophy, Religion, and Psychiatry*, ed. Hayes (London: Bloomsbury, 2017), 27.

this influence of Wittgenstein on Anscombe, and the centrality of Plato in her intellectual interests.

Second, Anscombe was trying to write the final draft of 'The Reality of the Past', what would become her first published philosophy paper (*Reminiscences* sec. 202). A year earlier, once he returned to Cornell from his Oxford sabbatical, Norman Malcolm had recommended her for inclusion in a book of essays on linguistic analysis by its leading and up-and-coming practitioners. The editor Max Black had written requesting a contribution, and Anscombe had agreed. Now, a year later, it was not done, and Anscombe was under pressure to get it submitted. The pressure was no doubt further increased by Anscombe's fear of Wittgenstein's possible reaction to it, knowing that Wittgenstein almost always got upset over attempts by his students to draw on his work in writing academic papers. In her fear (and perhaps recalling what Wittgenstein had said about her dissertation) Anscombe chose not to show the essay to Wittgenstein prior to sending it off for publication (see *Reminiscences* sec. 202).

Third, Anscombe's former tutor Raymond Klibansky, who was close to Anscombe's friend Lotte Labowsky, tried to assist Anscombe and Geach financially by hiring them to translate Descartes for his book series of primary sources in philosophy.[124] It was due that autumn, and while Geach was the primary translator, this may have been another source of stress.

Fourth, Anscombe had for some time been desperately trying to give up smoking. Among other efforts, she had gone to a hypnotist and undergone self-hypnosis to try to effect a cure (*Reminiscences* sec. 200–201). This was by no means a small problem for Anscombe.

---

[124] See letter from Lotte Labowsky to Raymond Klibansky, 12 December 1948. Courtesy of the Klibansky Archives at University of Marburg, Germany. While Anscombe and Geach would deliver the translation to Klibansky in 1948, and Alexandre Koyré would write a long introduction in 1950, the book was published only in 1954 as *Descartes: Philosophical Writings. A Selection Translated and Edited by Elizabeth Anscombe and Peter Thomas Geach*, with Introduction by Alexandre Koyré (London: Nelson, 1954), 303.

Fig 1.4 Capstan full-strength unfiltered cigarettes were Anscombe's cigarette of choice in the 1940s. *Wikimedia Commons*

According to John Hayes, Anscombe was at the time smoking 60 Capstan Full-Strength a day.[125] Capstans were unfiltered cigarettes, and were advertised to factory women during World War II as a means of relaxing at the end of a working day. Their cigarettes were

---

[125] See Hayes, ed., *Writings of Maurice O'Connor Drury*, 408.

later found to have the highest nicotine content of any UK cigarette, more than three times what is legally permitted today. By comparison, one would now have to smoke about 200 cigarettes a day to have ingested the nicotine that Anscombe was ingesting at that time.[126]

Fifth, Anscombe was beginning to be troubled by reactions to some of her unconventional behaviour. I have already discussed her perceived brashness and rudeness. Her friend Lotte Labowsky perceived in her a penchant for the theatrical, and her student Mary Warnock perceived in Anscombe a desire to shock: 'she had a most peculiarly beautiful speaking voice: but she liked to illustrate her points in lectures and seminars by obscene or scatological examples, the contrast between the language and its instrument forcing one's attention, in a matter that, to me at least, was painful'.[127]

In her poverty and with her addiction to cigarettes, Anscombe was sometimes observed picking up cigarette stubs from the gutter.[128] In addition, in October 1949, Anscombe would be arrested 'for wandering about with her hair down at 5 am, and refusing to give her name!'[129] Taken to the police station, they pressed for her to give her name, and Anscombe refused, demanding first to know the charge. Eventually she was released. Anscombe's anti-authoritarian streak also emerged in October 1948 when she began lecturing.

After her first lecture, Anscombe was reported by the Clerk of Schools to the Senior Proctor for lecturing in trousers; she was required to wear a skirt.[130] The Clerk of Schools maintained that

---

[126] In 1973 the UK government found that Capstans had 3.39 mg of nicotine (the next highest brand had only 3.2 mg). Since 2004 UK cigarettes are capped at 1 mg of nicotine.

[127] See Baroness Mary Warnock, 'In Memoriam: Professor G. E. M. Anscombe, Honorary Fellow', *St. Hugh's College Chronicle*, no. 72 (2000–2001): 13.

[128] Peter Conradi, *Iris Murdoch: A Life* (New York: W. W. Norton, 2001), 263.

[129] Iris Murdoch Journal #7, 31 October 1949.

[130] On 14 October 1948, the Clerk of Schools wrote to the University Proctor, 'A newcomer to the Schools as lecturer (Lecture list states Miss G. E. M. Anscombe, University Calendar Mrs. Anscombe), lectured to an audience of about 120 persons to-day

his main concern was that if a Lecturer was allowed to wear trousers (and non-academic dress more generally), how could they enforce the academic dress code for female undergraduates? The Clerk further claimed that 'women who lecture at Schools are very much in favour of as much as is possible being done to ensure that women undergraduates comply with the regulations'.[131] While these regulations strike us today as odd, trousers would not become an acceptable part of a woman undergraduate's academic dress at Oxford until the 1970s.[132] That year Anscombe and the Clerk played a cat-and-mouse game, the Clerk not allowing Anscombe to enter the Schools if she was not wearing a skirt.[133] Two years later, Anscombe would be at it again, and this time when she was reported to the Senior Proctor, she wrote the following letter with her tongue firmly-in-cheek:

On Sunday [21 January] I tore loose a ligament in my right shoulder, and today I found that I could not manage to dress otherwise than as usual, which, with my right hand and arm totally immobilized, is itself a sufficiently difficult and painful business. I may add that my trousers are subfusc, and my gown ankle length; so I hope the indecency is not too great.[134]

Surely not wanting to initiate a discussion of the relative ease of a female don donning trousers versus a skirt, the Senior Proctor gave Anscombe permission to wear trousers until her arm had recovered.

wearing trousers and the gown of a Master of Arts.' Files of University Proctor, Bodleian Library, QD/1.

[131] 14 October 1948 letter from the Clerk of Schools to the Senior Proctor, Files of University Proctor, Bodleian Library, QD/1.
[132] See Mac Cumhaill and Wiseman, *Metaphysical Animals*, 217.
[133] Pauline Adams, *Somerville for Women* (Oxford: Oxford University Press, 1996), 318.
[134] 24 January 1951 Letter from Anscombe to Senior Proctor, Files of University Proctor, Bodleian Library, QD/1.

Fig 1.5 Anscombe and Geach on the front stoop of 19 Fitzwilliam St., Cambridge, circa 1949–1950. *Photo by John Berkman, who took a picture of the original photo with the permission of Rebecca Morgan, GEM Anscombe's literary executor*

The aspect of Anscombe's counter-cultural behaviour that seemed to generate the most attention was her unconventional attire. In the postwar period, Britain was a conformist culture, with fairly strict societal expectations on appropriate attire, as among other things, it revealed where one fit in Britain's highly class-conscious culture.[135] The expectations of that time are largely

---

[135] In 1970, having been elected Professor of Philosophy at Cambridge, Anscombe showed up at the University's employment office. Anscombe was greeted with the

unintelligible for contemporary readers. But in the late 1940s, when Oxford's women's colleges were still on the margins and on a sort of probation in relation to the rest of the university, there was a particularly strong expectation that members of the women's colleges would conform to the university's written and unwritten norms, especially when it came to the attire of their dons and students.

While Anscombe's wearing trousers was, depending on the context, in defiance of either written or unwritten norms of appropriate attire at the university, it was not just the trousers. Claims have been made that Anscombe did not pay attention to her appearance more generally. For example, in something written many, many years later, Mary Warnock claims that Anscombe 'dressed in shapeless black trousers and a nondescript baggy sweater . . . her hair was longish, greasy and of no particular colour, held back in some kind of "bun" behind her head'.[136]

Although Anscombe's wearing of trousers at Oxford in 1948 was considered highly unconventional, it bears noting that women wearing trousers had become common during the war, as part of the uniforms of many women. No less than the future HM Queen Elizabeth II wore trousers as part of her war uniform. While at the time Anscombe was accused of dressing in men's clothes, according to John Geach, Anscombe always wore trousers made specifically for women.[137] Her trousers of choice were made of thick brown cotton corduroy, and had no zipper, but were buttoned up on both sides. With huge numbers of women's trousers made and worn during the war, they would have been widely and cheaply available in military surplus and second-hand clothing stores, especially since postwar women were expected to go back to wearing skirts and dresses.

question 'Are you the new cleaning lady?' 'No, I am the new professor of philosophy.' Apparently, Anscombe was not bothered by the question.

---

[136] Warnock, *A Memoir*, 75.
[137] Details on the kind of trousers Anscombe liked to wear is from John Geach in conversation with the author, September 2023.

Fig 1.6 Princess Elizabeth in trousers during World War II. While women wearing trousers during the war was pervasive and accepted, afterward British women were expected to go back to wearing skirts.

While Anscombe was unconcerned with bucking university regulations with regard to her attire, she took a very different attitude when her wearing trousers was attacked as a breach of appropriate piety in her attendance at Mass. In February 1949 Anscombe received a very unpleasant letter from a woman who objected to her wearing trousers to early morning Mass at St. Aloysius Church. Anscombe showed this letter to Iris Murdoch, who wrote in her diary: 'Elizabeth more nervous & unhappy seeming than I've seen her for a long time.

She talked of seeing a psychiatrist.' In any event, Anscombe searched out the priest at St. Aloysius, 'who seemed the oldest & most sober & most severe'. Murdoch reports Anscombe as telling her that the priest 'had said there was no objection to her clothes'.[138]

One of her closest friends at Somerville, Lotte Labowsky,[139] wrote about her concerns for Anscombe in a letter to her friend (and Anscombe's former tutor) Raymond Klibansky:

> Elizabeth Anscombe has been in a highly emotional crisis for the greater part of this term and I have been her rather unwilling confidante. But there is nothing amusing about her crisis, and she really is a volcanic person—even when one deducts a certain exhibitionism the difficulties inherent in her character are real enough for her. She has now gone off to Ireland and I hope that Wittgenstein will restore a certain balance in her.[140]

During this period Anscombe not only was being formed by Wittgenstein, but was also deeply influencing others. In the summer of 1947, Iris Murdoch visited Cambridge to look for lodgings, as she was to embark on a graduate scholarship at Newnham. Murdoch and Anscombe had been near contemporaries at Oxford, both reading Greats. In writing of her visit with Anscombe, Murdoch quotes from Psalm 25, 'I will wash my hands among the innocent and will compass thy altar, O Lord.' She then writes:

---

[138] Iris Murdoch Journal #6, entries for 26 February and 1 March 1949. KUAS 202/1/6, The Iris Murdoch Archive at Kingston University. All quotations from Iris Murdoch's unpublished journals are by permission of Kingston University.

[139] Miss Carlotta (Lotte) Labowsky arrived at Somerville in 1939 as a refugee scholar, and Somerville, together with the S.P.S.L. (Society for the Protection of Science and Learning), made a grant to her. Labowsky was a guest of Somerville throughout the war, and from 1942 to 1946 served as Somerville's Acting Librarian. Once Labowsky received her naturalization papers in 1945, Somerville elected Labowsky to the Lady Carlisle Research Fellowship. (See Pauline Adams, *Somerville for Women*, 70.)

[140] Letter from Lotte Labowsky to Raymond Klibansky, 13 December 1948. Raymond Klibansky Archive, Deutsches Literatur Archiv, Marbach.

On conversation with Elizabeth. 'No second rate philosophy is any good.' 'One must start from scratch—& it takes a very long time to reach scratch.' 'To discuss [Søren Kierkegaard] like receiving a tender anxious glance from a friend & then discussing it with an art critic.' (Wittgenstein) The ruthless authenticity of Elizabeth makes me feel more and more ashamed of the vague self-indulgent way in which I have been philosophizing. I must make a tremendous effort if I am to get any sort of philosophical clarity or truth out of the sea of fascinating dramatic, psychological, moral & other ideas in which I've been immersed.[141]

This was the beginning of a renewal of a friendship between Murdoch and Anscombe which grew in intensity over the next sixteen months. Murdoch clearly admired Anscombe both as a philosopher and as a person of great integrity. That year, with Anscombe commuting between Cambridge and Oxford, Murdoch spent most her time at Trinity College in the company of Hijab and Shah, both of whom had been studying with Wittgenstein until he resigned his chair, with Anscombe joining in on conversations on weekends or outside of term.[142]

Iris Murdoch's diaries are an unparalleled source for understanding what Anscombe was discussing on a day-to-day basis during the late 1940s. While Murdoch's diaries are typically about her 'private' life, her diaries from 1948 to 1950 are filled with Murdoch's philosophical discussions with Anscombe. From the summer of 1947, when her mentor Donald MacKinnon left for Aberdeen, Anscombe (and soon Yorick Smythies) would gradually replace MacKinnon as Murdoch's intellectual guides and heroes.

---

[141] Iris Murdoch Journal #4 (p. 24) 25 July 1947. KUAS 202/1/4, The Iris Murdoch Archive at Kingston University. All quotations from Iris Murdoch's unpublished journals are by permission of Kingston University.
[142] According to Hijab in 2001, during the course of the year the focus of Murdoch's affections transferred from Hijab to Shah.

There are well over 150 references to Anscombe in Murdoch's diaries in those years.

There is no doubt that Anscombe and Murdoch had a strong and ongoing friendship in the late 1940s and early 1950s. Murdoch was one of only a few persons to whom we know that Anscombe showed her copy of Wittgenstein's book. The years of Anscombe's closest association with Murdoch more or less encompass the years in which Murdoch identified as a Christian, prayed extensively, saw a spiritual director, went on retreats to monasteries, and so on. Both during these years, and later looking back on these years, Murdoch thought of Anscombe and Smythies as something like philosophical saints, in that they followed Wittgenstein in engaging in philosophy with utter seriousness and commitment, with a passionate desire—not to be clever or win arguments—but to search for the truth regarding the philosophical question at hand.[143]

Anscombe indicates she went to visit Wittgenstein in December of 1948 because she was 'in a bad way'. Anscombe left Oxford for Dublin on Friday, 10 December, the day after her final lecture on Plato's *Theaetetus*. According to her friend Yorick Smythies, Anscombe did not sleep at all the night before she left. However, Anscombe did not arrive in Dublin until the following Tuesday. To Wittgenstein's chagrin, she checked in at Ross's Hotel in Parkgate Street, where Wittgenstein was staying.[144] Shortly after Anscombe arrived, Wittgenstein wrote:

> Until yesterday I was still working a lot & very intensely. I know of course that this period will be followed by one of exhaustion & depression; but I want to make hay while the sun shines, & that's what I'm doing now, or was until yesterday. For this morning

[143] For more on Anscombe's relationship with Murdoch, see Lipscomb, *The Women*, 121–124, and Mac Cumhaill and Wiseman, *Metaphysical Animals*, 219–223.

[144] Story told by Rush Rhees to Michael Nedo. From Michael Nedo in correspondence with the author.

Miss Anscombe arrived & in rather a bad frame of mind, & I spent the whole day with her, I had to. What this will do to my work I don't know & I can't say that it doesn't worry me, but she is in need, & it's fate. (Please don't talk to anyone else about this.) Drury is going to see her tonight & I hope he may give her some good advice.

While in Dublin, Wittgenstein took Anscombe on a tour of his regular day, going from Ross's Hotel which was in the centre of Dublin near the Liffey River, going north up to the Great Palm House at the Botanical Gardens. This is where Wittgenstein would typically spend the middle of his day, alternatively sitting and walking, but in either case sniffing 'the good smell of the soil and the things that were growing there' while doing his work (*Reminiscences* sec. 200). Then he would take her to his favorite restaurant, Bewley's Café, which was located south of the river and on Grafton Street, one of Dublin's main commercial streets. There Wittgenstein would always eat his eggs with coffee, regular enough that the waitress brought it without Wittgenstein needing to order it.[145] It was also at Bewley's that Anscombe shared her troubles, telling Wittgenstein and Drury about her failed efforts at self-hypnotism and her alarming dreams (*Reminiscences* sec. 201).

Wittgenstein also took Anscombe to his favourite place, the Dublin Zoo, which was close to his hotel, and where the incident with the crocodile occurred (*Reminiscences* sec. 200) which Anscombe would later memorialize in her book *Intention*. Along with a trip to the cinema, resuming smoking, some medication from Drury, and some good nights' sleeps, Anscombe was feeling much better. Before Anscombe left, Wittgenstein had an extended discussion with Anscombe about the work he was doing there, and instructed Anscombe on particular work that he wanted to see incorporated into his book, the material which would become Part II of the published

---

[145] *Reminiscences* sec. 200; Monk, *Duty of Genius*, 536.

version of the PI. Why Wittgenstein had that conversation with Anscombe at that time we don't know, but he would give the same instructions to Rush Rhees when he visited him the following week.

At the end of Anscombe's visit, Wittgenstein wrote:

> Yes, Miss Anscombe arrived here last Tuesday & she was in a bad state. She is leaving to-day & she is better now; not thanks to any thing that I could do for her, & Drury, too, could only give her some sleeping-capsules; but the change of mental atmosphere & sleep have done her good; though she is not back to normal yet. That her coming at this particular moment greatly upset my work & me I will not deny; but her health is more important than my work. (All this, of course, is between you & me.) I have, in spite of everything /been able to/ do some work every day, though without the peace & joy I felt before. Perhaps some of it will come back. If it doesn't, it doesn't.[146]

In the spring of 1949, in an unprecedented move, and a year before her first three-year term was up, Somerville College granted Anscombe a second three-year term as Mary Somerville Research scholar. Up to that time, no applicant had ever been granted a second three-year term.[147] Not long after that, Principal Janet Vaughan seems to have enquired of Gilbert Ryle, at that time arguably the most influential philosopher in Oxford,[148] for an evaluation of the

---

[146] See Wittgenstein's letters to Ben Richards on 14 and 20 December 1948, in Schmidt and Citron, eds., *Der Briefwechsel zwischen Ludwig Wittgensteins und Ben Richards 1946–1951.*

[147] In the Anscombe file of Somerville College's records, there is a short CV of Anscombe during her time at Somerville. This CV, written after 1970 and probably at around the time of Anscombe's death in 2000, states that 'The [Mary Somerville Research] fellowship is normally held for 3 years only; Elizabeth's renewal for a second term is unique.'

[148] 'When at the end of the war [Ryle and Austin] found themselves the leading figures in a university flooded with mature and eager students, they set about, fairly self-consciously, building up what became known as the "Oxford" or "ordinary language" or "linguistic" school. Ryle did much to help found this school. His book *The Concept of Mind* was its flagship, the journal *Mind*, which he edited, became its official organ,

philosophers at Somerville. Regarding Anscombe, Ryle responded that he did not know her well, and that she had no publications, so instead he would comment on what he had heard about her, namely, that whenever she took part in a philosophical exchange, wrote Ryle, those who were not there would want to know 'What line did Miss Anscombe take?' Ryle was convinced that Anscombe was going to be a force in philosophy in the future.[149]

No doubt the reappointment came as a relief to Anscombe, though it meant that she was going to have to continue dividing her time between Oxford and Cambridge. This was clearly going to be difficult for the family both in terms of Peter's duties with the children, now six and three, and in terms of Barbara and John Richard's missing their mother. John Geach recalls his mother's regular departures from home as being very upsetting for him and his sister, and his father comforting them. After their mother left, Barbara and John Richard would each sit crying on one of their father's knees, with Peter wrapping his tweed jacket around the two of them so that they could snuggle up together.[150] At the same time, Anscombe was growing increasingly frustrated with Peter's not getting more regular employment, which prevented the family from being together in Oxford. Like her children, Anscombe was having a very difficult time being away from her family in Michaelmas of 1949. This would be a very difficult time for Anscombe personally, but Anscombe seems to have rallied once Wittgenstein returned to England, especially once she found out about Wittgenstein's cancer.

---

and the Oxford B.Phil. in philosophy, which he established after the war, served as its principal training ground, educating a generation of young students in what Ryle liked to call "The Revolution in Philosophy". Indeed, at an institutional level, Ryle reigned supreme, exercising an unparalleled power over philosophy appointments in Oxford and beyond." Ben Rogers, A. J. Ayer: A Life (New York: Grove Press, 1999), 254–255.

[149] Ryle's 10 November 1948 letter to Janet Vaughan can be found in the staff file for Anscombe, Folio 10–11, Somerville College Archives.

[150] John Geach recalls those moments in great detail, for example that his father characteristically wore a tweed jacket, starched white shirt, and corduroy trousers.

1949–1950: Act 6: Anscombe Goes to Vienna

Although Anscombe dressed unconventionally and is claimed to have taken practically no interest in her appearance, this did not keep people from noticing Anscombe's attractiveness. Mary Warnock said that 'her face was of astonishing serenity and beauty despite her having a noticeable cast in one eye. She had the look of an angel in a depiction of the Nativity. One instantly wanted, even expected, her sympathy, her blessing, and her care, as a believer might hope for the favour of the Holy Virgin. And what was even more striking was the beauty of her voice.'[151] Peter Geach noted that he had fallen in love with Anscombe's voice before he ever set eyes on her. Even relatively late in Anscombe's life, Rosalind Hursthouse said that her voice made one want to curl up in her lap and be told stories in it forever.[152]

While Bouwsma reported in late 1950 that Anscombe was 'stocky', any insinuation that Anscombe was more than average size at the time is hard to fathom. In late 1940s England, with food being rationed, one could not easily obtain an abundance of food. At the time, national kitchens—kitchens set up to feed the population at low cost—were common, but one still needed money to get a meal. Anscombe's poverty meant she did not have enough money to buy adequate food, much less an abundance of it.[153] Furthermore, she was a chain-smoker, and cigarette advertising at the time emphasized smoking as a means of losing weight! Anscombe's cigarette addiction was costing her about £50 a year, money she could not afford (*Reminiscences* sec. 215). Finally, as can be seen from the sculpture and from pictures of Anscombe from the late 1940s and early 1950s, Anscombe's face is thinner and more angular than the more rounded pictures of her face from her undergraduate years.

---

[151]   Warnock, *A Memoir*, 75.

[152]   Lipscomb, *The Women*, 137.

[153]   In correspondence with the author, 27 August 2024, Mary Geach noted that only a Cambridge grocer's generous offering of credit over a significant period of time in the late 1940s enabled the family to keep food regularly on the table at 19 Fitzwilliam Street.

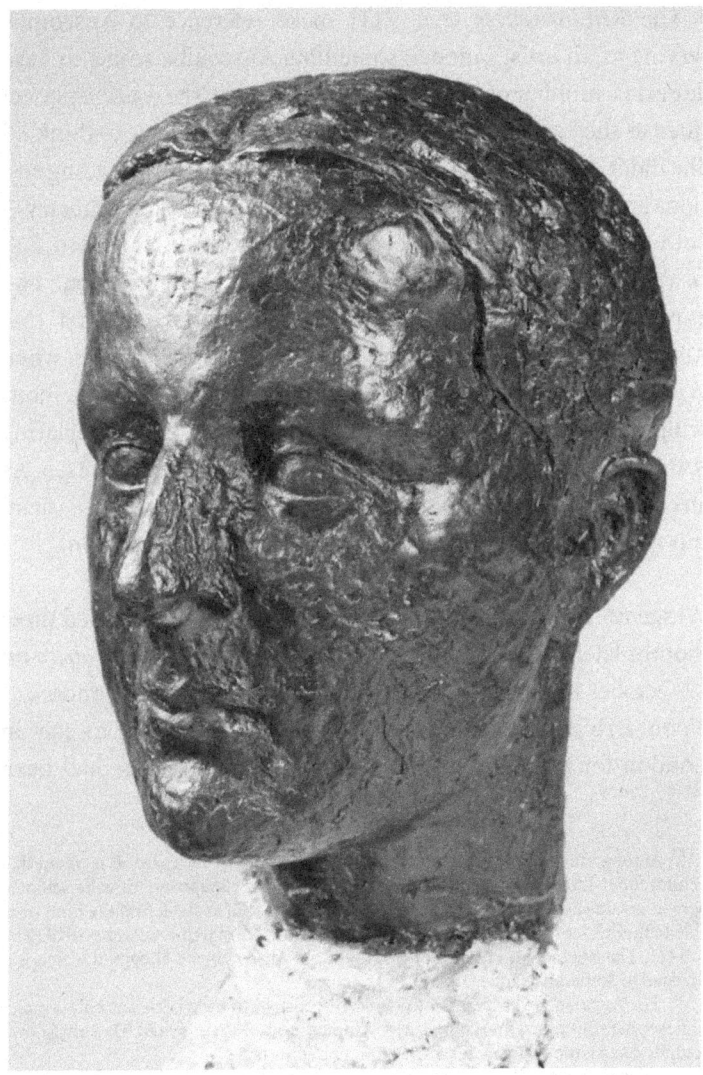

Fig 1.7 Anscombe's head sculpted by Sydney Sheppard in the late 1940s. *Image from Art UK, artuk.org*

The *Reminiscences* (sec. 211) make reference to Anscombe serving as an artist's model, something Anscombe seems to have done on a number of occasions. It was said that 'she was the perfect sitter, as she kept so still, as she found the time valuable to think'.[154] She did it often enough that Wittgenstein wound up attending sessions and debating with the sculptors about her facial symmetry—both a classical criterion of beauty and an empirically tested sign of attractiveness. Contra the sculptors, who thought no one had a perfectly symmetrical face, Wittgenstein demonstrated that Anscombe's face was indeed symmetrical.[155] Furthermore, when Wittgenstein took Anscombe to visit Michael Drobil,[156] a famous sculptor in Vienna, Wittgenstein showed her off to him, declaring Anscombe to have 'a beautiful head' (*Reminiscences* sec. 211). As any form of flattery would have been repugnant to Wittgenstein, this was no doubt Wittgenstein's and Drobil's honest opinion.

Wittgenstein had gone to America in July 1949 and returned three months later, arriving in Southampton on the *Queen Elizabeth* on 27 October 1949, with a 'boat-train' ferrying him up to London.[157] Upon arrival, Wittgenstein was seriously ill and had to stay in London for two weeks to recover. While in Ithaca he had been

---

[154] Among others, Anscombe sat for the sculptor Sydney Sheppard. It is noted that "Philosopher Elizabeth Anscombe used to sit for Sydney Sheppard while he sculpted her—it is said she was the perfect sitter as she kept so still, as she found the time valuable to think." See https://artuk.org/discover/artworks/elizabeth-anscombe-19192001-273425. The site includes photos of a sculpture of Anscombe by Sheppard which was donated to Somerville College, Oxford.

[155] The Austrian government considers Wittgenstein to have been not only a major philosopher, but also an accomplished sculptor, and has designated his only known sculpture as a national treasure which cannot be exported.

[156] Michael Drobil (1877–1958) was an eminent Austrian sculptor who often received commissions from the Wittgenstein family. Drobil represented Austria at the art competitions at the 1948 Olympics.

[157] Sometime shortly after his return from America, Anscombe met Wittgenstein at a train station. Gilbert Ryle's *The Concept of Mind* had recently been published, and Anscombe was reading it. However, when she met Wittgenstein at the train station, Anscombe felt obliged to conceal Ryle's book under a wrapper. But when Wittgenstein discovered what Anscombe was reading, he snorted with disapproval. Anthony Kenny, 'Elizabeth Anscombe at Oxford' (2015). Manuscript copy shared with me by the author.

diagnosed as hypo-thyroid. Despite taking thyroid (and liver and iron) extract, he remained anaemic, and was very weak and depressed. Although Wittgenstein wrote to Malcolm that upon arrival he was suffering from the flu, there were clearly larger medical issues at play. When Anscombe went to see him she 'had the greatest impression of hopeless misery and suffering he ever gave me' (*Reminiscences* sec. 230). But Wittgenstein's precarious health would not have been a surprise to Anscombe, for while he was in America, Anscombe was socializing with Ben Richards, who was getting regular reports on his health.

The previous spring, having been reappointed as a research fellow, Anscombe had enquired about the possibility of a travel bursary to learn German in Vienna. In her initial proposal Anscombe had indicated she didn't want to simply learn philosophical German—she was not interested in reading Kant or Hegel—but wanted to 'to read authors with a very wide vocabulary of abstract terms'. In June 1949 Somerville's classics professor Mildred Hartley testified to Anscombe's commitment to learning such a German, their having read Goethe together for two terms. Hartley also noted that 'having often discussed passages of Plato with her, I know what a good linguist she now is'.[158] Thus, Hartley strongly sympathized with Anscombe's desire to learn Germany in Vienna and hoped the committee would support her plan.

However, it was only after Anscombe's visit with Wittgenstein once he returned from America in late October 1949 that formal plans for Anscombe to go to Vienna were initiated. After seeing Wittgenstein, Anscombe made a formal request about a travel grant, and within two weeks Somerville granted Anscombe a £25 travel bursary 'to meet other philosophers and to learn German'.[159]

---

[158] 22 June 1949 letter from Mildred Hartley to Principal Janet Vaughan. Mary Somerville Fellowship Committee File, Somerville College Archives. Courtesy of the Fellows of Somerville College.

[159] Meeting of the Mary Somerville Research Fellowship Committee, 21 November 1949. Somerville College Archives. Courtesy of the Fellows of Somerville College.

After two weeks in London, Wittgenstein was sufficiently recovered to travel up to Cambridge in early November where he stayed at Straithard, the home of the von Wrights.[160] Upon arrival Wittgenstein was bed-bound. Dr. Edward Bevan paid a house-call and instructed him to stay in bed.[161] On 26 November 1949, Bevan gave Wittgenstein the diagnosis of prostate cancer, and confirmed it a day or two later.

As soon as Anscombe learned of Wittgenstein's diagnosis—along with the prognosis for Wittgenstein of six months to two years— she and Smythies travelled from Oxford to visit Wittgenstein.[162] While visiting Wittgenstein, despite the plan for her to go to Vienna, Anscombe tried to persuade Wittgenstein to come to Oxford and live with her or with Yorick Smythies. Upon returning to Oxford at the beginning of December, Anscombe told Murdoch 'if [Wittgenstein] dies like this he'll go to hell'.[163]

Meanwhile, Wittgenstein himself decided to go to Vienna. He wrote his sister Helene:

> I am turning over the idea of coming to Vienna some time in the
> near future. My health is fairly bad, and I am, for that reason,

[160] Malcolm, *A Memoir*, 122.

[161] Dr. Edward Bevan had been recommended to Wittgenstein by Drury. Drury had gotten to know Bevan while serving together in the Royal Medical Corps. Bevan was also the physician of most dons at Trinity College. Bevan indicates that this was the first time he met Wittgenstein. Bevan would remain Wittgenstein's physician for the final eighteen months of Wittgenstein's life (30 August 1966 letter from E. V. Bevan to Sr. Mary Elwyn McHale, held at the Cornell University Archives).

[162] In late November '[Barry] went with Yorick to stay with Elisabeth [at the Fitzwilliam Street house in Cambridge].... Yorick thought [Wittgenstein] dying.... Barry went because Yorick felt if Wittgenstein died there would be a terrible hole left, a vortex where he gone down, as if all the saints and devils would be gathered round [Wittgenstein's] bedside. Yorick in doubt whether to go to Cambridge, was frightened of going. B[arry] offered to go with him and, if necessary, see Wittgenstein.... B[arry] did not meet him [Wittgenstein]. Yorick went to see [Wittgenstein]. [Yorick] said he felt he must ask Wittgenstein to come to Oxford but didn't know what Polly would think. [Anscombe] was there and Yorick and Barry stayed with her at Fitzwilliam Street.' (From the papers of Frank Goodridge, quoted with the permission of Elizabeth Goodridge.)

[163] Murdoch Diaries, 7 December 1949. Courtesy of Iris Murdoch Archives at Kingston University.

unable to work. I'm hoping for some peace and quiet in Vienna
... I would probably have to lie down for part of the day.... Please
write or cable me whether my plan is possible ... assuming that
I obtain permission to enter from the authorities in London....
p.s. I can't travel just yet, but maybe in a few weeks.[164]

Whether Wittgenstein made arrangements for Anscombe in
Vienna prior to making his own we do not know. But the balance of
probability is that Wittgenstein only made concrete arrangements
for Anscombe's stay in Vienna either in December shortly before he left for Vienna, or after he arrived in Vienna, but before
Anscombe arrived on or shortly after 20 January.[165] The plan
was for Anscombe to spend five months in Vienna learning the
nuances of Wittgenstein's Austrian German, and learning of the
Viennese culture in which Wittgenstein's German was at home.
Once Wittgenstein and Anscombe agreed on the plan for her to go
to Vienna, Wittgenstein tried to get Anscombe to promise that she
would lie to Wittgenstein's friends and family in Austria if asked
about Wittgenstein's health (*Reminiscences* sec. 214).[166]

Anscombe departed for Vienna on 15 January, arriving some five or
six days later. Anscombe likely opted for the least expensive option,
even if it took longer. The £25 was a very small grant. The committee had earlier contemplated as much as a £100 travel grant.

---

[164] Ludwig Wittgenstein to Helene Wittgenstein, 28 November 1949. See Brian
McGuinness, ed., *Wittgenstein's Family Letters: Corresponding with Ludwig*, trans.
P. Winslow (London: Bloomsbury Academic, 2019).

[165] Wittgenstein's letter to Ben Richards on 19 January 1950 does not mention
Anscombe's arrival, but his letter on 24 January says that she had arrived and is getting
on well.

[166] Anscombe was not the only friend whom Wittgenstein tried to swear to secrecy.
On 11 December Wittgenstein writes Malcolm, 'My dear Norman, I want to ask a great
favour. It is simply that you do not under any circumstances let any one know about the
nature of my illness who doesn't already know about it. The same goes double for Lee.
This is of the greatest importance for me as I plan to go to Vienna for Christmas & not to
let my family know about the real disease.' Malcolm, *A Memoir*, 124.

In Vienna Anscombe got to know a lot about Wittgenstein, not only from Wittgenstein himself, but from conversations with his siblings and other family members, and from family friends such as the Hänsels and the Koders. Thus many of Anscombe's reminiscences about Wittgenstein come from her time in Vienna.[167]

Wittgenstein arranged for Anscombe to stay with the Hänsels, whom Wittgenstein liked very much and with whom he had spent Christmas Eve of 1949, right after arriving in Vienna. As Anscombe notes, if not for the fact that his oldest sister Hermine was dying, he would have had Anscombe stay in the Wittgenstein family's palatial home which was on the Alleegasse (now known as the Argentinierstrasse).

For the two months in which Anscombe and Wittgenstein were both in Vienna, Anscombe was meeting with Wittgenstein for discussions two or three times a week, and they socialized on numerous other occasions. This, however, still left Anscombe lots of time for her own work. In her proposal and report to her fellowship oversight committee, Anscombe said her goals for the year, which included her time in Vienna, were threefold—to improve her German, to meet Austrian philosophers, and to work specifically on two things: first, critically analysing passages from Plato's dialogues, especially his *Theaetetus*, to help her better understand Plato's account of knowledge, from which she hoped to deduce Plato's account of the nature of the soul; and second, to harness the significance of Wittgenstein's views on the 'openness and fluidity' of certain concepts, again with a focus on better understanding the concept of the 'soul'.[168]

While it was a clear goal of Anscombe in going to Vienna to improve her German, what is striking is that in *neither* her proposal

---

[167] During her time in Vienna, Anscombe become good friends with the Hänsels and the Koders, and corresponded with them over the next years. During the summer of 1951, when the family was moving from Cambridge to Oxford, Barbara was sent to Vienna to spend the summer with the Hänsels. (Conversation with John Geach, 2023.)

[168] From Anscombe's May 1950 report to the Mary Somerville Research Fellowship Committee, courtesy of the Somerville College Archives.

nor in her report does Anscombe say that she wants to improve her German *in order to translate Wittgenstein's work.* For example, in her report to the committee at the end of her time in Vienna she writes rather vaguely that her 'knowledge of German has enormously improved. . . . I shall be able to read and translate what I need for the future, so that the main aim of my visit will have been realized'.[169]

While numerous commentators writing after that fact about Anscombe's time in Vienna have claimed or assumed that she was learning German in Vienna to translate Wittgenstein's book, Anscombe herself never explicitly says that. And if not, why not? After all, Wittgenstein was a foremost philosopher, and Somerville was clearly very proud of Anscombe's association with Wittgenstein.[170] So if Anscombe's goal was to translate Wittgenstein's published work, why did she not say so? At that point, it seems likely that Anscombe had not formally spoken with Wittgenstein about translating his book for publication, and she avoided doing so, fearing Wittgenstein's possible reaction. It would only be in July 1950 that Anscombe would first put in writing her plan to translate Wittgenstein's book for publication.[171] But we have no *direct* evidence that Anscombe ever *explicitly* discussed her plan to translate the *Philosophical Investigations* for publication with Wittgenstein prior to his death.

Interestingly, on 11 January 1951, when Chadbourne Gilpatric of the Rockefeller Foundation visited with Anscombe and Wittgenstein in his room at 27 St John Street, Gilpatric described

---

[169] Anscombe's May 1950 report to the Mary Somerville Research Fellowship Committee, courtesy of the Somerville College Archives.

[170] 'It gave [Principal Janet Vaughan] immense pleasure to know that Wittgenstein was a frequent visitor to tea in the senior common room, the guest of Elizabeth Anscombe.' See Adams, *Somerville for Women*, 269.

[171] In her application for a University Lectureship on 15 July 1950, which would double her income, Anscombe was required to make a statement of her proposed research. At the end of her statement she notes, 'I should also like to make a translation of a book by Dr. L. Wittgenstein in German, to be published when that book is published.' (See Archives at Bodleian Library, Oxford, FA 9/2/21.)

him, and asked Wittgenstein about plans for publishing. Gilpatric writes in his formal diary:

In appearance and manner of expression, he makes a powerful impression. His face has an ascetic leanness, and his skin is remarkably fair with a kind of beauty most men would envy. His eyes dominate and control your attention. He speaks with great simplicity and compelling earnestness. At once you sense his intellectual power and moral force. He went on to describe how his thinking powers had failed and how for months he had felt no spark, no quick, fresh flow of ideas. He would say nothing about recent lines of thought because, as he said, he was bitterly dissatisfied with many attempts at formulation in the last two years. In response to a direct question about likelihood of finishing his work in book form—in progress for twenty years—he said that he was no longer able to work and expected he never could again.

Asked if he would publish any part of his writings, Wittgenstein said that he had a large number of manuscripts which showed the traces of constant refinement in expression. In many cases he has tried to express the same point in several different ways. Now he does not feel competent to choose which among alternatives is the better formulation. Therefore he will not edit or release anything he has written until he feels himself intellectually fit. If this happens, he will notify Chadbourne Gilpatric; if it does not, Elisabeth Anscombe will be his philosophical executor.[172]

While Wittgenstein may have had earlier discussions with Anscombe about making decisions as to which of his work should be published, could this be the first time Anscombe was being

---

[172] Chadbourne Gilpatric's diaries are located in the archives of the Rockefeller Foundation, Record Group 12, Officer's Diaries—Chadbourne Gilpatric. Thanks to Bethany Antos for making this material available to me.

told—indirectly—that she would be entrusted with the decisions about publishing Wittgenstein's work? And in what form? And with or without a translation? If so, despite her sadness with regard to Wittgenstein's failing powers, it must have been a comfort to Anscombe to learn that her efforts to learn German would not be limited to translating his work for her own understanding, but also to make his work publicly available in English.

The one thing we know about Anscombe was that she was always looking for opportunities for philosophical conversations. One reason Anscombe gave for going to Vienna was to become familiar with the work of Victor Kraft, and upon arriving in Vienna Anscombe began to attend meetings of the 'Kraft Circle'. At one of the first meetings she attended, Paul Feyerabend, one of the student leaders of the Kraft Circle, spoke on Descartes. 'I noticed an interesting looking lady in the first row and I asked afterwards who she had been. I was told she was a Miss Anscombe who stayed in Vienna to learn German so that she could translate Wittgenstein's work.'[173]

Knowing that Anscombe was familiar with Wittgenstein's later work, Feyerabend invited her to address the Kraft Circle. Anscombe's presentation did not go well, as the members thought her explanation of Wittgenstein reduced him to a 'particularly uninspiring kind of child psychology'. Disappointed with her efforts, Anscombe suggested to Feyerabend that he invite Wittgenstein. Feyerabend initially went round to Wittgenstein's residence to invite Wittgenstein, but being turned away, asked Anscombe for assistance in getting Wittgenstein to come.

---

[173] In his account Feyerabend continues, 'I rang her up and asked her for a meeting. I had read the Tractatus but I had no idea of Wittgenstein's later work. She explained it to me in discussions which sometimes lasted six to eight hours in a row'. See Matteo Collodel and Eric Oberheim, eds., *Feyerabend's Formative Years*, Vol. 1: *Feyerabend and Popper Correspondence and Unpublished Papers* (Cham, Switzerland: Springer, 2020), 28.

Elizabeth, who seemed to be familiar with Wittgenstein's peculiarities, suggested that I write a letter—'but don't make it too subservient.' I wrote roughly as follows: 'We are a group of students, we are discussing basic statements, and we are stuck; we hear you are in town—perhaps you can help us.' Wittgenstein seemed to like what I had written. 'I've received a rather nice letter', he said, again according to Elizabeth, emphasizing the 'rather', and was thinking of coming. Now the science students balked. 'Who is this guy?' they asked, 'and why should we listen to him? Anscombe was bad enough!' I calmed them down and reserved a room.

On the day of the meeting ... the hour arrived. Kraft was there, the philosophers were there—but no Wittgenstein. Afterward, Elizabeth told me how difficult it had been for Wittgenstein to negotiate this particular event. Should he come at the correct time, sit down, and just listen? Should he come a little late and enter with a flourish? Should he come very late, simply walk in, and sit down as if nothing had happened? Should he come very late and make a joke? ...

Wittgenstein was over an hour late. 'His face looks like a dried apple', I thought, and continued talking. Wittgenstein sat down, listened for a few minutes, and then interrupted: 'Halt, so geht das nicht!' ('Stop, that's not the way it is!'). He discussed in detail what one sees when looking through a microscope—these are the matters that count, he seemed to say, not abstract considerations about the relation of 'basic statements' to 'theories'.... There were interruptions, impudent questions. Wittgenstein was not disturbed. He obviously preferred our disrespectful attitude to the fawning admiration he encountered elsewhere. ... Wittgenstein, I heard, had enjoyed himself.[174]

---

[174] Paul Feyerabend, *Killing Time: The Autobiography of Paul Feyerabend* (Chicago: University of Chicago Press, 1995), 76–77.

Anscombe had conversations with Feyerabend throughout her time in Vienna, which 'occasionally proceeded from morning over lunch until late into the evening'.[175] Feyerabend notes that many of their discussions were discussions about Wittgenstein's book.

Her time in Vienna, perhaps surprisingly knowing her character, was not only about work. As a guest of sorts of the fabulously wealthy and connected Wittgenstein family, Anscombe soon was offered a variety of recreational activities, and was thought to have gone riding with certain members of the Viennese gentry.[176] In addition, she took time for sightseeing and travel. After four and a half months in Vienna, Anscombe started her journey home at the end of May. In her report, Anscombe had noted that with the exchange rate, her travel grant had gone much further than she had expected. So Anscombe took a sightseeing tour of northern Italy, focusing on the magnificent churches of the region. After travelling to Salzburg with Mrs. Koder, Anscombe continued on her own, spending nights in Venice, Verona, Milan, and Susa. A highlight of her trip, Anscombe relates, was falling off a Vaporetto (a water-taxi) into Venice's Grand Canal. Anscombe took an overnight train to Paris, spent a couple of days there, and then headed home to Cambridge to be reunited with Peter and the children, arriving around 8 June. A week later, Anscombe travelled to Oxford to see Wittgenstein.[177]

When Anscombe first returned to 27 St John Street on 16 June 1950, Wittgenstein had already been living there for close to two months. For while Anscombe stayed in Vienna until the end of May, Wittgenstein had returned to England in late March. After a month in London and at the von Wrights in Cambridge—where with his extreme sensitivity to noise Wittgenstein found the

---

[175] Paul Feyerabend, *Science in a Free Society* (London: Verso, 1982), 114.
[176] Roger Teichmann, correspondence with the author.
[177] Letter of Anscombe to Hermann Hänsel, 13 June 1950. With permission of Thomas Kott of Kott Autographs.

situation unbearable—arrangements were made for Wittgenstein to move to Anscombe's house in Oxford.[178] Key to Wittgenstein's choice to move to Oxford was to be close to and to be able to have conversations with two of his most devoted friends, Smythies and (upon her return) Anscombe.

When Wittgenstein arrived at the house at the end of April 1950, his new housemates included Peter Daniel, Frank Goodridge, and Barry Pink. All three were converts (or would shortly convert) to Catholicism, and were friends and devotees of Yorick Smythies (and to some extent Anscombe). Their devotion to Smythies mirrored the friendship and devotion of Anscombe and Smythies to Wittgenstein. Daniel and Goodridge had already been living at the house for more than two years. They had moved in while still undergraduates, but both had graduated the previous year. Having both fought in the war, Daniel and Goodridge were in their mid-twenties. Peter Daniel, the younger brother of Anscombe's friends Norman and Ruth Daniel, had like his older brother converted to Catholicism as a teenager.[179] Frank Goodridge had come up to Oxford as a Methodist to read English with C. S. Lewis,[180] but shortly after moving into the house came under Smythies' influence and was baptized a Catholic on 4 July 1950, with Smythies and Anscombe as his sponsors.[181] In the summer of 1949 Goodridge

---

[178] Wittgenstein flew from Vienna to London on 23 March 1950 and went up to Cambridge to stay with the von Wright family on 4 April 1950. Wittgenstein wrote to Anscombe to enquire about her earlier offer of accommodation, and Anscombe made the arrangements with her temporary house manager Frank Goodridge. Wittgenstein duly moved to Oxford on 24 or 25 April 1950.

[179] Anscombe and Norman Daniel privately published the pamphlet 'The Justice of the Present War Examined' in the spring of 1940. For details on this and Anscombe as an undergraduate, see John Berkman, 'The Influence of Victor White and the Blackfriars Dominicans on a Young Elizabeth Anscombe', *New Blackfriars*, September 2021, 706–722.

[180] Goodridge was secretary of the Socratic Club when Anscombe presented her critique of Lewis.

[181] Goodridge was clearly fascinated and absorbed into the philosophic community at Anscombe's house, where Smythies and Iris Murdoch were regular visitors. The year after he graduated (1949–1950), Goodridge would later confess that he spent most of the next year reading and discussing Dostoevsky with the 27 St John Street crowd

married Gillian Upton, who duly moved into the house. Barry Pink had moved in more recently, only four months prior to Wittgenstein. Pink was in his late twenties, and had come to Oxford to complete his National Diploma in Design at Ruskin College, which he had begun more than a decade earlier but had never completed.[182] A close friend of Yorick Smythies since he was a teenager, Pink learned of 27 St John Street while initially staying with the Smythies upon his arrival in Oxford, and moved in at the end of 1949. Pink did not move in on his own, but brought with him his six-year-old son Yorick Pink.[183]

Shortly after Wittgenstein moved in, he wrote friends that he found the lodgers nice, and one of them particularly nice. Wittgenstein is likely referring to Peter Daniel, the kind of kindhearted individual to whom Wittgenstein naturally gravitated. Daniel was generally characterized as extremely lovable by all those who knew him, both at that time and in his later years.[184]

The house at 27 St John Street was three stories, with a front and rear room on each floor. The house had a galley kitchen protruding into the garden from the rear room on the ground floor.

(Goodridge Archives). In the summer of 1949 Goodridge married Gillian Upton. The Goodridges occupied the two rooms on the ground floor. Anscombe was occupying the rooms on the first floor, and Peter Daniel had the room at the front of the second floor. Frank and Gillian would continue to live at 27 St John Street through the summer of 1951, when both Gillian and Elizabeth had new babies, with Gillian sometimes babysitting baby Mary Geach.

[182] Pink had begun the course of studies in 1935 (when he was fifteen) at the Chelmsford College of Art, but only did one year of full-time studies there. (Pink unpublished Autobiography, 55, 69, courtesy of Simon Pink.)

[183] When Pink arrived in Oxford, he was twenty-nine years old and married to Joyce 'Joy' Chandler, and they had three young children. However, Barry and Joy's marriage had just broken up, so Pink came to Oxford with his oldest child Yorick, who was then six, while the younger children remained with Joy.

[184] Frank Goodridge's son adds: 'Peter Daniel had a great sense of humour and great generosity of spirit. He was the one out of dad's circle whom we, as children, adored. My brother Pete was named after him and I believe he was Pete's godfather. He had lots of time for us too, a natural with children. We were more suspicious of Barry, and people like Yorick just seemed peculiar.' (John Goodridge email correspondence with the author 18 July 2024.)

Fig 1.8 27 St John Street, Oxford, Anscombe's residence in Oxford from 1946 to 1970.

The basement consisted of a shed for coal and storage of some foodstuffs. The front door opened on the right side of the house, and there was a narrow hallway on the right side of the ground floor halfway back, where one accessed the two ground floor rooms, a hallway to the garden, and the stairs. The second floor rear had a small bedroom and a large bathroom.

When Wittgenstein arrived, Frank and Gillian Goodridge occupied both rooms on the ground floor, Peter Daniel occupied the front room on the first, and Barry and Yorick Pink occupied the small rear room on the second. Wittgenstein was given the rear room on the first floor, the largest room in the house. Initially Wittgenstein was living below Barry and Yorick Pink, above Frank and Gillian Goodridge, and across from Peter Daniel.

Although married less than a year, Frank and Gillian Goodridge were already experiencing marital troubles. As Wittgenstein put it to Anscombe, 'she bickers soprano' (*Reminiscences* sec. 224). So shortly after moving in, Wittgenstein offered to change rooms with Barry and Yorick Pink. According to Yorick Pink, Wittgenstein thought that Barry and Yorick should have his (larger) room, since there were two of them. Wittgenstein gave a somewhat different account to Rhees: 'My room isn't very quiet & I'm going into another room in the same house where it's supposed to be more quiet.'[185] So Barry and Yorick happily changed rooms with Wittgenstein, thus moving from the smallest to the largest room in the house. For the next nine months, Wittgenstein lived in the small rear room on the second floor. When Anscombe returned, she moved into the front room on the second floor across from Wittgenstein, from where she attended to him.

Daniel characterized Wittgenstein's living space as follows: he 'lived there very simply with all inessentials pared away, in a small room, at his own wish very sparsely furnished, in which he sat in a deck chair; he ate his lunch off a copy of the *New Statesman* in lieu of a plate.'[186] Shortly before Wittgenstein moved to Cambridge, his

---

[185] Letter from Wittgenstein to Rhees, 7 May 1950, in B. McGuiness ed., *Wittgenstein in Cambridge*, sec. 424, p. 464.
[186] Peter Daniel, 'Afternoons with Wittgenstein', *Edinburgh Review* 89 (Spring 1993): p. 52.

room would be characterized similarly: 'his small room [was] furnished only with a bed, a table, a chair, and a small bookcase'.[187]

Once Wittgenstein was settled, in the evenings he would go over to the Smythies' house for conversations with Yorick. Once a week Wittgenstein would go for a walk along the canal, taking along his laundry to drop off with a woman who did his washing. For this walk, Peter Daniel explains, Wittgenstein would select one of his housemates to come along.[188] Goodridge concurs that conversations with Wittgenstein were almost always on walks with him. Goodridge tells the story of their being on a walk one time and hearing something coming from the Radcliffe Camera, they both pressed an ear against the doors, and listened to the choir inside.[189]

Conversations on walks with Wittgenstein were serious, but not like the walks that Anscombe, Malcolm, or Geach would take with him, since Wittgenstein recognized that he was not going for a walk with a philosopher. Nevertheless, the walks could be intense, especially with Frank Goodridge, who, being heavily under the influence of Yorick Smythies, was particularly eager to engage in philosophical conversation with Wittgenstein. But Wittgenstein clearly saw Goodridge's gifts as being in literature, and largely refused to engage in philosophical conversations with him. 'You should not try to think the same thoughts that Smythies thinks', Wittgenstein would tell him.[190] This would have been the kind of occasion when Wittgenstein might have used the French proverb to which Anscombe refers—'one cannot fart higher than one's behind.' This, however, did not put Goodridge off from wanting to engage in philosophical conversations. Goodridge indicated he spent an entire year while living at the house reading only

[187] Chadbourne Gilpatric's report for the Rockefeller Foundation. See Stephen Leach, 'Chadbourne Gilpatric and Ludwig Wittgenstein: A Fateful Meeting', *Nordic Wittgenstein Review* 9 (2020): 10.

[188] Daniel, 'Afternoons with Wittgenstein', 52.

[189] 'Frank Goodridge's Memories of Wittgenstein' at https://johngoodridgesite. wordpress.com/2018/05/26/frank-goodridges-memories-of-wittgenstein/.

[190] From the Frank Goodridge papers. Used with permission of Elizabeth Goodridge.

Dostoevsky, especially *Notes from Underground*, which Smythies was recommending to all of his friends.[191]

In the two months before Anscombe returned, Wittgenstein was often ill. Although he was fiercely independent, when he was too ill Polly Smythies would come by to see him and do his shopping for him.[192] Furthermore, in his illness it was more difficult for him to attend to his personal appearance. Yorick Pink recalls the first time he saw Wittgenstein in the house. He was so scruffy that Yorick took him for the gardener. In speaking to his father, Yorick referred to him as such and he recalls his father saying: 'That's not the gardener, that's Wittgenstein', with both of them laughing after that.[193]

As Anscombe indicates, Wittgenstein was capable of veering sharply from being intensely serious to revelling in 'low' culture, for example, going to whatever movie was showing—Wittgenstein's favourites were American movies featuring Betty Hutton or Carmen Miranda—and reading pulp detective stories for his light reading. Wittgenstein was able to engage in light conversation with Peter Daniel, whose kind heart endeared him to Wittgenstein. Daniel recalls a time when Wittgenstein told him that when he made a change from reading detective stories to reading Westerns, Yorick Smythies had told Wittgenstein that he had gone to a new 'low'. In response, Wittgenstein said that Yorick's (and Barry Pink's) predilection for reading 'Amazing Science Fiction' was 'really low'.[194]

When Wittgenstein moved into the house, Daniel, Goodridge, and Pink were suddenly confronted with their master's master, so to speak, and they were variously shocked and amused to find Smythies (and later Anscombe) behaving so differently than they

---

[191] Including Bouwsma, who discussed *Notes from Underground* with Wittgenstein. See Bouwsma, *Wittgenstein: Conversations*, 69.

[192] Polly Smythies interview with Peter Conradi, 1998. Courtesy of Peter Conradi archives, Kingston University.

[193] Yorick Pink, correspondence with the author, September 2023.

[194] Daniel, 'Afternoons with Wittgenstein', 52.

were used to when Smythies and Anscombe were in the presence of Wittgenstein. While as Anscombe indicates, this was to be expected, since Wittgenstein was so 'prickly', at some later point Goodridge took umbrage to this, and thought that it revealed a failing of Smythies and Anscombe, a lack of authenticity on their part.

There is little doubt that for a period Smythies was having too much influence over Goodridge. An example of this is that while Goodridge was engaged in 1948–1949, Smythies had tried to get Goodridge to reject a 'traditional' wedding. The extent to which each was at fault in terms of the dynamics of their relationship cannot be entirely sorted out. But Goodridge was clearly enchanted with Smythies, and while he was under the spell, it prevented Goodridge from imagining an alternative future for himself, one that he would eventually have to face. When the spell was finally broken, it clearly took some time for Goodridge to put his life back in order. Eventually, Goodridge came to see the influence of Smythies (and to a lesser degree Anscombe) to have been deleterious to his mental health.

1950–1951: Act 7: Anscombe Nurses a Dying Wittgenstein

The 27 St John Street house, full of fervent Catholics, also had its spiritual father, the Dominican priest Conrad Pepler. Fr. Conrad, who resided at Blackfriars Priory, a five-minute walk from the house, was a key figure in the lives of Anscombe and Smythies, and in part through his relationship to them became an important spiritual figure for Daniel, Goodridge, Pink, and Wittgenstein.

Although as an undergraduate Anscombe had been catechized and taught philosophy by two other Dominicans at Blackfriars, Fr. Conrad had become her favorite priest. Independently, Fr. Conrad had gotten to know Yorick Smythies and received him into the Catholic church 23 March 1944, and celebrating the marriage of Yorick and Polly four days later.[195] While it was Smythies who influenced Goodridge to become Catholic, it was Pepler who received Goodridge into the Church and baptized him on 4 July 1950. While Barry Pink had converted to Catholicism in 1947, Fr. Conrad was also the priest closest to Barry and Yorick Pink while they were in Oxford.[196] When Barry Pink had Yorick baptized as a Catholic at St. Aloysius parish on 21 February 1951, it was Fr. Conrad who baptized him, with Yorick and Polly Smythies serving as Yorick Pink's godparents.[197]

Thus, when Wittgenstein asked Anscombe to send him a Catholic priest (*Reminiscences* sec. 177–179, 231), she naturally sent along Fr. Conrad. According to John Steffen, Wittgenstein should be understood as having been a Catholic, what might be called a lapsed or 'bad' Catholic, but a Catholic nonetheless. Fr. Conrad relates his relationship with Wittgenstein:

> I was only introduced to [Wittgenstein] in the last six or seven months of his life. He wanted to talk to a priest as a priest and did not wish to discuss philosophical problems. He was of course originally Catholic and had some very good priest-friends in Austria. But he had not practiced as a Catholic for a long time. . . . When having to fill in forms during the war I understand he always put himself down as R.C. He knew he was very ill and wanted to talk about God I think with a view of coming back fully to his religion, but in fact we only had I think two conversations on God and the soul in rather general terms (he was already confined to bed) before he went off to Cambridge [on 8 February 1951]. . . .

---

[195] Dates of Yorick Smythies' reception into the Catholic Church and his marriage to Diana 'Polly' Pollard are courtesy of Fr. Dominic Jacob of St. Aloysius Parish, Oxford.

[196] Simon and Yorick Pink conversation with the author, September 2023.

[197] Courtesy of Fr. Dominic Jacob of St. Aloysius, Oxford.

After he had been in Cambridge for a little while I received an S.O.S. from Yorick Smythies and Elizabeth Anscombe to go over quickly as he was dying. He had said before that he would very much like to continue our talks, etc. But although I went immediately I arrived when he was already in a coma from which he never emerged. We therefore decided that in view of his expressed wish regarding talking to a priest we would give him conditional absolution. This I did. He died that evening as far as I recollect and the parish priest at Cambridge agreed to give him a Catholic funeral and he was buried I think in the Catholic cemetery in Cambridge. . . . I had to return to Oxford and could not be there.[198]

Apart from any spiritual influence that he had individually on the denizens of 27 St John Street, Fr. Conrad also seems to have influenced those in the house to consider living in an intentional Catholic community. Fr. Conrad had grown up at a very famous intentional Catholic community named Ditchling. His father Hilary Pepler, along with famous artist Eric Gill, had founded it forty years earlier.[199] In the late 1940s Fr. Conrad was involved with and regularly visiting a lay Christian community in Gloucestershire known as the Taena community. In the late 1940s the entire Taena community gradually converted to Catholicism, with Fr. Conrad as one of their spiritual guides.[200]

---

[198] Letter from Fr. Conrad Peplar to Sr. Mary Elwyn McHale, 11 August 1966. Courtesy of the archives of Cornell University.

[199] The importance of lay Catholic communities for Fr. Conrad is attested to by Mary Geach, who recalled hearing 'Fr. Conrad give a sermon the text about the seven pillars of wisdom, and naming the movement for establishing lay communities as one of the pillars on which the renewal of the church was being built' (Mary Geach email correspondence with Christopher Coope, 16 January, 2019).

[200] Founded by George Ineson, the community included both families and single people; the main occupations of the community were farming and pottery, and the community recited the Benedictine Day Hours (in English). Each family lived separately except for a communal meal in the middle of the day. The larger story of the Taena community is told in George Ineson, *Community Journey* (London: Sheed & Ward, 1956).

In the latter part of 1950 Anscombe, Smythies, Daniel, Goodridge, and Pink were all very interested in moving to the Taena community, but the spouses of Smythies, Anscombe, and Goodridge were not. Christopher Coope writes that 'Peter [Geach] told me that he had once been alarmed at the thought that Elizabeth would join a small religious community which had settled in the vicinity ... of Gloucestershire—taking with her (it would appear) the whole family.'[201]

In the autumn of 1950 Anscombe had conversations with Wittgenstein about moving to the Taena community. Wittgenstein himself had pursued the possibility of life in a religious community in Austria in the 1920s. As late as 1949 Wittgenstein had visited a Benedictine abbey, and in 1950 Fr. Conrad attempted to make arrangements for Wittgenstein to live at a Dominican priory in Staffordshire. As Anscombe was agonizing about the possibility of joining the Taena community, at one point Wittgenstein said, 'Leave the bloody thing alone.' Apparently, she did not pursue the possibility further. Anscombe's considering joining the Taena community has come down in Geach family lore, because Wittgenstein's exclamation 'leave the bloody thing alone' was endlessly repeated by various family members over the years as a kind of in-house joke. Whenever a family member was suggesting something another family member thought unwise, out would come 'leave the damn thing alone!'[202]

---

[201] Christopher Coope, email correspondence with the author.

[202] Both John Geach and Mary Geach told virtually the identical anecdote, with this 'aphorism' originating with the possibility of moving to the Taena community as the origin of this expression. Mary Geach added, 'It stinks!' From separate conversations with Mary Geach and John Geach. NB: it is not clear that this was Wittgenstein's intended meaning. Norman Malcolm writes, 'One of Wittgenstein's favourite phrases was the exclamation, "Leave the bloody thing alone!" He delivered this with a most emphatic intonation and mock solemnity of expression. It had roughly the signification that the thing in question was adequate and one should not try to improve it. He used it on a variety of occasions: one time meaning that the location of his bed was satisfactory and it should not be moved; another time, that the mending that my wife had done on a jacket of his was sufficient and that she should not try to make it better' (Malcolm, *A Memoir*, 69).

Although Anscombe never moved to the Taena community, other members of the house did. In the spring of 1951, Barry Pink reconciled with his wife Joy, and along with their three children moved to the Taena community in May 1951 and lived there for a year.[203] It was while Barry Pink was living at the Taena community that Anscombe commissioned him to carve Wittgenstein's gravestone. George Ineson writes about working with Barry Pink and Peter Daniel to transport Wittgenstein's gravestone from the Taena Community to Cambridge:

> 12th February [1952]. A strange interlude. Barry has just finished carving a large tombstone to be placed on the grave of Professor Wittgenstein, the Cambridge philosopher who has died recently. We borrowed Peter's large car, rolled the heavy stone on to the trailer and motored across country to a cemetery near Cambridge where we placed it in position. We discussed . . . Barry's suggestions on 'associate membership' and the building up of a 'village community'.[204]

While living at Taena, Pink not only carved the gravestone, but also built a house for his family to live in. During that year (1951–1952), the schoolteachers for the children were Barry's wife Joy and Peter Daniel. In the spring of 1952, Yorick Smythies made at least two lengthy visits to Taena with the desire to join the community. Long after the rest of the group had moved on to other things, Smythies would continue to make extended visits to Taena.[205]

---

[203] Conversations and email correspondence with Simon Pink, September and October 2023.

[204] See Ineson, *Community Journey*, 181.

[205] In a long, unpublished document about Yorick Smythies by Peter Daniel that he shared with a number of people, he writes, 'Without becoming members, Yorick, Barry Pink and I stayed for some months with the [Taena] community after previous shorter visits. [Yorick] continued such sojourns longer than I did. Yorick was deeply attracted by the community and would have joined it but for the opposition of his wife Polly. . . .

The interest in the Taena community at 27 St John Street was discussed sufficiently that various people who dropped by the house found out about it. Denis Paul, who got to know Anscombe when he was president of the Aquinas Society (Anscombe and Murdoch were faculty advisors to it), was a regular visitor at 27 St John Street, and because of his knowledge of German, was eventually assisting Anscombe with her efforts to translate Wittgenstein's book.[206] Paul was also a student of Isaiah Berlin, and he gossiped to Berlin about Anscombe and the 27 St John Street community. Berlin wanted to see Wittgenstein's book, and was frustrated that he could not get access to it. He seems to have taken out some of his frustrations in a private letter, making jokes about Anscombe and the goings on at 27 St John Street:

> The Wittgenstein intimates—Miss Anscombe, her husband Geach, and others—were thinking of founding a colony in order to live, think, eat and be like Ludwig. Originally it was intended to invite L. himself, but now that he is dead they propose to establish it anyhow. A great deal of violent artificial neurosis, not washing etc., anyhow you can imagine—hideous stammering in place of articulate speech, perverted Catholicism and all the other delicious attributes.[207]

Yorick understood his wife's objections, and told me it was for her a "stunt" like some other departures from normal with which he had confronted her. The Taena people regarded him as almost a saint, while amused by his wild unpracticality. I agreed with him in regarding them as the best lay Christians I had ever met. They received recognition and some direction by becoming oblates of Prinknash Abbey.'

[206] Anscombe would acknowledge in the prefatory translator's note to the *Philosophical Investigations* that Denis Paul, along with Rush Rhees, Georg Henrik von Wright, Peter Geach, Iris Murdoch, Lotte Labowsky, and Georg Kreisel, all 'either checked the translation or allowed me to consult them about German and Austrian usage or read the translation through and helped me to improve the English'. Wittgenstein, *Philosophical Investigations*, iii.

[207] Berlin, *Enlightening Letters 1946–1960* (London: Chatto & Windus, 2009), 229.

Like a lot of gossip, Berlin's was wrong on most of the details and infused with nasty hyperbole.[208] But Berlin was not misinformed by Denis Paul about the 27 St John Street group's interest in becoming part of an intentional Christian community.

While this letter by Berlin making fun of Anscombe is widely cited, what is not cited is Berlin's serious and considered view of Wittgenstein and Anscombe, which was of a high order. With regard to Wittgenstein, at this time Berlin contributed the entry on Wittgenstein to Brittanica's Book of the Year. There he writes that Wittgenstein

> practiced a technique whereby more light was thrown on some of the most tormenting problems of modern philosophy than the older and more mechanical methods had succeeded in doing. This new and more flexible method required qualities of imagination and insight, and even a kind of poetical genius. . . . His teaching was the most fruitful contribution to the abstract thought of the day made by any single human being.[209]

Similarly, despite his evident personal dislike of Anscombe, Berlin's considered opinion of her was that she was brilliant. In late 1950, he was asked by Anna Kallin of BBC radio to recommend philosophers to put on the air. She notes:

> The best thing in [Berlin's] view would be to ask a few people, who would be able to expound the English philosophical thought of the last twenty years. . . . He suggested . . . Hampshire, possibly Urmson, Toulmin. . . . He also though we should try out Wittgenstein's pupil Elisabeth Anscombe, a brilliant woman who

[208] On Berlin's propensity for gossip, see Leach, 'Chadbourne Gilpatric and Ludwig Wittgenstein', 7.
[209] Leach, 'Chadbourne Gilpatric and Ludwig Wittgenstein', 14–15.

would represent Wittgenstein's views faithfully, but has as well her own Catholic angle.[210]

Berlin's recommendation was seconded by Hampshire himself in response to a similar enquiry:

> You once asked me about Miss Anscombe of Somerville College, Oxford, as a possible broadcaster and I think I was rather discouraging about the possibility of persuading her or of getting her to confirm to the conditions. Wittgenstein being dead, she remains as literary executor and chief disciple and is preparing his book for the press. I am told that she is now much less inhibited about speaking in public than she used to be, and I think it would be very worth while to try to persuade her to broadcast—but not, I suggest, about Wittgenstein, unless she wants to. Her style and method would be something new to listeners to philosophy talks & ought to be represented.
>
> She is of course a Roman Catholic and *very* unlike Freddie Ayer or me or other 'analytical' philosophers who broadcast. But she is even more unlike Barnes, Copleston etc. Of course everybody is disapproved of, but I think you would be amused and would enjoy 'producing' her. Yours, Stuart[211]

So Prudence Smith of the BBC duly wrote Anscombe on 18 November 1951, and two days later she replied, saying, 'I shouldn't refuse to do something if I thought I could do it, but I do not believe I could. It's not worth a journey to see me, but if you are in Oxford and want to pursue it, we might talk about it. But as I say, I am very

---

[210] 14 December 1950 notes by Anna Kallin on her conversation with Isaiah Berlin. Elizabeth Anscombe file at the BBC Archives at Reading.

[211] 12 November 1951 letter from Hampshire to Prudence Smith. Elizabeth Anscombe file at the BBC Archives at Reading.

doubtful—just of my capacity.'[212] While Anscombe declined at the time, a year later she agreed to go on the BBC, and in the summer of 1953 she gave her first talks on the BBC, on the philosophy of Wittgenstein.

In the months leading up Wittgenstein's death, Anscombe would be saddled with considerable health problems. In October 1950 she was going blind in her left eye, and in early November physicians operated on it to try to save her sight. Anscombe's friend Lotte Labowsky reported that after the operation she would have to lie on her back in a darkened room for ten days. On 26 November Wittgenstein wrote, 'I saw Miss Anscombe to-day. She is up and can go out for a short time and she's all right except that she still sees double if she looks through the operated eye, and that makes her feel sick. But if one talks to her she forgets about it and doesn't feel the nausea.' Anscombe would have to wear an eye patch for some months to avoid the nausea. In the end, the operation was not a success, and she became effectively blind in her left eye.

It was around this time that Wittgenstein started suggesting to Anscombe that she should eat less, that she was looking 'fat all over'. It was at this point that Anscombe revealed to Wittgenstein that she was three months pregnant.[213] Wittgenstein was unusually observant regarding Anscombe, since as late as March 1951 when Anscombe was a full six months pregnant, her pregnancy was still a secret, with almost no one outside a small circle of friends and family aware of it.

---

[212] 18 November 1951 letter from Prudence Smith to Elizabeth Anscombe. Elizabeth Anscombe file, BBC written Archives at Reading. A little over a year later, on 20 January 1953, Anscombe would again write Prudence Smith, this time to say that if Smith still wanted her to talk about Wittgenstein, she 'might be able to work something out'. And indeed, Anscombe submitted her talk on 2 April, and recorded it at the BBC studios on 23 April 1953. It was an hour-long programme, thirty minutes of Anscombe reading from Wittgenstein, and thirty minutes of Anscombe commentating on what she read.

[213] Anscombe was not the only one at 27 St John Street who was pregnant at the time. The Goodridges' first child arrived on 19 April 1951, six weeks before Anscombe gave birth to Mary Catherine Geach on 5 June 1951.

On Sunday, 21 January 1951, Anscombe tore a ligament in her right shoulder, the arm with which she wrote. Just two days later, she began her 'Readings in Plato' lectures which she gave on Tuesdays and Thursday at noon at Schools (the main lecture building in the university). It is not clear how Anscombe would have managed to give her lectures that term, being unable to use her right arm to write them out. Anscombe was to have given a paper at Oxford's Philosophical Society on 2 February 1951, but cancelled because of her injury, presumably because she was unable to write out a paper for the occasion.[214]

By early February, Wittgenstein's condition was worsening, and he decided to move to Cambridge to live at the home of his physician Dr. Edward Bevan and his wife Joan. Many months earlier, after Bevan had diagnosed Wittgenstein's prostate cancer, Wittgenstein had told Bevan that he did not want to die in hospital. Dr. Bevan kindly invited Wittgenstein to come and live with him and his wife Joan for the final days of his life.

So on 8 February, Anscombe accompanied Wittgenstein to Cambridge, going first class to make the trip more bearable for Wittgenstein. On the trip, Anscombe read Kleist's *Prinz von Homburg* to Wittgenstein, in which he delighted (*Reminiscences* sec. 225). Within weeks of arriving in Cambridge, Wittgenstein's health and his ability to work took a sharp turn for the better. When Dr. Bevan had diagnosed Wittgenstein with prostate cancer back in November 1949, Bevan had prescribed Wittgenstein a treatment of hormones to try to slow the development of the cancer. Unfortunately, a side effect of the treatment was that they made Wittgenstein mentally sluggish, and hard to do the work he wanted to do. It was this reason that in early 1951 Wittgenstein was saying that he had not been able to do serious work since 1949. However,

[214] See the minutes of the Philosophical Society, MS. Top. Oxon. E. 392/2, p. 45, held in the Archives of the Bodleian Library.

once Wittgenstein was settled in at Bevan's home, Bevan stopped Wittgenstein's hormone and X-ray treatments. Wittgenstein noted at once it was like a veil had been lifted from his mind, that he was suddenly able to do work at the highest level.[215] As Wittgenstein put it in March 1951: 'I am going to work now as I have never worked before.'[216] The impact of Wittgenstein's going off the medicine can be seen in *On Certainty* sec. 300–676, which he wrote in the last six weeks of his life, and which reads unusually fluently. Wittgenstein was feeling so much better that by early March he was thinking that he would soon be well enough to travel or go back to Oxford.[217] Unfortunately, this feeling of wellness only lasted a couple of weeks.

Since Anscombe was lecturing in Oxford from mid-January to mid-March, and not being able to use her right arm, was undoubtedly struggling to keep up, she could not easily get back to Cambridge to see Wittgenstein until the end of term. And then, shortly after arriving back in Cambridge, during the night of 22 March (Holy Thursday) Anscombe was rushed to hospital for an emergency appendectomy. She remained in hospital for ten days.[218] At the time, she was over six months pregnant with her third child Mary.

Once out of hospital, although she was needing to rest and recover, she would see Wittgenstein a number of times before returning to Oxford for Trinity term, to teach a seminar on Proclus with Lotte Labowsky.[219] Having known Wittgenstein for a little

---

[215] Malcolm, *A Memoir*, 134.

[216] Joan Bevan, 'Wittgenstein's Last Year', in Flowers and Ground, *Portraits of Wittgenstein*, 1031.

[217] On 9 March Wittgenstein writes to Rhees, 'I'm up every day a bit & often the whole day. I'm very weak physically & mentally & have all sorts of discomforts but <u>very</u> little pain.—I should <u>very</u> much like to see you around April 8th. I don't know yet where I shall be then. Whether here or in Oxford. We can arrange details of place & time later.' See Wittgenstein to Rhees, 9 March 1951, in B. McGuinness ed., *Wittgenstein in Cambridge*, sec. 434, p. 474.

[218] Correspondence between Geach and Anscombe and the University Chest (about pay deductions while off work). Archives of Bodleian Library, Oxford.

[219] For details of this seminar, see Mac Cumhaill and Wiseman, *Metaphysical Animals*, 249–256.

more than six years, Anscombe's last extended conversation with Wittgenstein was on Sunday, 22 April, when they went for a walk, before she caught the train back to Oxford.

Wittgenstein was active right up until two days before his death, writing and going for walks. On the weekend he saw Anscombe, he had been to visit von Wright at Trinity College the previous day, and also met with Geach the same day he went for a walk with Anscombe. A couple of days later, Drury visited Wittgenstein on the way back from his honeymoon in Italy. When Drury headed for the train station, Wittgenstein insisted on accompanying him, against Drury's protests.

On Friday, 27 April, the temperature dropped suddenly, and when Wittgenstein went out for his late afternoon stroll to the neighbourhood pub with Joan Bevan, he was not properly clothed for the cold weather. Not long after his return from the pub, Wittgenstein was violently ill with stomach flu (i.e. gastro-enteritis), accompanied by severe vomiting and diarrhea. In his terribly weakened condition, Wittgenstein was succumbing to a flu bug. The next day, realizing that Wittgenstein was close to death, Dr. Bevan called Wittgenstein's closest friends (which Wittgenstein had earlier instructed him to do) to be with him. Meanwhile, Joan Bevan sat with him on the Saturday night, and at one point before Wittgenstein lost consciousness, she told him that his friends were coming. Wittgenstein replied, 'Tell them I've had a wonderful life.'[220] Anscombe, Smythies, and Fr. Conrad came from Oxford, Ben Richards came from Derby, and Con Drury flew over from Dublin. On the Sunday Wittgenstein was mostly asleep or unconscious. Periodically, he would awaken and take some water, but he could not speak. Wittgenstein wanted his friends to hold his hand, and they did that throughout the day. At about 5 p.m. Wittgenstein seems to have realized that he was close to death. At that point Fr. Conrad gave him conditional

---

[220] Joan Bevan, 'Wittgenstein's Last Year', 1031.

absolution, and remained with his friends saying prayers at his bedside until his death.

Wittgenstein's biographer Ray Monk implies, and others have repeated, that Wittgenstein's friends *decided* whether Fr. Conrad should give conditional absolution and whether Wittgenstein should be buried as a Catholic.[221] In one account, Drury merely notes that Dr. Bevan was complaining that 'no one will decide whether the priest should say the usual office for the dying and give conditional absolution', perhaps assuming that his friends needed to decide the matter. In fact, in one place Drury writes that he replied, 'whatever was customary should be done'.[222] As such, Drury was handing the decision to Fr. Conrad, which was appropriate on a number of levels. Monk's narrative extrapolates a number of assumptions, which taken together give the unfortunate impression that Fr. Conrad—who was Wittgenstein's priest—as craven and feckless, and who did what Drury, a non-Catholic, directed him to do or not to do. But this is not how a Catholic priest at that time would have operated. Fr. Conrad would have to consider Wittgenstein a Catholic in order to give conditional absolution, and if the Catholic was unconscious, according to Canon Law the priest must presume that the Catholic would request it.[223] As another Dominican priest, Fergus Kerr explains, 'Fr. Conrad would never have set out [to Cambridge on 29 April] unless he believed that Wittgenstein wanted him called; and he would not have given conditional absolution unless he believed that Wittgenstein was a Catholic'.[224] The one context in which Dr. Drury may have been directing Fr. Conrad was in

---

[221] 'Drury recollected Wittgenstein's remark that he hoped his Catholic friends prayed for him. . . . this decided the matter, and they all . . . kneeled down while Conrad recited the proper prayers' (Monk, *Duty of Genius*, 579).

[222] M. O'C. Drury, 'Conversations with Wittgenstein', in Hayes, ed., *Writings of Maurice O'Connor Drury*, 144.

[223] See Steffen, *A Cool Temple*, 318.

[224] See Steffen, *A Cool Temple*, 318.

his capacity as a medical doctor, as Drury implicitly indicates elsewhere: 'I arrived at Cambridge to find him unconscious and obviously dying. . . . I asked this priest to say the usual prayers for the dying in which we all joined.'[225]

Two day later, on 1 May 1951, with Fr. Conrad having had to return to Oxford, the parish priest gave Wittgenstein a Catholic burial at St. Giles Cemetery in North Cambridge, surrounded by Anscombe and a few other of Wittgenstein's closest friends. In the days following Wittgenstein's death, Anscombe was overcome with grief, weeping so bitterly and violently that Peter was worried that Anscombe would miscarry Mary, with whom she was eight months pregnant.[226]

After Wittgenstein's death, according to the will he had executed in Oxford on 29 January 1951, Anscombe, Rhees, and von Wright were announced as Wittgenstein's literary executors. Their first order of business was to prepare Wittgenstein's 'book' for publication, and Anscombe and Rhees were appointed editors. While what constituted Wittgenstein's book evolved from 1938 to 1948, getting progressively larger, Anscombe and Rhees were in full agreement about Wittgenstein's last statements about what should be in the volume. It was to consist of the last typescript version he had made, which he had left with Anscombe in November 1948, plus the material he instructed both Anscombe and Rhees to be added to it in discussions with them in Dublin (known by the executors as the Dublin MSS[227]) in December 1948.

[225] Dr. M. Drury to Sr. M. Elywn McHale, Letter of 1 April 1966. Courtesy of Cornell University Archives.

[226] This is according to Mary Geach, communicated in emails from Rebecca Gormally, 22 and 26 August 2024.

[227] 26 November 1951 letter from Anscombe to von Wright, which can be found in Erbacher and Krebs, 'The First Nine Months of Editing Wittgenstein: Letters from G. E. M. Anscombe and Rush Rhees to G. H. Von Wright', *Nordic Wittgenstein Review* 4, no. 1 (2015): 212.

On 28 May 1951 Anscombe invited von Wright to come from Cambridge to see her in Oxford as soon as he was able (he was hobbled by an injured knee). She further indicated, 'I hope so much not to be locked up when you do', referring implicitly to the possibility of her being in hospital for the birth of her third child. As it came to be, Anscombe would indeed be hospitalized when von Wright came to see her. On 5 June she left a note on her front door for von Wright:

> Dear Professor von Wright, I am afraid it is necessary for me to leave for the hospital (Radcliffe Maternity Home): this involves a breakdown in hospitality for which I am very sorry.
>
> If it were at all possible to see you . . . I should be extremely glad . . . you could come and see me, say about or towards 12 tomorrow morning.
>
> It is now 3:30 [unclear if a.m. or p.m.], and I believe this business will be over before many hours.
>
> If you feel like it, do make yourself some coffee and help yourself to such food as there is. A pint of milk on the front-door step is mine & at your disposal.
>
> I'm so sorry. Yours, Elizabeth

Indeed 'this business' was completed later that day with the arrival of Mary Catherine Geach. She would shortly be baptized at St. Aloysius Church in Oxford, with Yorick and Polly Smythies as her godparents.

Anscombe would devote most of the next two years to preparing a translation of Wittgenstein's book for publication, which would go on sale on 1 May 1953, almost exactly two years after Wittgenstein's death. For the next five years, her salary being paid by the Rockefeller Foundation, Anscombe would devote the vast majority of her time to editing and translating other works from Wittgenstein's *Nachlass*. Anscombe would emerge not only as a leading interpreter of Wittgenstein's work, but also as a formidable philosopher in her own right. Over the last six decades, Anscombe's reputation as a major twentieth century philosopher has only continued to grow.[228]

[228] My thanks to Roger Teichmann and especially Erin Green for their editorial comments on earlier versions of my paper. My thanks also to John Anscombe, Christopher Coope, Charles Geach, John Geach, Mary Geach (Gormally), More Geach, John Goodridge, Liz Goodridge, Luke Gormally, Rebecca Gormally, Jane Heal, Fr. Dominic Jacob, James Klagge, Michael Kremer, Michael Nedo, Simon Pink, Yorick Pink, Roger Teichmann, and Kitty Warnock, and the archivists at the BBC written archives, Collegium Institute Archives at the Kislak Center, University of Pennsylvania, at the von Wright archives, Thomas Davies at King's College, Cambridge, Dayna Miller at Kingston University, Sabina Brtnik at the Deutsches Literaturarchiv at Marbach, Frieda Midgley at Newnham College, Matthew Chipping, St. Hugh's College, and Kate O'Donnell, Somerville College, all of whom spoke to me and/or provided otherwise unavailable documentation or personal information for this paper.

2

Anscombe's *Reminiscences*: Portrait of a Philosopher

Roger Teichmann

The document here published under the title *Reminiscences of Wittgenstein* was written by Anscombe in a series of notebooks over some period of time. As she herself puts it, 'I write down from time to time quite stray recollections of Wittgenstein as they come back to me, if I have the chance when they do; hence they are quite rambling and disorganised' (sec. 172). A reader of the original manuscript can indeed feel thrown about from one topic to another; at the same time one quite often encounters an extended series of remarks dwelling on a particular theme or point. Probably it was the disorganized nature of what she was writing that led Anscombe to give the manuscript the rather modest title of *Anecdotes about Wittgenstein*. But the picture of Wittgenstein that emerges from this document has surely more than enough first-hand, thoughtful, and vivid detail to qualify it as a memoir of the philosopher worthy to stand comparison with the others that have already been published. It is a memoir penned, moreover, by one of the people who knew him best and whose own philosophical acumen enabled her to ponder and reflect on the thought as much as on the man.

That Anscombe intended her reminiscences for posterity seems clear from her telling the reader how she came to write them, as well as from such cautionary asides as we get concerning whether a memory is clear or more of 'an impression'. Part of Anscombe's

Roger Teichmann, *Anscombe's* Reminiscences: *Portrait of a Philosopher* In: *Anscombe on Wittgenstein*. Edited by: John Berkman and Roger Teichmann, Oxford University Press.

motive for writing the document was presumably to correct the 'grim and cramped' picture of Wittgenstein that seemed to her to be conveyed in particular by Malcolm's memoir (sec. 172). But I feel sure we would still have these reminiscences even if Malcolm had never published his book. There are other writings of Anscombe's in which she refers to her conversations with Wittgenstein or more generally to the sort of mind she perceived him as having,[1] but only in the *Reminiscences* do we get a rounded, often subtle, and distinctly human portrait of the person.

For that portrait to emerge as coherent, such that the main psychological and intellectual contours can be taken in and the reader get a sense of the unity of Anscombe's subject, it was necessary to reorder the remarks. (The case is somewhat similar to that of Wittgenstein's ordering and reordering of his *Bemerkungen* to achieve what he wanted in the *Philosophical Investigations*.) Whether Anscombe herself meant to carry out a reordering at some stage is not known.[2] But the need for, or at any rate permissibility of, such editorial intervention was recognized by Anscombe's daughter and literary executor, Mary Geach, who has approved the version of the *Reminiscences* here published.[3]

The principle of ordering which I have adopted is broadly thematic, as the six subtitles attest. Only through such a thematic approach, it seemed to me, could the latent coherence and power of

---

[1] See, e.g., 'The Simplicity of the Tractatus' and 'On the Form of Wittgenstein's Writing', both in M. Geach and L. Gormally, eds., *From Plato to Wittgenstein: Essays by G. E. M. Anscombe* (Exeter: Imprint Academic, 2011).

[2] In an email to me (5 February 2022) Luke Gormally wrote: 'There could be some claim to authority for your proposed ordering—thematic—if my earlier impression is correct that a loose insert (a scrap of paper) in one of the small volumes listed themes which I speculated at the time I handled the volume were probably intended as a key (complete or incomplete—I don't know) for reorganising the Anecdotes. So it would be worth getting a hold of a copy of that scrap of paper; it was left in the volume by me.' Unfortunately a search for the scrap of paper by the current curators of the MS has turned nothing up.

[3] This version is a complete transcription of the MS but for two minor omissions: an anecdote which Anscombe inadvertently repeats (see *Reminiscences* fn. 80), and a short sentence which has been left out at the request of Mary Geach.

Anscombe's portrait be realized. The original manuscript is divisible into paragraphs or sections of varying lengths; the transcription first made by Luke Gormally[4] (Mary Geach's husband) as far as possible retained these sectional divisions, and the numbers in square brackets which I have placed after each section correspond to the original ordering in Luke's transcription. Hence the reader can, if he or she chooses, reconstruct that original ordering. It was, by the way, from Luke Gormally that I first heard of the existence of the 'Anecdotes' and of his transcription of them. Luke sadly passed away in April 2023. To him, as to Mary, is owed a great debt of gratitude in connection with the publication of this important document.

I have spoken of the *Reminiscences* as a memoir or portrait of Wittgenstein. They are also something else: a portrait of a relationship—that between Wittgenstein and his younger pupil and friend, Elizabeth Anscombe. Anscombe was no mere observer or stenographer; she engaged with Wittgenstein both philosophically and personally, if not as an absolute equal then at any rate as a person capable of and intent on thinking for herself. Like others, Anscombe could feel a sort of dumbfounding fear of his intellectual wrath, but with her this evidently wore off:

> Looking back, I can see that the disagreeable relation of fear and stupefaction was for the first four years or so of our friendship, and largely in connection with philosophy; about other things and in practical communications I had no difficulties of that kind. (sec. 204)

So even in the early years she seems not to have been in awe of him in non-philosophical matters. And as the notes from their discussions 1946–1947 published in this volume show, whether or not she was susceptible of 'stupefaction' Anscombe was, or became,

---

[4] I have been able to check Luke's transcription against the original MS: only one or two minor corrections had to be made.

able to discuss philosophy with Wittgenstein with the serious-ness and honesty which he himself will have desired and which he aimed to inculcate or encourage in his students. The result is that a reader of these *Reminiscences* quite often has the impression of lis-tening in on discussions between what were, after all, two giants of twentieth-century philosophy.

But the conversations between Anscombe and Wittgenstein were by no means confined to philosophy. Religion, literature, art, history—these all came into their discussions, as did more bio-graphical matters relating to family, friends, and colleagues. In the *Reminiscences* Anscombe also recounts events in Wittgenstein's life that she witnessed or that she heard about from others; moreover we learn about Wittgenstein's manners, tastes, habits, and moods. (Anscombe had ample opportunity to observe these things, es-pecially when he was staying with her in 27 St John St, Oxford.) Finally, there are the last days and hours of Wittgenstein's life, simply but poignantly described by Anscombe, who was one of those by his bedside when he died.

What sort of man was Wittgenstein? In reading memoirs written by those who knew him, one can be struck by how differently he comes across in the different accounts: to some extent, it can seem as if his character has been refracted through that of the writer. He surely didn't present a completely different face to each of the various people around him, being in fact a person who was *ut-terly himself*—but it may have been that such was the complexity of his personality that different aspects, different facets, impressed different people more or less strongly (and sometimes the same person on different occasions).

Something that does come through in Anscombe's *Reminiscences* is this complexity. On the one hand, deeply serious—on the other, someone who could be 'speechless with laughter' (according to Ben Richards; sec. 172). On the one hand, highly cultivated—on the other, fond of what is simple and down to earth (in food, furniture, human beings). And so on. It would be impossible to present any sort of résumé of the man's personality. In what follows I want to look at just some of Wittgenstein's character traits as they emerge from the *Reminiscences*, part of my aim being to address the question: are there parallels to be drawn between features of Wittgenstein's character and features of his philosophy?

A good place to start is Wittgenstein's great sensitivity to the particularity of a case (person, predicament, etc.), to its idiosyncrasy, the way or ways in which it differs from other cases of the same general type. This of course is a well-known theme in his later philosophy. He considered prefacing the *Philosophical Investigations* with a quotation from *King Lear*: 'I'll show you differences.'[5] The craving for generality is to be resisted, but not only when doing philosophy: for to understand the human beings around us we likewise need to have an eye (or ear or nose) for the idiosyncratic—for nuances and subtle differences.

> He once said to me after using a w.c. in my house which was idiosyncratic: 'Sometimes you must pull the plug [sc. chain] again at once if it doesn't work, in other cases that is just what you must not do, you must wait till all is quiet; sometimes a half pull at first is right and so on. These differences apply to people too!' (sec. 43)

This observation also illustrates another notable characteristic of Wittgenstein's, his capacity to come out with telling similes and metaphors. The best way to deal with a person, like the best way to flush a loo, varies from instance to instance. It is something you must just learn through experience, and the skill that you thereby learn may be one that you yourself cannot articulate in words. (That last thought isn't explicit in the remark quoted but is one that Wittgenstein elsewhere expresses.)

---

[5] Here at least was something from Shakespeare of which he'd have to approve; for his general attitude to the bard, which Anscombe describes as 'grumbling'; see sec. 70.

If Anscombe is right, Wittgenstein's own capacity to register or 'intuit' people's idiosyncrasies was highly developed:

> He appeared to perceive things about people—sometimes one could not see what he could be getting at. 'Don't worry about that child, she's all right'; but 'That's the one you should be concerned about—he will be a problem to bring up'. He said of Georg Henrik's boy when he was only three 'I see hell in that child's face'. (sec. 44)[6]

Such sensitivity is obviously important for human relationships and for friendship in particular, and there are various places in the *Reminiscences* where Anscombe alludes to Wittgenstein's friendly attentiveness, not to mention generosity. It was also important for Wittgenstein's mode of pedagogy, the aim of which was to help his students towards individual *understanding*. That I understand such-and-such is a matter of my own capacities—to move around the terrain smoothly, not get stuck in dead ends, nor sit still through inertia or complacency, and so on. Understanding is not manifest in coming out with approved formulas—for of course there will always be the question whether I understand those formulas, not to mention the possible further question whether they are of any use to man or beast. This itself is a conceptual, and so philosophical, point: to understand is to be able to *do* certain things, it is not to *have* something, e.g. inside me (like a ghostly or neural telephone directory). But it is also a point by which a teacher, especially of philosophy, needs to be practically guided. You need to be sensitive to what is hindering *this* person in seeing something, to what picture it is that is dominating *that* person's thinking. For only then will you be in a position to help them to a place where they can see

---

[6] It is true that Anscombe is here non-committal about whether what Wittgenstein perceived was real, but in the context of her overall portrait it seems that she would lean that way.

a way out of their particular thicket and begin to move and think smoothly.

> Once in a lecture I said 'But I want to say: "blue is *there*!"' and he said: Now let me find the medicine which is the right one for you *now*; and then came out with the idea of 'pain-patches' on fruits and plants. This was certainly effective. I have always since understood better the Locke idea about secondary qualities. (sec. 128)

Note Wittgenstein's emphasis on 'you *now*'. Such was his focus on the individual mindsets of those he was talking to that he

> very often seemed to understand one's philosophical thoughts and problems better than one did oneself. One would say what one thought—then he would amplify it, make it seem more convincing, carry it deeper—and then undo it. (sec. 129)

These remarks about Wittgenstein's pedagogy lead naturally to another point in the vicinity. As well as stressing the importance of seeing the particular in people, Wittgenstein—connectedly—would note how words and sentences must often be understood as having been uttered or written by such-and-such a person, in such-and-such a situation. Again, the craving for generality needs to be resisted. The picture of words as carrying their meaning around with them from utterance to utterance is one of the objects of a sustained critique in his later philosophy, but the thrust of that critique is not recondite or technical—it is not the preserve of professional philosophers:

> He particularly liked a story of Bismarck's being told some remark and asked his opinion on it; his reply was 'It depends who said it.' (sec. 34)

The point is further illustrated by Wittgenstein's approach to religious judgements and to such questions as whether they are true/false, whether they can be justified, etc.

> Rush Rhees told me about Wittgenstein's saying of proofs of the immortality of the soul: 'If it's something you can prove, I don't want it!' [...] 'A theory does nothing for me.' Anyone *saying* something religious is—or ought to be (?)—*doing* something religious in saying (cf. the remark about 'filling reasoning with religious content'[7]). *What is he doing, saying that?* is Wittgenstein's question and he is not moved by the question: Is it *true*? because to say p is true is to say p and so the original question remains: *what is he doing* in saying that? (But not at all in the sense of 'speech-acts'.) (sec. 104)

That last parenthetical remark of Anscombe's is not a mere puff of impatience directed at a notion closely associated with one of her *bêtes noires*, J. L. Austin, as one might naively think. The notion of a speech-act might be a good one but it is not the one we need here. After all, differentiation of utterances by type of speech-act is differentiation into *types*; what primarily interests Wittgenstein in connection with religious utterance really is the question 'What is this person here doing?' To be sure, one can also ask and address a question like 'What are these people doing?' or indeed 'What are we doing?'—such questions are to be found addressed by Wittgenstein, for example in his remarks on ritual.[8] But those more general questions would not have as much interest for us as they do if the answers to them did not enable us to tackle particular concrete questions like 'What does he mean? What is he up to? What are *you* up to?' Such questions are particularly pressing in the case

---

[7] See sec. 94.
[8] See, e.g., the *Remarks on Frazer's Golden Bough*.

of religious utterances because (for Wittgenstein) their being religious must consist in their relating in some way to how the person leads his or her life, something that is evidently a personal and so to speak biographical matter.

To return to Wittgenstein's sensitivity as to what is the case with another person: it has to be said that this feature of his make-up had its downside, however much it contributed to his capacity for friendship and his skill as a teacher. For he could in fact be hypersensitive, make too much of something, take offence too readily.

> The impression that Wittgenstein gave one sometimes was of an instrument that was extremely sensitively gauging a number of things; exactly what, however, one didn't know.
>
> This feeling of his being unavoidably equipped with a whole lot of antennae, registering one did not quite know what, in connection with every slight thing, this was I think what made him seem a difficult person to be with. —His comments on people often seemed accurate but could he not just have disregarded what so-and-so said, as a casual remark which did not deserve to be bothered about? (sec. 40, 41)

'*Unavoidably* equipped': here Anscombe hints at the dimension of suffering or strain. It's clear that Wittgenstein was often not at ease with other people, and his relations with others could come under strain owing to his 'demandingness'. Even a good friend like Malcolm could be cut off for some while as a result of a (to us) innocent-seeming remark: this occurred after a conversation between the two in which Malcolm invoked British national character as ruling out the likelihood of a British plan to assassinate Hitler in 1939.[9]

---

[9] N. Malcolm, *Ludwig Wittgenstein: A Memoir* (Oxford: Oxford University Press, 1984), 93. Wittgenstein wrote to Malcolm: 'what is the use of studying philosophy if all that it does for you is to enable you to talk with some plausibility about some abstruse questions of logic, etc., & if it does not improve your thinking about the important questions of everyday life?'

Anscombe relates how some of her own remarks could provoke similarly indignant responses, although Wittgenstein doesn't appear to have cut off relations with her ever. 'He more than once ticked me off for being "cock-sure". He used to blow me up for any manifestation of this' (sec. 186). In the *Reminiscences* there are several examples. There are also examples of Wittgenstein getting annoyed or offended for other sorts of reason, less 'intellectual'; on occasion Anscombe could feel ill-used (see sec. 227).

One instance of Wittgenstein's annoyance is of interest both for its denouement and for the ground of his annoyance:

> [H]e got violently angry with me for having told Miss Deneke he was too ill to see her—he feared it would get back to his family. 'It was bloody of you, it was absolutely bloody of you!' he kept on saying. I didn't feel particularly badly treated on that occasion, but when I saw him again he said 'You've got an apology coming from me!' That was the apology. (sec. 227)

This particular apology may have been grudging, but we must remember the lengths to which Wittgenstein could and did go in that department. I have in mind his trekking to the Austrian village of Otterthal in 1936 in order to apologize to the former pupils of his whom he had mistreated when a schoolmaster in the 1920s.[10] But perhaps these latter apologies should be seen as of a piece with the 'confessions' he was making to various friends at that time, i.e., as attempts to achieve a certain truthfulness and integrity of character, and to overcome the cowardice that stood in the way of that. It does seem that in 1926 he had not been completely up front with people about the details of his behaviour. In other words, Wittgenstein may have been more concerned with his own relationship with truth than with his relationships with the individuals to whom he offered apology.

[10] See R. Monk, *The Duty of Genius* (New York: Penguin, 1991), 370–372.

This brings me to another set of questions about Wittgenstein's character having both personal and philosophical overtones. I referred above to the *ground* of Wittgenstein's annoyance at Anscombe's having mentioned his illness to Miss Deneke. He wished to keep from his family the fact that he was, mortally as it turned out, ill. So far, such an attitude is not in itself in tension with a habit of truthfulness; but consider the following passage:

> I had a scruple when he asked me to tell a lie if anyone asked about his illness in Austria. I said I couldn't make that promise. He was a bit put out and later returned to the subject— 'You're saying you can't tell a lie'. 'Nothing is more likely than that I should tell a lie' I said, 'It's only that I can't make you that promise. I tell lies, I think, about twice a week. I mean quite straightforward ones.' 'Good!' he replied. 'I would find it difficult to be friends with someone who couldn't tell a lie.' He didn't ask me to explain the objection I felt; but he was very discerning, and probably guessed. How could I pray for him to God who hates lies and coolly undertake to tell lies for him? My prayers were feeble as it was. (sec. 214)

'I would find it difficult to be friends with someone who couldn't tell a lie.' This is surely a remarkable thing for Wittgenstein to have said, and it is so striking that I am sure that Anscombe is reporting it more or less, if not exactly, verbatim. But what of that almost obsessional desire for honesty which was manifest in, among other things, his 'confessions' of 1936? Surely Wittgenstein of all people had a strong attachment to, even reverence for, the truth?

> At another time, and more than once, he said to me that he could not understand the idea of loving God. Once he added 'I *do* understand loving the truth. I have loved the truth—by which, mind, I do *not* mean that I think I *have* the truth.' (sec. 92)

The picture is evidently complicated. We might ask: what did Wittgenstein mean by 'someone who couldn't tell a lie' in the remark quoted in sec. 214? Did he mean 'someone who couldn't tell a lie when a lie was called for'? Did he mean someone who *sets their face against* lying, whose attitude to lying might be expressed in 'I just can't tell a lie', understood as a sort of declaration? Or is he imagining some genuine impossibility, akin to the impossibility of flying?

When Anscombe told him she lied regularly he replied, 'Good!' It seems unlikely that this answer amounted to 'Good! For those lies you told will, I'm sure, have been ones that were actually called for in the situations; hence it's your good judgement I'm approving of.' I suspect that what Wittgenstein had in mind was something like this: to err is human—in one's friend one wants to recognize a shared humanity. That you do lie (present tense frequentative) enables me to love you as someone in the same boat as I'm in, just as does the fact that you get drunk sometimes or go in for minor acts of vengefulness. If someone who couldn't tell a lie is someone who doesn't in fact lie, then *someone who couldn't tell a lie* might actually be a chimera, precisely because to err *is* human and occasions for lying beset every one of us in all sorts of circumstances. Language use is part of our form of life in a way in which drinking alcohol isn't; and while angels and brute animals might be incapable of lying,[11] human beings are neither angels nor brute animals, as those Scholastics recognized who placed us in between the two categories in the Great Chain of Being. You could not *befriend* an angel or a dog, however affectionate you might feel towards the latter (and in spite of the adage that a dog is a man's best friend).

These thoughts suggest a philosophical parallel. If Wittgenstein is right, philosophical problems have their source in human confusion (a broad notion)—the confusion arising from our

[11] Cf. *Philosophical Investigations* 250: 'Why can't a dog simulate pain? Is he too honest?'

'bewitchment by language' (*Philosophical Investigations* 109). That we are language users means not only that going astray through lying is a perennial feature of human life but also that going astray through muddled thought is such a feature. And you and I can only do philosophy together if we can both see what is tempting in various seductive lines of thought, lines which however lead in the end to nonsense or at least aporia. If you are (so to speak) an angel or an animal, then the phantasms and castles in the air which language throws up will be invisible to you and my philosophical questions will either sound like the ravings of a madman or appear to be continuous with the rest of my chatter, just more of the same. But you are neither of these: you are a human being. In doing philosophy with you I in a sense recognize our shared humanity, just as I do if I befriend you.

In response to Wittgenstein's well-known dictum that his aim in philosophy was to show the fly the way out of the fly-bottle (*Philosophical Investigations* 309), Gilbert Ryle once asked, 'What about the fly that never finds its way *into* the fly-bottle?' Ryle's fly would be either an angel or an animal, or alternatively would be a human being very deficient in the use of language. (Or simply immature, like a baby.) If we are talking of people who speak (write, sign) a language, then even those who eschew all 'intellectual thought' will at certain points in their lives inadvertently let false analogies, reifications, equivocations or the like lead them to say things which can only be sorted out by some patient philosophizing.

Wittgenstein wrote: 'Never stay up on the barren heights of cleverness, but come down into the green valleys of silliness [*Dummheit*]' (*Culture and Value* 76e). His reason for this exhortation? 'For a philosopher there is more grass growing down in the valleys of silliness than up on the barren heights of cleverness' (*Culture and Value* 80e). Good philosophy can only be done by parties who are not afraid to talk nonsense—not for its own sake, nor to shock and titillate, but in the hope (e.g.) of seeing where sense leaves off and nonsense begins. One can imagine Wittgenstein saying: 'I would find it difficult to do philosophy with someone who couldn't talk nonsense.' But the ultimate *motive* of the one cavorting in the long grass of the valley of silliness is really that love of truth which Wittgenstein ascribed to himself, even while confessing that he couldn't understand what it would be to love God.

For Anscombe the love of truth was intimately connected with the love of God; this is hinted at in her rhetorical question 'How could I pray for him to God who hates lies and coolly undertake to tell lies for him?' In an essay posthumously published as 'Truth: Anselm and Wittgenstein', she writes: 'Looking at my title ["Truth"] I am sometimes awed by it, for what leaps out of the page at me is one of the names of God.'[12] Whether she would have at all sympathized with Wittgenstein's 'I would find it difficult to be friends with someone who couldn't tell a lie', even under the interpretation of that remark which I have suggested, seems unclear.

I have already touched on Wittgenstein's attitude to religious judgements, his homing in on the question 'What is he doing, saying that?' (as Anscombe puts it) and his impatience with theories and proofs when it comes to religion. In the *Reminiscences* the difference between Wittgenstein and Anscombe on such matters is a recurring theme. One could say of Wittgenstein's conception of religion not just that it was anti-theoretical but that it was in a certain sense anti-rational. Thus he says to Anscombe: '*You* may be able to fill reasoning with religious content; I never could' (sec. 94). And there is the following exchange:

> Very early on in my acquaintance with him we had some discussion, the rest of which I have forgotten, about people of different

[12] Geach and Gormally, *From Plato to Wittgenstein*, 71–76; 71.

religions denying each what the other said—was there a real disagreement here? Wittgenstein's arguments will have tended to throw doubt on this, and I said 'I thought of the difference as *propositional*' and he said 'You are talking like a bloody scholastic.' (sec. 183)[13]

And yet it appears that Wittgenstein felt a certain sort of respect for Anscombe's religious outlook, a feeling in which we might even discern something akin to envy. Consider the following two passages:

Once in my house on the landing he caught me with Tolstoy's version of the gospel in my hands. 'Oh!' he said, 'that is not something for you. It can only disgust you. It is true that it meant a *great* deal to me once, but you see, you know the real thing. I did not, at that time.' (sec. 75)

The idea that *every* thought was open to anyone of enough intelligence seemed alien to him. He spoke contemptuously of Russell's speaking as if he might have embraced, if any religion, Buddhism. He said of the New Testament once that these were mountain slopes a long way away from where he was. I remember now that that was when he said 'I am a frog in a pool'. (sec. 95)

'You know the real thing' means 'You know the Gospel (i.e. the New Testament)'. No need for Tolstoy's version if you know the real thing. And yet for Wittgenstein the New Testament was like mountain slopes a long way away from where he was. He felt as cut off from, and as little before, those mountain slopes as a frog in a pool. It wasn't that he didn't *understand* the New Testament so much as

---

[13] It is interesting that Anscombe appends to this anecdote the following parenthesis: 'Cf. his remarks in the pre-Tractatus notebooks about his best work coming from his most strongly *scholastic* feeling.' Is she perhaps siding with the earlier Wittgenstein against the later?

that he felt incapable of living his life in accord with its message and spirit. He could think this of himself while regarding others as having managed what he could not. And it seems to me that he (at least sometimes) looked on Anscombe as having managed this.

Let me here quote from a letter which he wrote to Yorick Smythies (a fuller version of which appears in the Appendix), having heard from Smythies of his conversion to Roman Catholicism:

> If a friend of mine were to take up tight-rope walking and told me that in order to do it he thinks he has to wear a particular kind of garment I should say to him: If you're serious about that tight-rope walking I'm certainly not the man to tell you what outfit to wear, or not to wear, as I've never tried to walk anywhere else than on the ground. Further: your decision to wear that kind of garment is, in a way, terrible, however I look at it. For if it means that you're serious about the thing it's terrible, even though it may be the best and greatest thing you can do. And if you're dressing up and then don't do the tight-rope act it's terrible in a different way.[14]

At the risk of rendering prosaic what has been expressed figuratively: someone who adopts the Christian way of life is like a tightrope-walker, and someone who does so by joining a particular church is like a tightrope-walker who feels he must don a special garment. 'I've never tried to walk anywhere else than on the ground,' writes Wittgenstein; that is, he has not adopted (or: been able to adopt) the Christian way of life, however much he esteems and admires it. If Smythies is 'serious about the thing it's terrible, even though it may be the best & greatest thing you can do'. Terrible because what is at stake for a tightrope-walker is huge—he could

---

[14] B. F. McGuinness, ed. and trans., *Ludwig Wittgenstein and the Vienna Circle* (Lanham, MD: Rowman & Littlefield, 2008), 363.

plummet to his death—but possibly 'the best & greatest thing you can do' because the successful tightrope-walker is somewhere far above the heads of those walking on the ground.

An inability to embrace Christianity, or to embrace it fully, was not for Wittgenstein a matter of insufficient intelligence but if anything a failure of the will. Indeed, 'cleverness' was something he was generally suspicious of or even derogatory about, particularly in connection with religion but also in connection with philosophy. I have already mentioned his exhortation to come down from the barren heights of cleverness into the green valleys of silliness; and we have also this:

> What makes a subject hard to understand—if it's something significant and important—is not that before you can understand it you need to be specially trained in abstruse matters, but the contrast between understanding the subject and what most people *want* to see. Because of this the very things which are most obvious may become the hardest of all to understand. What has to be overcome is a difficulty having to do with the will, rather than with the intellect. (*Culture and Value*, 17e)

Bad philosophy Wittgenstein regarded as resulting typically from complacency and laziness, rather than from lack of intellectual talent. Anscombe writes:

> The first time he detained me after his lectures—in October 1944, he said: 'It's not lack of talent that mostly makes people into bum philosophers. Look at Ewing. Do you think his trouble is lack of talent?' (sec. 164)

This view of things (in which, I think, there is a lot of truth) helps to explain the kind as well as the degree of self-criticism which Wittgenstein went in for, both as a philosopher and as a human being. To accuse oneself of failure of will, of (e.g.) moral laziness, can for some people take on a self-lacerating aspect which is lacking from self-accusations of lack of talent. No doubt there is something to be said here about the very high standards of behaviour, taste, work, etc. with which he and his siblings were inculcated as children; let us not forget that at least two of his brothers committed suicide. Of course having high standards is in itself a good thing, and Wittgenstein so regarded it:

> [W]e talked of bad writing in philosophy and he remarked: I had good luck; I was very well brought up. I believe he was referring, not to his philosophic training but to his home; certainly all his family had very exacting standards—e.g. in music. (sec. 192)

It may however be that the inculcation of such standards, and later the self-imposition of them, need to be tempered with love if an individual is not to be miserable. That naturally explains why someone as prone as Wittgenstein was to crippling self-criticism should yearn for a forgiving love of the kind which Christianity teaches can be shown us above all by God; and here, I think, is perhaps the main source of Wittgenstein's religiosity.

> I don't know from when his idea that he was lost stemmed. Possibly this always was his tendency [. . .] When he gave expression to that belief of his it was depressing to an extreme degree. He was as it were unapproachable about it. I remember his parting from me once with the words 'Only the Deity can help me'. Except that it was depressing, I did not know what to make of him, of those utterances. (sec. 113, 114)

And yet

> in his last days he spoke of his life as having been one of on the whole cheerful music—the grave and solemn and terrible notes had not been played through him. (sec. 236)

Might the approach of death have induced in Wittgenstein a lessening of that feeling of being lost or damned which had so often afflicted him? It is hard to guess; his character was surely harder to fathom than most.

> I did not understand him. I think I told him so once, for I remember him saying in answer 'How should you understand me?' and something about his life being different. (sec. 234)

But perhaps these thoughts are in danger of producing an impression of Wittgenstein that is too 'grim and cramped'. One of the most attractive features of the *Reminiscences* is their conveying how much of laughter and humour there was in Wittgenstein's company. Here the connection with philosophy is very strong: it can almost seem as if the main source of humour for Wittgenstein lay in the surrealism of thought to which philosophizing so naturally lends itself. Malcolm reports Wittgenstein as saying that 'a serious and good philosophical work could be written consisting entirely of jokes.'[15] And it's clear that his lectures could be peppered with jokes and with humorous fancies. At the same time when a philosophical enquiry was underway to get distracted by the merely ludicrous was grounds for rebuke:

> I don't remember his jokes at all, except that his lectures had a good many in them and one would be desperate with laughter—desperate because once the joke had flowered, so to speak, he so often suddenly stopped laughing or smiling, as he might laugh or smile leading up to it, and assume a serious, even a savagely serious, air and say 'It's not a joke.' (sec. 138)

The jokes to which Anscombe refers will not have been mere asides or ways of keeping his audience entertained (as they typically are

---

[15] Malcolm, *Ludwig Wittgenstein*, 28.

in philosophy lectures); they will have arisen in the course of following through those so seductive lines of thought that ultimately peter out in nonsense—taking this or that path through the undergrowth in the valley of silliness. (Anscombe makes this clear in sec. 139.)

Outside the philosophy lecture, Wittgenstein's taste still lay especially in the direction of what might be called semantic humour: word play, nonsense, etc.

> He liked the riddle: What is the difference between a hairdresser and a sculptor?— the first curls up and dyes, and the second makes faces and busts. The collapse of meaning, I mean the revolution in the transition from noun to verb. He got that from Ben Richards, on whose affection, with that of Con Drury, he so much relied in the last years of his life. Ben was mostly rather silent but he enjoyed many of the same sorts of things as Wittgenstein and particularly the same sorts of jokes. (sec. 161)

It was Ben Richards who described Wittgenstein as on occasion being speechless with laughter. But it is a smiling rather than a laughing Wittgenstein that we more often encounter in the *Reminiscences*. An example which will entertain philosophers is at sec. 225; I won't spoil it for the reader by giving it here.

I remember that in Anscombe's philosophy lectures in Cambridge (which I attended as an undergraduate) there were often displays of humour emerging out of the following-through of some line of thought, just as she describes happening in Wittgenstein's. Apart from anything else, these moments tended to get engraved on the memory, ideally along with the accompanying philosophical point. With Anscombe there was also sometimes a quasi-theatrical element. I think it was Michael Dummett who recalled how during a lecture—possibly one of those which were together to become the monograph *Intention*—Anscombe pronounced the words 'I'm going to be sick' (an utterance of interest because it *isn't* an expression of intention) with alarming realism; no doubt she coolly followed them up with 'That is an example of …' or similar. In a lecture I attended in the 1980s, Anscombe talked about the capacity some people have to waggle their ears, saying of herself that she believed she lacked this capacity. She nevertheless (sitting behind her desk) had a go, appealing to her audience to confirm whether or not she'd actually succeeded in waggling her ears. At this distance of time I think the point may have related to simple bodily actions of which the agent does not have non-observational knowledge (hence the need for a mirror or other people's testimony). Or it may have had to do with the concept of trying: typically when you try to do X (in particular when you try and fail), you in fact do Y (successfully), *thereby* trying to do X—as when you push on a door, thereby trying to open it. But Anscombe's trying to waggle her ears didn't consist in some other intentional action, Y. In fact it consisted in her pulling various odd faces. Under the description *pulling that odd face*, what she did could hardly be called intentional; and in fact the only description under which her action was intentional would seem to be *trying to waggle her ears*. For she was right: she couldn't waggle her ears.

Anscombe's sense of humour had a distinctly mischievous streak. I don't know if that was true of Wittgenstein's—nothing of that sort seems to come through in the *Reminiscences*. One day, I think at a meal, Anscombe turned to me and asked: 'Did you know, Roger, that some trees have sex?' Knowing her as I did, and also knowing the relevant botanical facts, I was able to reply, 'Yes: you mean in some species there are males and females.' I could see from her smile that I had deftly avoided the trap laid for me. That she could be something of a prankster is attested in many other anecdotes.

The friendship between Anscombe and Wittgenstein was a close one. It's sometimes said of Wittgenstein that his attitude to women was generally negative and that he made a special exception of

Anscombe, perhaps because he found it possible to regard her as a sort of honorary man. After all, as she herself reports, he used to address her as 'Old man', although in later years he dropped what she refers to as 'this ludicrous habit' (sec. 180). In fact there are several instances in the *Reminiscences* where Wittgenstein speaks positively about women, either with admiration or with affection. He advised Anscombe to 'listen to Frau Hänsel' (sec. 24) whose intellect was so superior to her husband's. Similarly, though he didn't particularly like Polly Smythies, he 'conceded "She has sense", which Smythies had not' (sec. 175). It was enough to dispel his worries about his friend Rudolf Koder's fiancée, Lisl, for him to see a photo of her: he then said, 'Oh well, that's all right', and they went on to be good friends (sec. 170). When someone spoke disparagingly of a paper given by Martha Kneale he came to her defence, uttering the (from his lips) unlikely sounding verdict 'She was nice'[16] (sec. 169). So it seems fair to say that he didn't harbour any general prejudice against women; and indeed that conforms with his being attuned to the individuality and idiosyncrasy of people in the way I have already described.[17]

But his relationship with Anscombe was of course special. In the very early days there may have been some distrust:

It was round about then that he told Smythies that he had had some good conversations with me, but would not see me

[16] I don't think this can mean 'She made nice, i.e. fine, distinctions.'

[17] On the other hand there is Peter Geach's view: 'Each year at the beginning of his course of lectures Wittgenstein would have a great many listeners, largely female; this crowd would rapidly shrink to a hard core of regular attenders by the third or fourth lecture. This happened in particular during one year's attendance by Elizabeth; noticing this shrinkage, Wittgenstein looked round the room with gloomy satisfaction and remarked: 'Thank God we've got rid of the women!' His anti-woman attitude, from which he dispensed Elizabeth, amused me but also rather alarmed me; I knew that at least one woman formerly his pupil had had it made brutally clear to her that she was no longer in his good books and I feared for the effect on Elizabeth if she should thus be rejected' (P. T. Geach, K. J. Shah, and A. C. Jackson, eds., *Wittgenstein's Lectures on Philosophical Psychology 1946–47* [Chicago: University of Chicago Press, 1988], xii).

anymore, because he did not just want to be a thinking shop; however he must later have changed his mind about my attitude towards him, which indeed wasn't that at all. (sec. 184)

But before long Wittgenstein was taking Anscombe seriously as a philosopher, and in contrast to his early assessments of her writing ('Bought for a farthing' and 'Shit on the floor'; sec. 188), his later assessments were encouraging. The following will have taken place in 1949:

> I was anxiously preparing the last version of an essay called 'The reality of the past' and was in a bad state for concentrating on it. Wittgenstein said he was keen that I should finish it and get it out; I asked why and he said 'Because it will be good for your reputation'. But he added 'I am taking it for granted that it will be good'. This assumption seemed to me a very doubtful one and I did not take the risk of showing it to him; I was too cowardly. (sec. 202)

Wittgenstein's reference to Anscombe's reputation shows something additional, namely that he wanted her career to go well. Indeed to that end in 1945 he went so far as to don a necktie—hateful to him—when visiting the Principal of Newnham in order to urge her to give Anscombe a post at that college (sec. 189).

In 1946 Anscombe started learning German with a view to being able the better to read and understand Wittgenstein.

> I told Wittgenstein, and he said 'Oh, I am very glad. For if you learn German, then I can give you my book to read'. This had been my hope, and it spurred me on. We read the introduction to Frege's *Grundlagen* [*der Arithmetik*] together. (sec. 199)

Not only did Anscombe and Wittgenstein read Frege together; the list of works they read together and discussed, especially in German, is long and almost all of it is not academic philosophy in the usual sense of that phrase. It includes Goethe, Schiller, Dürer, Weininger, Kleist, and others. In several instances Wittgenstein gave Anscombe a particular book to read, and she also gave, or at least showed, him works she was interested in, for example Kafka (who was not to Wittgenstein's taste; sec. 58). The purpose of all this reading and talking was clearly not simply that Anscombe's grasp of the German language should improve but also that she should learn about German culture—and indeed that the two of them should be able to discuss the themes and ideas implicit in the texts. (Wittgenstein's choice of Weininger surely falls into this category.) Their discussions of literature ranged wide, as the *Reminiscences* make clear, and although the emphasis was on German literature we encounter also such figures as Joyce, Dostoevsky, Shakespeare, Cowper, and Newman.

I mentioned a moment ago Wittgenstein's desire to help Anscombe in her career, and this helpfulness on his part became a feature of their relationship. When she was pregnant with her second child Wittgenstein paid for Anscombe to be able to have the child in a private maternity home (the pregnancy was a difficult one), insisting that the payment be regarded as a gift and not as a loan. In the *Reminiscences* we read of several instances when he gave her things. Among these were a waste paper bin, a mackintosh, two chairs, and a toy for Barbara. Apart perhaps from the last, these were items which he felt she would need, which would be of some good to her. In fact this trait of Wittgenstein's was rather general:

I found Wittgenstein a kind and considerate man. If he heard of someone in trouble, he would ask 'Can I help?' If one was in trouble oneself, it was possible to go to him and get help and advice, even though this was obviously interrupting him in work. He was not carelessly amiable or carelessly generous; there was a good deal of thought in what he did for people. (sec. 216)

Anscombe in her turn looked after Wittgenstein at her Oxford home when his health was failing, until the time when he received an invitation from his doctor, Edward Bevan, to come to Cambridge to be looked after by him and his wife Joan (sec. 224–225). The description Anscombe gives of Wittgenstein's final hours is simple and affecting:

Once he opened his large and fierce looking eyes, flung out his hands, and shut them again. Edward told him we were there and that Conrad Pepler was coming. Ben and I held his hands; he groped to have his hand held if it was not. (sec. 231)

The priest whom she'd recommended to Wittgenstein when he wished to talk to a priest, Conrad Pepler, arrived and gave the unconscious Wittgenstein conditional absolution. After Wittgenstein had died it was Con Drury who proposed that he have a Catholic burial; it seems that, Yorick Smythies and Ben Richards having agreed to this idea, Anscombe was not asked, perhaps on the assumption that she would concur. Anyway she did not object. Wittgenstein had been raised in a nominally Catholic household and had never formally renounced his faith. And for a man who said in all earnestness, 'Only the Deity can help me', a Catholic, or at any rate Christian, burial doesn't seem inappropriate.

Wittgenstein's death was a great blow to Anscombe. Her husband Peter Geach would later recount how her weeping for her lost friend and teacher was so intense that he, Peter, became worried that, being pregnant with their third child, she might do herself and the baby a mischief. Such grief must have been extreme indeed;

Anscombe was not in general a lachrymose person and the picture Geach presents is almost alarming. It is certainly very affecting.

Wittgenstein was buried in a plain grave in the Ascension Parish Burial Ground, near to where Dr Bevan lived, and in 2001, when Anscombe died, she was buried next to Wittgenstein.

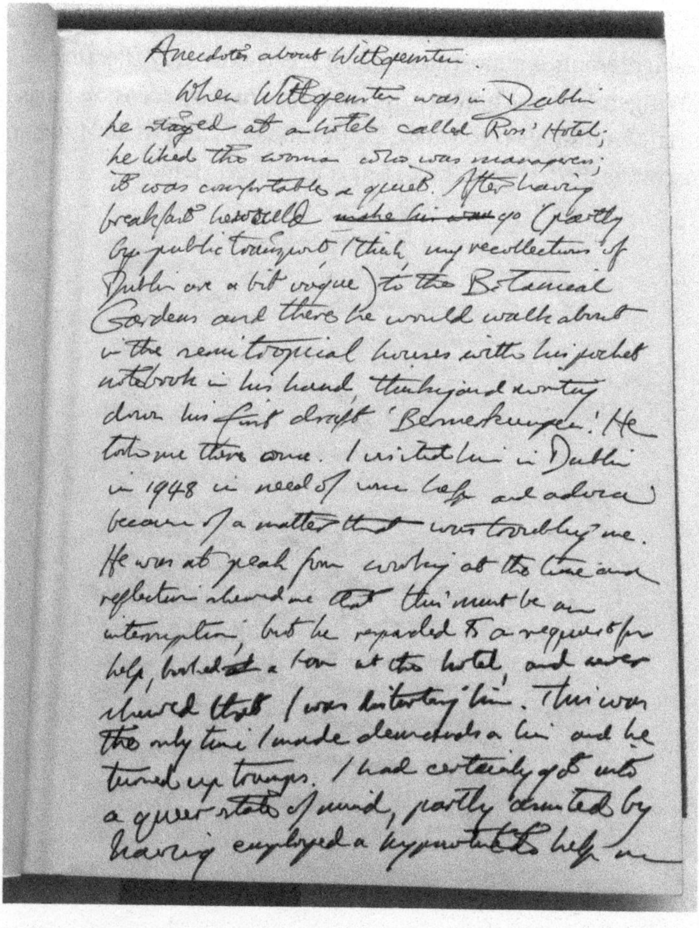

Anecdotes about Wittgenstein.

When Wittgenstein was in Dublin he stayed at a hotel called Ross' Hotel; he liked the woman who was manageress; it was comfortable & quiet. After having breakfast he would ~~make his way~~ go (partly by public transport I think, my recollections of Dublin are a bit vague) to the Botanical Gardens and there he would walk about in the semi-tropical houses with his pocket notebook in his hand, thinking and writing down his first draft 'Bemerkungen'. He took me there once. I visited him in Dublin in 1948 in need of some help and advice because of a matter that was troubling me. He was at peak form working at the time and reflection showed me that this must be an interruption, but he regarded it as a request for help, booked a room at the hotel, and never showed that I was disturbing him. This was the only time I made demands on him and he turned up trumps. I had certainly got into a queer state of mind, partly dominated by having employed a hypnotist to help me

Fig 3.1 First page of the smaller of Anscombe's two sets of 'Anecdotes about Wittgenstein'. *Photo by John Berkman, File 212, Box 6, Collegium Institute Anscombe Archive at the University of Pennsylvania, Kislak Center for Special Collections, Rare Books and Manuscripts, used by permission of the Collegium Institute*

3

Reminiscences of Wittgenstein

Elizabeth Anscombe

Family and the Family Circle

1. When Wittgenstein was going to join the army (or something of the sort) he couldn't remember the names 'Johann' and 'Joseph' with which he had been supplied, but knew there was something of the sort, so he came home and asked his father: then his mother came into the room. His father told her 'This fellow doesn't know his name!' She looked at him and said 'That's Ludwig'. He told me this story. [1]

2. He said he had not a happy childhood, and a *most miserable* youth. [2]

3. He told me his mother was a wonderful daughter, and a wonderful wife, but he thought not so good at being a mother. She had not any appreciation of her children till they were grown-up. She would brush them aside, so that to their ears 'the children of the house' was a contemptuous expression. He told me a story of how they ran into some royal party somewhere and someone said 'Won't you play with the arch-duchess?' and one of the Wittgenstein children said 'Aber wir sind doch nur die Hauskinder'.[1] [3]

---

[1] 'But we are just the house children.'

Elizabeth Anscombe, *Reminiscences of Wittgenstein* In: *Anscombe on Wittgenstein*. Edited by: John Berkman and Roger Teichmann, Oxford University Press. © Oxford University Press 2025.
DOI: 10.1093/9780197648988.003.0003

4. His father feared they would value money and value people according to money too much—a mistake, for none of them had such thoughts at all. [4]

5. His sister, Frau Salzer,[2] told me that when he was a boy they used to say that he had just come out of a band box, he was so funny and smart. [5]

6. He told Smythies[3]—or so Smythies told me—that when he was about nine he and his brother Paul decided that the Christian religion (the Catholic one which they were taught) was all a swindle. [6]

7. From the same source: when he was about 14 he (and his brother) had no use for any composer but Wagner. [7]

8. His father was terrifying. When he came home, his first cry was to know where their mother was. His anger was dreadful. Once it was heard when the girls were having a sewing lesson; the young woman whose task it was to teach them went under the table at the sound of it. [8]

9. Endless tutors and governesses came to the house to teach the children all sorts of things. [9]

10. Wittgenstein objected to Polly[4] fussing about good taste (she used to say her father's taste was bad)—what did it matter; his father had not had good taste and he had never thought anything of it. [10]

11. Paul Feyerabend[5] told me he had met an old schoolmaster from Linz[6] who had had to reason with Wittgenstein when he was at school there—Wittgenstein had locked himself in a

---

[2] Helene; see Appendix.
[3] Yorick Smythies; see Appendix.
[4] Polly Smythies, wife of Yorick Smythies; see Appendix.
[5] Paul Feyerabend (1924–1994), Austrian-born philosopher of science. Anscombe first met Feyerabend in 1950 during her visit to Vienna; Feyerabend was a student there and the director of the Kraft Circle. Anscombe gave a paper to the circle and later persuaded LW to attend one of its meetings.
[6] From 1903 to 1906 LW attended the technically oriented K.u.k. Realschule in Linz, a small state school with 300 pupils in Upper Austria.

room and threatened suicide. He persuaded him to give it up for the time. [11]

12. When Wittgenstein entered a room—in Cambridge, say, at meetings of the Moral Science Club—everyone present became tense and self-conscious. His middle sister Frau Salzer[7] once said to me 'I don't think anyone is ever quite natural in my brother's presence'. [30]

13. He told me that listening to people's talk—e.g. in a family circle—gave him a hazy feeling, sent him into a haze. This he told me about the general family conversation in Ben's[8] family. He added that it had been the same in his own, so that sometimes he would be asked 'Why did you have such a terrible expression?' He was regarded with some awe in his own family. [31]

14. Mrs Sjogren (his niece)[9] told me of a family council before a wedding—the wedding of her elder sister I think—about how Ludwig must be told to wear a tie at the wedding. One of his sisters undertook to persuade him and was successful.[10] [32]

15. I once asked him how his family happened to be called 'Wittgenstein' and he said that they had been court-Jews to the princely family.[11] —On the other hand he had no feeling of being Jewish, no associations. [50]

16. He told me he was the only person who would tell his sister Gretl[12] to 'come off it' and so that they were not on quite good terms towards the end of his life; she was offended by this. (Only I have not quite got this right.) [118]

---

[7] Helene; see Appendix.
[8] Ben Richards; see Appendix.
[9] Clara Sjögren, Helene's daughter; see Appendix.
[10] Cp. the tie anecdote at sec. 189.
[11] More details can be found in Appendix, under 'Karl Wittgenstein'.
[12] Margarete; see Appendix.

17. He took me to see her in Vienna, in the house he built.[13] She had always had people at her feet. She always wanted to interfere with people and tell them how to put their lives right—her brother, I think, only with his friends and some-times pupils, and not always. I did not very much like her for these qualities; we argued, I remember, about advising people and trying to change them. (This was much later.) But she told me an interesting thing about Freud, who was a friend of hers; how he said one must proceed (in trying to do things about people) 'nur ohne Affekt'[14]—the prohibition on Affekt was repeated very strongly. [119]

18. Her brother told me that Freud had cured her son[15] of stammering by analysing him—but worse things had come in place of the stammer. [120]

19. He was once with Koder[16] in the country in Austria (I have this from Ben) and they heard a man singing in a house they passed by. It was so good that they stopped and went in and spent time with him talking and singing. The man was a miner or something of that sort, and he came to Vienna in search of Wittgenstein, wanting to work for him. Of course Wittgenstein couldn't employ anyone, being poor, but Postal (that's who he was) got a job with his sister, Mrs Stonborough.[17] I gather that was a very strong friendship. [137]

20. He told me about his brother Paul's quarrel with his sisters. That was the occasion on which he said 'Courage when

---

[13] Haus Wittgenstein. Margarete Stonborough commissioned the architect Paul Engelmann (a student of Adolf Loos) to design a townhouse for her, and LW became deeply involved in the project. Engelmann later said that he regarded LW as the au-thor of the final product. The building itself is modernist in the manner of Loos and his followers and must have presented a striking contrast to the buildings that originally surrounded it. After World War II and again after Margarete's death Haus Wittgenstein suffered various vicissitudes; it now houses the Cultural Department of the Bulgarian Embassy, although much of the original interior has been conserved or restored, espe-cially on the ground floor.

[14] 'Only without affect'.

[15] Thomas Stonborough (1906–1986).

[16] Rudolf Koder; see Appendix.

[17] I.e. Margarete.

no one respects you for it is very different from courage when everyone respects you for it—it demands a quite different range of qualities'. He said 'My brother Paul is a good man, but he did not have courage at a moment when it was needed, and he was much humiliated.' In consequence of the quarrel Paul would never see his sisters even though he came to Vienna every year and visited the Koders.[18] He demanded that Ludwig too should break with the sisters, or rather with Mrs Stonborough, who had so much wounded him; 'naturally, I wouldn't do that, so I don't hear from him.' (So far as I know, this was the ground of the break with Hermine Wittgenstein[19] and Helene Salzer too.) [138]

21. Wittgenstein liked to give people things and put a lot of thought into doing so. —I remember his telling me a story of how his eldest sister Hermine was with her parents in Paris and went out to look for a present—perhaps it was for her youngest sister (Mrs Stonborough) who was the great beauty of the family, and one of the great beauties of the day. She came back to them and said: 'There's nothing!' [177]

22. When Wittgenstein arranged for me to stay with the Hänsels in Vienna, he said of Dr Hänsel[20] 'He isn't intelligent'. And I thought probably this was nonsense, that Wittgenstein would have 'absurdly high standards'; anyone with whom he was on such friendly terms must be intelligent. But indeed I found it was as he said: Dr Hänsel was a wonderfully good and lovable man with a face which looked as if he had purity of heart and had been through quite a lot; but his intellect was like a cultural weekly so that one kept on feeling a bit embarrassed talking to him; the terms in which he thought of things seemed to be so blunted and dull. Yet

---

[18] Rudolf and Lisl; see Appendix.
[19] LW's oldest sister; see Appendix.
[20] Ludwig Hänsel; see Appendix.

it didn't matter, I suppose because his thoughts were what Wittgenstein called 'bum' *only* from lack of talent. [55]

23. He sighed to me over Dr Hänsel: 'He keeps on speaking of Catholic culture'. [123]

24. He told me to listen to Frau Hänsel. She was a completely unpretentious person with a fine expressive face who thought nothing about herself and thought the world of her husband; but she was much more intelligent than he—what she said was what came out of her own understanding, and her German was expressive and beautiful. [104]

25. He told me once how Ludwig Hänsel came to see him on a train as he was passing through somewhere (or perhaps he had to catch a connection). Dr Hänsel told him of how his elder daughter, whom Wittgenstein knew well and had liked very much, had been killed in a car crash. And they were moving fast, and Dr Hänsel went on running. Wittgenstein stood still and said 'Good Heavens! What are you doing?' And Dr Hänsel said: 'You have to catch your train'. Wittgenstein found this amazing. [178]

26. He told me of how his family were worried about the proposed marriage of one of his great nieces to someone whom they did not like at all. They asked his advice what to say to her since she was, it seemed, hopelessly fixed on the man. He told them not to try and change her by pointing to his faults—that there might be a chance of causing her to reflect if they asked her to consider whether she felt confident of his kindness. (This didn't work, as a matter of fact.) [179]

27. When Hermann Hänsel[21] went to see him in Norway,[22] troubled about faith (which he was feeling he could no longer

---

[21] Ludwig Hänsel's son.

[22] Between 1914 and 1918 LW designed and built a hut at Skjolden in Norway, on an isolated hillside spot overlooking the Lustrafjord. Here he would spend months at a time alone and working.

hold to) Wittgenstein said: Don't concern yourself with your father's *arguments*. He wished him not to be affected by the fact that his father used bad arguments [sc. for religious belief]. [180]

28. Of his first brother's suicide,[23] Wittgenstein told me: He was alone in the world, with not one person to turn to, in Berlin. — I can't remember whether it was he or other members of his family who remarked on the lack of effect that this had on his parents; I mean, they did not think it was a sign that they need be especially concerned and thoughtful in relation to the other ones. —I know it was someone else, at least I think so, maybe Frau Salzer or Mrs Stonborough, who told me of their mother's taking one of the young boys for some examination, and some examiner or teacher warning her that the child was in a bad state nervously, and her telling this as a curious and funny story—it never occurred to her to take this seriously.[24] [198]

29. I remember Wittgenstein saying something which indicated that *of course* his sister lived a life of perfect sexual probity: this consorted with the dignified standards that lay in his background. An example of the inconsistent mixture of attitudes—clearly he would have been indignant if anyone had suggested otherwise; yet he would have reproved or expressed disagreement, I suppose, with someone speaking as if disorderly sexual behaviour deserved condemnation.

---

[23] Two of LW's brothers definitely committed suicide, Rudolf ('Rudi') and Kurt. (The eldest, Hans, might have done; the circumstances of his death remain mysterious.) Anscombe here refers to Rudi; see Appendix.

[24] Hermine Wittgenstein wrote: 'When my seven-year-old brother, Rudi, had to take his public school entrance examination, he was so unhappy and afraid that the examining teacher told my mother: "He is a very nervous child; you should be careful with him." I have often heard this sentence repeated with irony, as if it were nonsensical. My mother could not seriously consider that one of her children could be overly nervous; that, for her, was out of the question.' (*Familienerinnerungen*, 96; quoted in A. Waugh, *The House of Wittgenstein: A Family at War* [London: Bloomsbury, 2008], 24.)

But probably, as usual, it would have depended *who* it was and *how* he spoke. [200]

30. On telling people they were going to die: we spoke of this in Vienna and he said with him it would depend quite on the person. His sister Hermine rightly was informed; but he would not so inform his other sisters. 'If she had been all right when you came you would have stayed with her; that would have been A1', he said, speaking of the arrangement he'd made for me to stay with the Hänsels. I very intensely regretted not having known Hermine Wittgenstein. I assumed that like all the others she was 'riesig kritisch'[25] but when I said this to Lisl Koder she said, 'Nein, sie war *gar* nicht kritisch'.[26] And Frau Hänsel said to me that she was a person who worked on herself to become better always. That in some way she was 'gar nicht kritisch' was an *amazing* piece of information about someone belonging to *that* family in that generation ... and I remembered the story of her saying 'There's nothing!' when she went to the jewellers in Paris with any amount of money at her command, to buy a present for her younger sister;[27] and how much her parents respected her and relied on her advice. [201]

31. More than once I heard (I think from him and from someone else) how Wittgenstein once exclaimed in the family circle: 'Listen to Hermine! It is like a piece of marvellous machinery that creaks!' [202]

32. He used to go to the house where his family was not, to work, say. Thus in the summer he'd stay in the house in the Argentinierstrasse and sleep under the porte-welière [post-delivery] entrance for the sake of coolness. [203]

---

[25] 'Hugely critical'.
[26] 'No, she was not *at all* critical'. Lisl Koder was wife of Rudolf Koder; see Appendix.
[27] See sec. 21.

Culture and Sensibility

33. He once remarked that when he was a young man, in *his* country it had long ceased to be the case that anyone worthy of respect occupied himself with politics and government, though in England that was still happening then—but now no longer. [26]

34. He much liked Bismarck and said 'That was a *man!*' about him.[28] He particularly liked a story of Bismarck's being told some remark and asked his opinion on it; his reply was 'It depends who said it'. [27]

35. Another thing he liked was a story of, I think, the cricketer Grace who became a missionary:[29] 'What God wants is a heart—any old turnip will do for a head'. [28]

36. Many of the people he liked best had a very plain, bald, simple sort of affectionateness which shews in their letters to him. I believe he wanted this from people very much and valued it enormously when he got it. [54]

37. I can see now that one of the things he was very sensitive to was goodness of heart, which made him speak very appreciatively of people. He would say that someone was nice at once because he could see that; and if it had been positively built up so that what a person thought and thought of doing was impregnated with it and shewed discernment

---

[28] Cp. Bismarck's own description of Disraeli: 'Der alte Jude, das ist der Mann' ('The old Jew, he is the man'). In a letter to Malcolm (5 February 1948), Wittgenstein wrote: 'I am not reading much, thank God. I read in Grimm's fairy tales & in Bismarck's *Gedanken & Erinnerungen* [his autobiography] which I admire greatly. I don't mean, of course, that my views are Bismarck's views. It's written in very excellent, though rather difficult German, as the sentences are very long. Otherwise I'd recommend you to look at it.'

[29] W. G. Grace did not in fact become a missionary. Anscombe is probably referring to the cricketer C. T. Studd (1860–1931), who did become a quite famous missionary, having been a notable cricketer. Studd played in the original Test against Australia at which the Ashes were first named and his own name appears in a poem inscribed on the Ashes urn.

too, he would say 'So-and-so is colossal'. But he would react very critically and not enjoy what was done for him in ways which he somehow registered unfavourably. [114]

38. He told me of a time when he was teaching in Austria,[30] had little money and not always enough to eat and of a parish priest at some distance whom he used to go and visit. If when he arrived the housekeeper asked him if he would have anything the priest would say '*Don't ask! Give!*' That he found tremendous. [103]

39. I remember Smythies telling me about Wittgenstein telling him of a negro family—father, mother and one or two children—whom he had seen on a journey. They had made a great impression on him because everything had seemed right about them; dignity in the father, control and kindness, all the relations right. It is likely that he often looked at people and mostly saw most things about them as wrong; rather, it is certain. [105]

40. The impression that Wittgenstein gave one sometimes was of an instrument that was extremely sensitively gauging a number of things; exactly what, however, one didn't know. [111]

41. This feeling of his being unavoidably equipped with a whole lot of antennae, registering one did not quite know what, in connection with every slight thing, this was I think what made him seem a difficult person to be with. —His comments on people often seemed accurate but could he not just have disregarded what so-and-so said, as a casual remark which did not deserve to be bothered about? I once said something like this to him, and he explained what it

---

[30] Between 1920 and 1926 LW taught in four successive primary schools in Lower Austria, at Trattenbach, Hassbach, Puchberg and Otterthal. Malcolm reports LW as having related this story of a preacher in Wales, not Austria, and of its being the preacher's wife that asked LW if he would have something, not his housekeeper (Malcolm [1984, 61]).

would have been for the remark in question to have been 'a casual remark' and how it was *not* that! He convinced me at the time. [115]

42. It was difficult to generalise. I remember his once saying: with one person you find everything in disorder, and it is awful, with another, everything is in disorder but it doesn't matter at all. I.e. his judgments about people were only individual and if he disliked something, it wouldn't follow that he would object to it in something [sc. someone] else. [116]

43. He once said to me after using a w.c. in my house which was idiosyncratic: 'Sometimes you must pull the plug [sc. chain] again at once if it doesn't work, in other cases that is just what you must not do, you must wait till all is quiet; sometimes a half pull at first is right and so on. These differences apply to people too!' [117]

44. He appeared to perceive things about people—sometimes one could not see what he could be getting at. 'Don't worry about that child, she's all right'; but 'That's the one you should be concerned about—he will be a problem to bring up'. He said of Georg Henrik's[31] boy when he was only three 'I see hell in that child's face'. [87]

45. At some time in the years 1944–46 Wittgenstein was invited by a student of English at King's, whose name was Butler,[32] to give a talk to a society, I think a literary one, that Butler belonged to. He would not do that but went to at least one meeting of the society, was disgusted with what he heard, and arranged with Butler to have some meetings in his room with two or three other people—one was a man

---

[31] G. H. von Wright; see Appendix.

[32] John Butler (1923–1958) was a student at King's College 1942–1945, where he proceeded from Part I of the Moral Sciences degree to Part I of the English degree. From 1943 to 1945 he lived in the east wing of the Bodley Building (room S4); this apparently is where the meetings took place. (Information on Butler and his accommodation courtesy of the archivist of King's College.)

called Stern who, Georg Henrik tells me, later wrote a book on Lichtenberg.[33] Wittgenstein asked me to join in these meetings, which quickly moved to King's, since Butler would smoke and Wittgenstein did not like the smell in his rooms. The discussions were about aesthetic matters. I missed part of them because women had to leave undergraduate rooms in King's then at 10.30 [p.m.]. Wittgenstein's main theme was the lack of a tradition now *in* which you knew what to do and how to do things. He said that not one of us would know how to paint a plain black cross on a white wall, if we were given the task: we would not know *where* to put it, or the proportions to adopt. He pointed to the young men who were lounging or sitting in various ungainly positions and said: you do not know how to sit; no one knows how to sit! Look at a photograph from the last century and you will see how once people did know how to sit. [57]

46. He liked to look at the work in photographers' shops. He once took me to look at a large photograph of Lord Rutherford[34] in Ramsey and Muspratt in Cambridge:[35] this he thought very good, very fine. (It looked *extremely* old fashioned, dignified.) Mostly he was contemptuous—especially in Oxford, looking at the poses with thoughtful expressions, intense looks, etc. 'This is the psycho-analytic series!' he said, pausing in the passage at Ramsey and Muspratt's Oxford

---

[33] Joseph Peter Stern (1920–1991), FBA, was educated at St John's College Cambridge, completing his doctorate with a thesis on Lichtenberg in 1949. He taught at St John's, Cambridge, 1952–1962, and then as professor at University College London 1972–1986. The book referred to is his *Lichtenberg: A Doctrine of Scattered Occasions, Reconstructed from His Aphorisms and Reflections* (Bloomington: Indiana University Press, 1959).

[34] Ernest Rutherford (1871–1937), 1st Baron Rutherford of Nelson, OM, FRS, Hon FRSE. New Zealand physicist. Rutherford became director of the Cavendish Laboratory at the University of Cambridge in 1919. The photograph by Ramsey and Muspratt dates from 1937 and is now owned by the National Portrait Gallery.

[35] Lettice Ramsey (F. P. Ramsey's widow; see Appendix) and Helen Muspratt opened their first joint studio in Cambridge above a row of shops in 1932. In 1937 Muspratt married and expanded the studio to Oxford, whilst Ramsey remained in Cambridge and continued to run the original studio until the 1970s.

shop. Further up the Cornmarket there was a place where the style was different. I remarked on this. 'Yes, these are the extroverted types' he said. He made it clear that the idea of having one's photograph taken by these people, and assuming the sort of appearance they photographed, struck him as disgusting—no one decent could join in such a debased activity. [58]

47. He had once tried to have some good photographs made of himself and thought them not quite bad. He gave me one of them (saying with a slightly grim smile 'Don't publish it'). It was made in Vienna I *think*, about 1935. —Once he tried to take a photograph of me, saying: 'Now don't try not to look self-conscious'. But it must have been a failure as I never heard anything more of it. [189]

48. In the King's discussions I remember he used to speak of the influences of what was admired and respected on constructions to which it was irrelevant—times when edges of balconies would suggest a ship's construction, and now stream-lining, even to 'baby prams'. [59]

49. Butler (the King's meetings) once said he liked the University Library (architecturally).[36] Wittgenstein congratulated him on his courage in saying so. [127]

50. He was entirely pessimistic about the impossibility [sic] of doing anything good in art or literature now—unless someone was an utterly new genius, and did something really new; his example of this *sort* of thing was Tolstoy's fables. But the possibility of doing good work otherwise depended on a culture, a tradition, and that we had not got, because all had gone rotten. So that there was no possibility of someone being a good craftsman and knowing how to design a chair,

---

[36] The University Library building, designed by Giles Gilbert Scott, was constructed between 1931 and 1934. It is a Grade II listed building. The building bears a resemblance to Scott's industrial architecture, including Bankside Power Station (now Tate Modern). The library tower stands 157 feet (48 m) tall.

say, which would be a good chair. I think it was not at King's but at my house in Oxford that he pointed to a very ordinary upright wooden armchair: the armchair version of a very common sturdy sort of kitchen chair, they are mostly in dark wood with a rather solid square seat shaped for sitting on, round front corners to the seat, the back leaning back a bit with the two upright pieces turning over at the top and a flat piece going across nearly at the top between them, and in the middle another piece going across with a very characteristic shape[37] always found in these chairs; the legs slightly splayed, with two pieces going from back to front one at each side and a cross piece; a most ordinary chair which has still not become rare enough to cost anything noticeable, one may pick up a couple for a few shillings in a sale room. —Wittgenstein pointed to the armchair of this pattern and remarked: 'No one can make such a chair now.' (So far as I can see what he said was true, one would be surprised to find someone doing it and if someone (through whim, say) started reproducing the pattern it wouldn't look the same.) [60]

51. He said 'It's no good trying to walk with a gait, no one can walk with a gait and if you try to have one you will be disgusting; all you can do is to crawl—any bloody how.' [61]

52. Shoddiness in materials and construction and impatience so that bad work was let pass were unacceptable to him. When he was building his sister's house[38] he'd spend ages on a hinge and compel everyone to be patient, to do it again, to hold up the work, to get it right. His attitude towards every sort of product was like what one hears of Toscanini as a conductor. Modern English people talk about 'perfectionism',

---

[37] There is a drawing in the MS here depicting this shape.
[38] The Wittgenstein Haus in Vienna. See sec. 17 and fn. 11.

but Toscanini is reported as saying he was 'just an honest musician'. [135]

53. At those meetings in King's on aesthetics I remember he said: 'All decent people are nomads now'. And he tried to convey his impression of a young man, a farmer somewhere—I believe in Austria—laughing; someone who hadn't had to 'be a nomad'. [122]

54. About the evil deeds of the Russians his reaction was merely that one might have to go a certain distance in the wrong direction to take an aeroplane in the right one.[39] He felt extremely black about our times. I once cited to him someone (either Teresa or St John of the Cross) saying that all the devils were not more one's enemies than one's fellows in one's convent. He was interested in, pleased by the remark, but apparently rather disconcerted at the source; he wanted to connect it with troubles arising from the horrible plight of people in modern Western culture. [107]

55. English pacifism gave him a 'stomach ache'. Above all, he thought English people talked with *no* grasp of what it was for your country to be in danger of being overrun by an enemy army. — (I suppose that just as there are some things a man shouldn't survive, I mean can't survive with honour, so there are others he can't stand on one side from, like there being a band of marauders attacking his village and his village defending itself as well as it can.) [142]

56. I heard from Rudolf Koder after the first war, when Bertrand Russell[40] was running a society for Peace, Freedom and something else (Justice or Brotherhood) and trying to sell the idea to Wittgenstein, *he* expressed great disgust and wouldn't have anything to do with it. Russell said: 'Really,

---

[39] Presumably the 'evil deeds' referred to were those of the post-revolutionary Bolshevik government.

[40] Bertrand Russell; see Appendix.

Wittgenstein; I believe you would rather I started a society to promote War, Slavery and (whatever the third thing would be)!' Wittgenstein nodded emphatically and said: 'Rather that! Rather that!' [143]

57. He used to say (so people in Vienna told me) that the tram-stop or bus-stop shelters were the only decent things built in that time. [108]

58. I got Wittgenstein to read some Kafka. He did not like him. He thought the stuff ought not to have been written. He said: 'He had a great deal of trouble, *not* writing about his trouble.' I told him of Kafka's instructions to burn it all, and he said 'I wonder why?' I suggested because it was not brought to the form he wanted. He said with great emphasis: 'Oh no! That is a reason why one does not publish in one's lifetime. It is not a reason for wanting one's work burnt'. He added: 'I think he may have had the right idea.' [62]

59. I once showed him some Leon Bloy (I forget what). He was disgusted. 'He gesticulates', he said. [63]

60. A consequence of the Kafka episode was that he gave me Weininger, both *Geschlecht und Charakter* and *Über die Letzen Dinge*; he bought these in Vienna and gave me them when we were both there in 1950. He gave me Weininger as a man who had done what Kafka ought to have done—written about his trouble. (He meant Kafka's writings were an elaborate *pretence* of writing about what he was in fact failing to write about.) [64]

61. He spoke once of the scene in *Crime and Punishment*, the scene of the murder, and how clearly it causes one to visualise the room. [101]

63. I believe the first thing he gave me was a book of Dürer's *Little Passion*,[41] which we used to take to Church with the

---

[41] This is a series of thirty-six woodcuts with frontispiece by Albrecht Dürer on the life and Passion of Christ. It was produced in 1511; its title distinguishes it from Dürer's earlier *Great Passion*.

young children for years. —Something, half of which has got lost, to my sorrow, Grimms *Märchen.* [228]

64. I still have, I think, a strip of paper on which quite early in our acquaintance he wrote out a quotation from Goethe for me: 'Edel sei der Mensch, hilfreich und gut; denn das allein unterscheidet ihn von allen Wesen.'[42] [144]

65. We read Goethe's *Faust* (Part I) together, and I remember his quoting someone who spoke of the electric character of the verse. [145]

66. He said he could not appreciate much English poetry because of the stiffness, the courtly diction. (Blake was the great exception of course.) I was struck by the way in which German poetry could be of the utmost grandeur and *yet* have something nearly homely about it; or indeed quite, as in Gretchen's speech about the jewel case.[43] [146]

67. We also read part of *Eduards Traum* by Wilhelm Busch but I did not enjoy it very much and we didn't go far with it. Something I did enjoy extraordinarily was Kleist's *Marionettentheater.* [147]

68. About the time of Wittgenstein's last journey to Cambridge (February 8th 1951) we were reading Kleist's *Prinz von Homburg* together. I felt sympathy with the 'Er will den Brutus spielen' speech and we disagreed over the attitude of the prince's uncle—Wittgenstein said I did not understand. He had a respect for the ideal represented there. [25]

69. He made me read a poem of Schiller's of which he said that it was in poetry what variations on a theme were in music. — One of the things I most admired that he showed me was a

---

[42] 'Let man be noble, helpful and good; for that alone distinguishes him from all other beings.' The first verse of Goethe's poem *Das Göttliche.* The original is slightly differently punctuated and there is an additional (final) line: 'die wir kennen' ('that we know').

[43] In Goethe's *Faust.*

sonnet of Keller: 'Es ragt ein Haus . . .'[44] He had previously given me the plot of this sonnet and that of itself made a great impression on me and the sonnet corresponded to the hopes of it his account raised. —I remember he also read me Mörike's 'Denk Dir, O Seele'.[45] This was in Vienna when I was trying to get more German inside me than when I had started to learn it in England. [151]

70. He used sometimes to read Shakespeare but grumbled at him. Though I remember his reading me a couple of lines (it was from one of the Henry IV–V plays, and I think I'd recognise it, but can't remember it for the moment) and saying: 'That inclines me to say: "What wisdom!"' I don't know of his ever having read the Sonnets. [152]

71. About James Joyce—Wittgenstein remarked to me 'It's a different culture': he mentioned Joyce's phrase 'the snot-green sea', something to say which was unimaginable in the culture that he grew up in. Kreisel[46] once told me (though he's such a liar one does not know if what he says is true, though I don't know why he should have made this up) that Bruce Hunt[47] asked him whether Wittgenstein had the obscene sense of 'Eier'[48] ('balls') in mind at all in his example of someone punning on 'weiche'[49]—the whisper. Do you like your eggs hard boiled or soft and the singer had to reply 'Weiche, Wotan, Weiche'.[50] Kreisel said he reported this question to Wittgenstein who was horrified: 'Would he think *that* of me?' —Kreisel had another story about a limerick graffito

---

[44] This would appear to be the sonnet by Gottfried Keller (1819–1890) whose first line is 'Ich weiß ein Haus, das ragt mit stolzen Zinnen.' The 1851 version of this sonnet is titled 'Der Schein trügt'; another version by the poet is titled 'Jeder Schein trügt.'

[45] Presumably Mörike's poem 'Denk' es, O Seele!'

[46] Georg Kreisel; see Appendix.

[47] Bruce Hunt (1924–1884), Trinity College, became a Benedictine monk. Mentioned also at sec. 107.

[48] Literally, 'eggs'.

[49] Soft, softly.

[50] Erda's aria in scene 4 of Wagner's *Das Rheingold*.

that Wittgenstein had seen, which he called 'distinctly pleasant'. [199]

72. I once pooh-poohed *Finnigan's Wake*[51] to him—what was the good of something only scholars working at it could make anything of? He said: 'For all you know, this will become the regular form in which people write'. [227]

73. He spoke once of Virginia Woolf and said there was something about her that he liked—a hint of a culture that wasn't university culture, but came from her home. [148]

74. I told him how much I liked reading Montaigne, and he said he never had, though an uncle of his had been very keen on him. He added, I think, that the same uncle (if I am not wrong) had had a passionate admiration for Molière, a thing he did not enter into at all. He manifested no temptation to read Molière. [170]

75. Once in my house on the landing he caught me with Tolstoy's version of the gospel[52] in my hands. 'Oh!' he said, 'that is not something for you. It can only disgust you. It is true that it meant a *great* deal to me once, but you see, you know the real thing. I did not, at that time.' He was right enough that I didn't get much out of the Tolstoy. [171]

76. I had not read Tolstoy's fables, which he thought 'something completely new', something that was not dependent on a tradition;[53] and he told me some of them before I read them; in particular I remember his recounting the story 'How much earth does a man need?' and also 'The Candle' and 'The Two Old Men'. I am not sure whether he also told me 'The Three Old Men'. [189]

77. We once exchanged a few words about the *Sickness unto Death*. He compared it to someone looking at you with a very grave face. —I heard from Smythies that he grumbled

---

[51] *Finnegans Wake* by Joyce.
[52] Tolstoy, *The Gospel in Brief*.
[53] Cf. sec. 50.

about Kierkegaard's way of going on in general. That it was like someone who wanted you to see that there was an orange you could take, or wanted you to take it. But instead of saying 'Here is an orange' he made infinitely roundabout observations from which no one could readily get that there was an orange to take. Smythies asked what I thought, and I said it was possible a man just wouldn't be able to take it in if you said 'Here is an orange'. [172]

78. Of William James Wittgenstein said 'He was a *man!*'[54] He spoke with admiration of James writing down what he *crudely* wanted to say. (He was never interested in subtlety in philosophy.) Again, he called him 'illustrated turns of speech'.[55] [173]

79. He greatly liked Desmond Young's book on Rommel,[56] partly because Young did not accuse Rommel for being a general in Hitler's armies. [176]

80. I heard from Smythies that he thought of visiting German P.O.W.'s. [prisoners of war], but that he made the point that he wasn't going to treat them as if they were criminals.[57] [175]

81. I looked at the Four Courts[58] and asked 'Is that modern?' 'No! Of course not' he said. 'You don't think people can build like that in this century.' I remained very puzzled about it till I learned it had been rebuilt after destruction in the troubles; it was the newness of the stone I had noticed. [213]

82. Once I remember (this was in Cambridge) we talked about Yiddish. He said he found it very unpleasant to hear. [214]

---

[54] Cp. LW's saying about Bismarck, sec. 34.

[55] 'Him' is presumably shorthand for 'his writing'. The phrase 'illustrated turns of speech' (*illustrierte Redewendungen*) appears in *Philosophical Investigations* sec. 295, where LW is discussing the pictures we create or adopt when doing philosophy: 'not facts; but as it were illustrated turns of speech'.

[56] *Rommel: The Desert Fox* (1950).

[57] Malcolm tells of going with LW on a visit to a camp for German prisoners of war on the outskirts of Cambridge, after which 'I believe that Wittgenstein subsequently provided some musical instruments and music for the prisoners.' (Malcolm [1984, 56].)

[58] In Dublin.

83. He was vituperative about 'basic English'.[59] 'I'd as little take it into my mouth as dirt.' [215]

84. 'I know what I want, and I want little' he said about his domestic arrangements. I remember Shah[60] was rather shocked at the domestic work he had to do in Ireland on the West Coast; but, as Rush Rhees[61] remarked to me, that was not something *he* complained of. —He did complain of how uncivilised the people were—not even washing the shit off the eggs he bought from them; and also there were people who could have offered a bit of neighbourly helpfulness to someone living alone out of the way without transport; and they did not. [224]

85. Of course he liked the *manner* of the nice sort of Irish people; pleasanter than the English. But the standard of *manners* very low. [225]

86. He told me how once before the first world war he was in a railway carriage with two bishops of the Church of England who had evidently been at (or were going to) some meeting of bishops. They addressed one another as 'my lord' and their whole conversation with one another was enormously soigné. I asked him if he hadn't wanted to laugh. He looked amused and said 'I was rather impressed'. [134]

87. His ideal for a culture, a world, I don't have much inkling of; his desires about how *people* should be are [were] plain and straightforward; what he appreciated (not necessarily made friends with). It is an extraordinary fact about England or whatever the area concerned was, that this wasn't visibly the reasonable and ordinary need: it is

---

[59] Basic English (British American Scientific International and Commercial English) was the invention of C. K. Ogden, translator with F. P. Ramsey of the first edition (1922) of the *Tractatus Logico-Philosophicus*. It was intended to be an international auxiliary language and aid for teaching English as a second language.

[60] Kanti Shah; see Appendix. Shah had visited LW in Ireland in the spring of 1948.

[61] Rush Rhees; see Appendix.

obviously what one wants, that people should be helpful and give thought to what they did and what was going on and to the person they were addressing. If someone was like that, Wittgenstein would praise him. And people used to retail *stories* about this, as part of the unfathomed mystery of his personality! I don't say that was not a mystery—I do not believe I understood or understand him—but *that* preference was like preferring food over starvation and clothes over nakedness in the cold. [226]

88. He once spoke of the impression made upon him by Poland when he was there—which can only have been the time in the first world war, I think, when he was in Cracow. It was a real culture, but a rancid one, he said—like genuine butter which has gone rancid. [238]

Religion

89. Wittgenstein once said to me that he thought he could not be great friends with someone wholly lacking in something religious. I said what about Russell. He said that when he realised Russell was so lacking, he ceased to be friends with him; that he had thought that Russell had something of this in him. He added: 'You may not think much of 'A Free Man's Worship' but it at least shows that *something was going on.'* [14]

90. I once mentioned this conversation to Kreisel, who seemed a trifle disconcerted (unusual for him). [15]

91. I once shewed Wittgenstein Cowper's Supplices 'Hatred and Vengeance etc'.[62] He was displeased with the title 'Lines

---

[62] William Cowper's poem, *Hatred and Vengeance, My Eternal Portion*, known also as *Lines Written during a Fit of Insanity*. Anscombe's term 'supplices' is Latin for 'suppliant'. The poem does not contain the phrase 'Just God'.

in his 2nd period of insanity' (if I remember it right) but I told him I thought it was Cowper's own. He said the poem expressed thoughts which I knew which were his own—except for 'Just God'—*he* wanted to say 'Hard God'. [21]

92. At another time, and more than once, he said to me that he could not understand the idea of loving God. Once he added 'I *do* understand loving the truth. I have loved the truth—by which, mind, I do *not* mean that I think I *have* the truth.' [22]

93. 'What are these thoughts to me? I am like a frog in a pool.' (I *think* we had been speaking of something religious.) [23]

94. '*You* may be able to fill reasoning with religious content; I never could.' [24]

95. The idea that *every* thought was open to anyone of enough intelligence seemed alien to him. He spoke contemptuously of Russell's speaking as if he might have embraced, if any religion, Buddhism. He said of the New Testament once that these were mountain slopes a long way away from where he was. I remember now that that was when he said 'I am a frog in a pool'. [40]

96. When I went to Oxford in 1946 I thought I would come back for his lectures, but he persuaded me not to do that but to join in some discussions he was having with Hijab.[63] Some of these were about religion, but I did not remember them very well, perhaps understanding them rather little. I do remember that he liked the story of a character in Keller[64] who, when asked what his religion was, said he didn't know that he had any particular religion, except that when things went well for him they didn't have to go well. —Wittgenstein used to discuss *what* was religious

---

[63] Wasfi Hijab; see Appendix. The meetings referred to here were those some of which Anscombe took notes on, notes that are included in this volume.

[64] Gottfried Keller, mentioned also in sec. 69.

about that. If the man meant that because of this or that feature of the situation they might go badly this would not be a religious thought. If my memory does not deceive me, he was driving at the idea that any explicable content would *disqualify* it as a religious thought. [67]

97. We talked about the existence of the world too; from this I carried away only the strong impression that he still had the idea of 'the feeling for the world as a—limited—whole'.[65] He contrasted the scientific attitude with this. [68]

98. He also talked about what it could mean to say 'God will not tempt you beyond your strength'—or 'God does not tempt a man beyond his strength'. —He spoke of one person saying 'I can't' and another 'you won't'; and all we can say is 'he doesn't', —or rather, then he perhaps must say 'I don't'. [69]

99. The difficulty about not being tempted beyond your strength was (I believe) not having any criterion except what happened for what was within your strength—so if you are in danger of succumbing how can it be information to say God will not tempt you beyond your strength? *What* is being said? [70]

100. I remember talking with him at this time too about Newman[66] and miracles and George Fox.[67] He detested the idea that a set of reasonable men could decide that something was a miracle. So if George Fox called something a miracle, that was that he had it in him to call it that.[68] He

---

[65] See *Tractatus Logico-Philosophicus* 6.45.

[66] John Henry Newman (1801–1890). English cleric, theologian, and author, associated with the 'Oxford Movement'. He was originally an Anglican priest but converted to Catholicism, subsequently being made a cardinal and in 2019 being canonized. He wrote extensively on the nature of miracles.

[67] George Fox (1624–1691). English Dissenter and a founder of the Religious Society of Friends, commonly known as the Quakers. His *Book of Miracles* contains numerous accounts of miracles for which he himself was allegedly responsible.

[68] In the MS the word 'just', before 'was', has been crossed out; perhaps the whole sentence could be paraphrased: 'So if George Fox called something a miracle, that meant that he had it in him to call it that.'

spoke of Newman's saying a miracle was a sign, not just an extraordinary event. 'I see what he means. If my stick jumps in the air, goes into several pieces, says ha-ha and then comes together again, that's impossible or extraordinary, but is not a *miracle!*' [71]

101. 'What is it to me if a set of fools say something could not happen in the course of nature?' (This was about having panels of medical experts at Lourdes.) I said 'Must they be fools?' 'All right—what is it to me if a *set of very clever men* say something could not happen?' —I wondered what he would think if he *saw* an extraordinary event of a kind to be against the course of nature. He said his present thought was that it would be 'So what?' —He did not *despise* belief in miracles; only 'rational' belief in miracles. He would not despise the man whose taking something as a miracle was a sort of 'Aeusserung',[69] a confession wrung from him. What he could not stand was the suggestion that a reasonable man could see as a matter of reasonable consideration that such and such miracles happened. He thought this a stupid misunderstanding. [72]

102. He used to call Ludwig Hänsel a 'Giftmischer',[70] so Dr Hänsel told me. The phrase surely came from the Apostles in Cambridge, which he joined (I think he was faintly ashamed, in later life, of their oath; or perhaps he was only amused).[71] *They* spoke of poison-mixing, so far as I know,

---

[69] 'Expression', 'avowal'. The term is famously made use of in the *Philosophical Investigations*.

[70] 'Preparer of poison' (also 'chemist').

[71] Those joining the Apostles were (are?) required to swear an oath of secrecy. In his *Autobiography*, Russell, quoting from one of his letters, writes: 'My friend Wittgenstein was elected to the Society, but thought it a waste of time, so he imitated henry john roby and was cursed.' In a footnote Russell explains: 'Henry John Roby was elected a member of the Society, but wrote to say he was far too busy to attend the meetings and was therefore ritualistically cursed and his name was spelt thenceforth without capitals. Ever after when a new member was elected the curse was solemnly read out.' Of LW's decision Russell writes, 'I think he did quite right, though I tried to dissuade him' (B. Russell, *The Autobiography of Bertrand Russell* [London: Unwin Paperbacks, 1975], 231).

meaning anything religious or parsonical. But he thought about the phrase and put a peculiar construction upon it. He would think the arguments of apologetic, which were supposed to prove beliefs of religion, were a case of 'poison-mixing'—i.e. a poisonous mixture produced from ingredients that ought not to be put together. (Or that is my *impression* of his idea. In any case I have only impressions. But here there is some effort at understanding and construction out of *vague* memories, rather than recording of utterances, and so I warn that it is an impression.) [73]

103. I once asked him what he would say to someone who came to him troubled by doubts in religion. He replied: 'I should probably raise doubts about his doubts'. [75]

104. Rush Rhees told me about Wittgenstein's saying of proofs of the immortality of the soul: 'If it's something you can prove, I don't want it!' I think it makes this a bit more intelligible to read some of the remarks in Waismann's records of Wittgenstein's talks with him and Schlick.[72] 'A theory does nothing for me.' Anyone *saying* something religious is—or ought to be (?)—*doing* something religious in saying (cf. the remark about 'filling reasoning with religious content').[73] *What is he doing, saying that?* is Wittgenstein's question and he is not moved by the question: Is it *true?* because to say p is true is to say p and so the original question remains: *what is he doing* in saying that? (But not at all in the sense of 'speech-acts'.) [81]

105. This accords well with all I remember hearing him say. I remember once walking with him by the river in Cambridge,

---

[72] Friedrich Waismann (1896–1959), Austrian philosopher. Between 1927 and 1936 Waismann had many conversations with LW on topics in philosophy of mathematics and philosophy of language. These conversations, recorded by Waismann, were eventually published in McGuiness 1979. Moritz Schlick (1882–1936), Austrian philosopher and one of the founders of the Vienna Circle. Waismann studied under him.

[73] See sec. 94; also sec. 96.

and his talking about truth. Here again Wittgenstein used the fact that to say ' "p" is true' is to say 'p', to shew that 'there are as many different sorts of truth as there are different sorts of proposition'. — (This is certainly a long way from what people mean when they speak of different sorts of truth. —E.g. description of a room, description of a sensation; these are different kinds of proposition.[74]) [82]

106. 'One makes cultural demands', 'One has cultural requirements', he once said— 'of course I know that's nothing that counts as religion.' [88]

107. He was worried about Bruce Hunt; 'so green.'[75] It was Hunt who said to him, 'I'm afraid I do believe in natural rights'; and Wittgenstein said to him (what he did not say only to him) 'Never be proud of seeming a fool—you may be one.' Hunt tried to become a Dominican. Wittgenstein thought this a very bad idea because of all that philosophy; but he was concerned when Hunt was not accepted and asked me whether it meant that Hunt would so to speak be blacklisted for joining some other order. I told him it would not. [89]

107. 'One should not think one has the true philosophy because one has the true religion.' [90]

108. I remember trying to tell him about a book by an American lady on fanatical sects and vagaries; unluckily I called it a 'survey'. 'I hate these surveys!' he said. I said 'But they really did do ridiculous things, like expecting divine guidance for whether to put on the right stocking first or the left.' He rebuked me for not knowing what I was talking about. [91]

109. Once I asked him whether, if he had a friend who came from a witch-doctor part of the world and was inclined to believe in witch doctors and adopt corresponding practices, he would try to stop him. He thought briefly and

[74] Cf. *Philosophical Investigations* sec. 291, 292.
[75] An epithet LW also applied to Kreisel; see sec. 159.

said, 'Yes, but I don't know why'. He always detested sayings like 'But modern science shews...'. [92]

110. On attempts to make sense of, to reconcile apparent contradictions in, religion, he said: 'It's like enclosing something jagged in smooth glass. I prefer to have it jagged.'[76] [93]

111. He felt some interest in Newman. He was however annoyed by Newman's defending trans-substantiation by saying we didn't know much about substance. He bought a volume of Newman's sermons but gave it away to us because its controversial character displeased him. He liked a saying of Newman's that the Trinity was 'unus' not 'unum'[77] and it seemed to say something to him, which I tried to grasp but couldn't. [149]

112. I told him that when I was sixteen/seventeen I had read à Kempis[78] with great appetite. He exclaimed that there must be something in the idea of an *anima naturaliter Christiana*[79] but I turned the conversation by telling him that that phrase didn't mean in Tertullian anything of the sort, but was a statement that the soul is (i.e. all souls are) so, as shewn by the general intelligibility of greetings, 'God bless you', and so on. He said nothing to that and after a while we talked of something else. [150]

113. I don't know from when his idea that he was lost stemmed. Possibly this *always* was his tendency; but possibly from the time in the nineteen twenties when he thought God

---

[76] Cf. Anscombe's account of a meeting of the Moral Sciences Club at which Wittgenstein referred to Augustine: 'The Question of Linguistic Idealism', *Collected Papers*, Vol. 1, p. 122.

[77] 'Unus' is the masculine form of the Latin word for 'one'; 'unum' is the neuter form of that word.

[78] Thomas à Kempis (c. 1380–1471), German-Dutch theologian and author of *The Imitation of Christ*.

[79] 'Naturally Christian soul'. The phrase is coined by Tertullian (c. 155–c. 220), the early Christian theologian; see *Apologeticus* 17.6, *Patrologia Latina* 1:377.

called him and what he had to do to obey the call was—
from then on without calculation or consideration to do
whatever came into his head. He had not the courage,
or resolution, or obedience to face this prospect. I heard
of this, not from him but from Ludwig Hänsel, and
I connected it at once with that anger he had shewn me
when I spoke of those sectaries who have the idea of doing
whatever occurs to them at the bidding of the Holy Spirit.
I had not understood that anger, it had seemed extraordinarily personal, not like when he was reproving me for
being 'cocksure'. [164]

114. When he gave expression to that belief of his it was depressing to an extreme degree. He was as it were unap-
proachable about it. I remember his parting from me once
with the words 'Only the Deity can help me'. Except that
it was depressing, I did not know what to make of him, of
those utterances, I didn't know *how* serious they were. I believe in fact he was quite serious whenever he appeared serious. I have often thought about a time when he said to
me—more than once indeed— 'If someone asks me if I believe in the devil, I believe in the devil *in man*. But I think
I should not torment myself with a bogy'. Now this was the
utterance of a man who really was in danger, or had been in
danger, of being frightened by the thought of the devil; but
it *could* have been the utterance of one who was *not* really
at all inclined to torment himself with that thought. That is
the shallowness of the time, that you get people saying one
should not repine about past bad actions, who really are in
no danger of doing so and probably a bit of that if it really
happened to them would be just what they need to have.
So I heard Wittgenstein in puzzlement because I was un-
sure of answering him as I would answer someone else who
said a thing like that, indeed pretty sure it would be a mistake, but I did not really grasp that he meant it and I would

usually be silent. I never knew anyone who said so little that he did not mean. In his writings there aren't, I think, careless words. [165]

115. I once reported to him the argument of Pascal's Wager, which he received from me as if he did not know of it. 'A queer argument' he said, but no more:[80] [169]

116. 'There is such a thing' Wittgenstein once said to me 'as being born with a rotten character, and I suppose that the doctrine of original sin means that everyone is born with a rotten character. I do not agree.' [188]

117. On one occasion in my house at Cambridge we were talking and he said: 'It may be *necessary* for a man to make confession to someone.' I asked 'Necessary for what?' He replied 'For his own peace of mind'. [194]

118. The idea of 'testing the spirits to see whether they are from God'[81] was alien to him, something he seemed to reject. I did not ever make that Pauline quotation to him; I wish I had, to learn what he would make of it. But the idea that one could criticise, enquire into, doubt, assess, when one received as one thought a divine call, *seemed* to be something he quite rejected. The whole idea of 'rationality' here, of thinking one could have reasons against a man's claim of this sort, seemed offensive to him. Of course, he granted it could be mere silliness and affectation, but after that, no reasoned considerations. (What I have said in this paragraph, except for what he granted, is more interpretation than report on my part.) [195]

---

[80] In the MS this anecdote is repeated later on: 'I told him once of the argument in Pascal, the wager—which surely he had heard of before? but he heard it as if it were new to him. 'A queer argument' he said, but no more.' [197] This has not been included in the present text.

[81] See 1 John 4:1.

119. Once he spoke to me at this time[82] of the way the world treated God. I asked what he meant. 'Why, that no one obeys him, no one cares, no one has the slightest respect for him'. [131]

Thought and Work

120. If one—as one might think—only slightly altered the words of something Wittgenstein said, he would be utterly puzzled and reject the thought. It was unsafe to draw vague inferences as to the *sort* of thing that he thought, from one's assimilations of what one heard from him to some more or less commonplace or easy run of thought on a subject. [29]

121. The moves of thought that Wittgenstein made were not usually predicted accurately. [43]

122. One such move, very powerful in the right place: 'But *surely*', one says, 'I *know* such and such, quite apart from any words!' Wittgenstein replies: All right—but how do you know that 'such-and-such' is the verbal expression of what you know? Such a comment opens the ground up before one's feet, quite suddenly. [44]

123. Early on in our acquaintance Wittgenstein quoted to me with great approval a French proverb: 'On ne peut pas chier plus haut que la queue'.[83] [45]

124. He sometimes made people stupid, I believe, as when Hijab suggested that knowledge was more intense than belief.

---

[82] The original position of this paragraph (after sec. 212 [130]) shows that Anscombe is referring to the time when she and Wittgenstein were in Vienna.

[83] 'One can't shit higher than one's tail'. The more usual French phrase is 'péter plus haut que son cul', i.e. 'to fart higher than one's arse', generally applied to someone who has a too high opinion of himself.

Wittgenstein was angry at that, he thought Hijab must be pulling his leg, to say something so silly. [46]

125. At another time he exclaimed in class that we were all intelligent people but left our intelligences outside in the market place, and it was this market-place intelligence that he wanted. It is quite true that one would sometimes timidly suggest the obvious, or timidly put the obvious construction on his words, for fear he meant something much more difficult. [47]

126. Sometimes I believe he made one stupid because one was afraid of being stupid—so one would choose a different way of saying something from the way it first occurred in one's mind, thinking this other way would go down better with him—only to find that he had objections which did not apply to what one really meant. [35]

127. He made one feel that it was very difficult to look in the right direction. [76]

128. Once in a lecture I said 'But I want to say: "blue is *there!*"'[84] and he said: Now let me find the medicine which is the right one for you *now*; and then came out with the idea of 'pain-patches' on fruits and plants.[85] This was certainly effective. I have always since understood better the Locke idea about secondary qualities. [48]

129. Wittgenstein very often seemed to understand one's philosophical thoughts and problems better than one did oneself. One would say what one thought—then he would amplify it, make it seem more convincing, carry it deeper—and then undo it. [49]

130. I remember saying I couldn't make anything of the mouse passage.[86] He laughed and said 'I like the mouse. It is a

---

[84] In the MS the first two words of 'blue is there!' are underlined, the third is double underlined.
[85] Cf. *Philosophical Investigations* sec. 312.
[86] *Philosophical Investigations* sec. 52.

good passage.' That reminds me of a story of Rhees saying something made something else so much clearer—well, Wittgenstein thought that ground for crossing it out. — This sort of thing must be the ground for Professor Price's[87] story that he wrote it in English first and then translated it so that fewer people should understand it. 'That makes it intelligible' probably = 'That produces an illusion of understanding'. [230]

131. I remember his blaming Kierkegaard as a man who wanted people to take an orange but tried every way of getting them to do it but saying, 'Here's an orange, have it.'[88] [231]

132. [This] Consorts curiously with his own stuff about therapy and a sickness of the understanding not being terminated (I suppose like terminating a pregnancy). But fits with the stuff about having his feet on the ground, a *healthy* understanding, home baked thoughts. He never that I can remember spoke of *plain* thinking but I believe he might well have done so, it was what he wanted. *Of course* his name is one of the names invoked in the cult of *anything but plain thinking*. [232]

133. I once said to him 'But of course everybody understands that in such and such a way' (I am sorry that I forget the topic). 'If everybody understands a thing in a certain way that is sure to be false!' he said. He quoted to me Nietzsche's saying: 'If something true receives public

[87] H. H. Price (1899–1984), Welsh philosopher. From 1935 to 1959 he was Wykeham Professor of Logic and Fellow of New College, Oxford; among those who attended his lectures on perception was the young Anscombe who later recorded: 'I found them intensely interesting. Indeed, of all the people I heard at Oxford, he was the one who excited my respect; the one I found worth listening to. This was not because I agreed with him, indeed I used to sit tearing my gown into little strips because I wanted to argue against so much that he said. But even so, what he said seemed to me to be absolutely about the stuff' (G. E. M. Anscombe, *Ethics, Religion and Politics. The Collected Philosophical Papers of G. E. M. Anscombe*, Vol. III [Oxford: Basil Blackwell, 1981], Introduction, viii]).
[88] Cf. sec. 77.

acknowledgement, ask in the interests of what lie this has happened'. [233]

134. He once asked me why people so commonly took some line or other and I said that I thought it was really true that people were like sheep, that hardly anybody actually thought anything on his own account but they took up things to think because they heard them and everyone was saying them. 'I believe you are probably right', he said, and we started talking of something else. [234]

135. In remembering him, I am struck by his capacity to break off his consideration of a matter—quickly to take in how things were, accept it without comment or reaction— though with full attention—and then not dwell on it. It was probably *this* that enabled all his remarks to seem so attentive and discussions to seem so high-powered. *Either* the full blaze of attention, *or* leave it alone, having taken it in. No vaguely blathering on about what had come up. I remember he once spoke of 'chatting' and I was amused, thinking to myself 'Chat? You never chat!' But that was not true. We did chat, have desultory conversation; he made many casual remarks. But they lacked emptiness, the emptiness of exchanges people make for the sake of going on talking. I know other people whose conversation has slightly this character who do not in the least resemble Wittgenstein. I don't think I know anyone who does this very definite switching off, leaving the thing. [235]

136. Wittgenstein often said that he did not like writing in which people did his chewing for him, as one would not like chewed food. He liked authors who gave one what they had to give and one chewed and digested it. I am not clear about this: William James would be a *clear* example. I believe this was not for him an expression of *his* taste (like not liking light-hearted Gothic). [236]

137. Wittgenstein once told Kreisel (so Kreisel told me) that he devoted more time and thought to questions of style than Kreisel could well imagine. [42]

138. I don't remember his jokes at all, except that his lectures had a good many in them and one would be desperate with laughter—desperate because once the joke had flowered, so to speak, he so often suddenly stopped laughing or smiling, as he might laugh or smile leading up to it, and assume a serious, even a savagely serious, air and say 'It's not a joke'—but I wish I could remember examples. The only one I can remember concerned the king who wanted his wife to weep—What did he want? Tears to come out of her eyes? Then an onion would do—but they were mostly funnier and more unexpected than that. [77]

139. Once in a lecture at Cambridge, with a very small group of students, I remember only that Lewy[89] and I were there, he was pursuing some matter very closely, and making very ludicrous suggestions (the 'patent nonsense' of the thoughts one was tempted to have[90] revealed in examples that made one want to collapse laughing) when suddenly he said with great ferocity 'Whoever laughs I *hate*!' Astonishingly, this was actually intimidating, not embarrassing. [124]

140. I remember finding him embarrassing early on, I think in the autumn of 1944. He'd not been put down as chairman of the Moral Sciences Club but Broad[91] had; I think this

---

[89] Casimir Lewy (1919–1991), Polish-born philosopher. He studied philosophy at Cambridge under John Wisdom, graduating in 1939, and attended LW's lectures from the late 1930s until 1945. Anscombe could well be referring to the lectures of Michaelmas 1944, when LW's audience numbered just six. See J. Klagge and A. Norman, eds., *Ludwig Wittgenstein: Public and Private Occasions* (Lanham, MD: Rowman & Littlefield, 2003), 355.

[90] Cf. *Philosophical Investigations* sec. 464: 'My aim is: to teach you to pass from a piece of disguised nonsense to something that is patent nonsense.'

[91] C. D. Broad (1887–1971), English philosopher. From 1933 he was the Knightbridge Professor of Moral Philosophy at Cambridge. Although he found LW's way of doing philosophy antipathetic, he did not oppose LW's election to a professorship at Cambridge; he apparently said that 'to refuse the chair to Wittgenstein would be like refusing

was because he wasn't expected back, merely, but he took it as an indication of non-confidence and made a long speech about it, explaining that he was willing not to come if they didn't want him.[92] [125]

141. On the famous occasion when Joad[93] attacked Cambridge philosophy and Wittgenstein made a long reply, saying that Plato had called sophist the man who made money out of peddling shoddy second hand wares, and that was Joad—'the slum landlord of intellectual slums'—Moore[94] was nodding energetically in agreement with it all. (I have this by report, it was before my time.) Wittgenstein asked Wisdom[95] later what he'd thought of it. Wisdom said he'd been rather bored. Wittgenstein was angry with him. He told me of this later: 'I thought he hadn't the *right* to be bored!' [126]

142. Of Norman Malcolm[96] he said 'He would give his right arm for philosophy'. That was when Norman was attending Wittgenstein's last lectures. [41]

143. Of Plato: 'What is so good about him is that it is clear that these questions are a matter of life and death to him'. [18]

144. Once in my kitchen at Cambridge after a meal we were looking at Plato's *Ion*. Wittgenstein read the end and

---

Einstein a chair of physics' (M. Drury, 'Some Notes on Conversations with Wittgenstein', in *Ludwig Wittgenstein, Personal Recollections*, ed. R. Rhees [Oxford: Blackwell, 1981], 156). For LW's thoughts on this, see sec. 148.

[92] LW was duly elected chairman.
[93] C. E. M. Joad (1891–1953), English philosopher and broadcasting personality. Joad read his 'Appeal to Philosophers' at a meeting of the Aristotelian Society at Trinity College on 23 January 1940. For details of Joad's paper and Wittgenstein's response see G. Citron, 'Wittgenstein's Personal Conversations with Rush Rhees (1939–1950): From the Notes of Rush Rhees', *Mind* 124, no. 493 (2015): 56–57. Interestingly, Joad was invited to read the same paper at the Jowett Society on 31 October 1945, the first Jowett meeting after the war.
[94] G. E. Moore; see Appendix.
[95] John Wisdom (1904–1993), English philosopher. He succeeded LW as Professor of Philosophy at Cambridge in 1952.
[96] Norman Malcolm; see Appendix.

said 'And so say I' and shut the book up. He spoke in an unemphatic conversational tone—not, as I remember, a very common one with him. I remember his using it again on another occasion in Lotte's[97] rooms in Somerville (we were using them for some reason) when I showed him (without comment) a piece by Lichtenberg[98] which had struck me as absurdly like Wittgenstein himself both in ideas and in style. (It was[99]) Wittgenstein read it and said 'Yes, I might have written it myself'. [78]

145. That summer in Oxford he was walking downstairs with me in the Smythies' house and said 'It is easier to go upstairs than downstairs'—then he added 'You know, that is the sort of remark that might get preserved, when everything else one produced was lost, and then people write endlessly about this one remark'. [79]

146. Once, when we were sitting in a train he said: 'I wouldn't want what I have written to be consulted as ...' I can't remember the phrase he used, but my impression of the gist of it was something like 'an authoritative book'. Or like a collection of dried flowers ... 'It may be that you will some day lose interest entirely in these thoughts.' [167]

147. We spoke once of his perhaps giving up philosophy, which he did not want to do just as a profession—it had to be living work, or he was not happy to do anything in it—and I said it might revive as it did before. He said 'And I'll stage another comeback, when I'm completely ga-ga'. [221]

---

[97] Carlotta ('Lotte') Minna Labowsky (1905–1991), German-born classicist who (being Jewish) left Germany in 1934 and eventually became a Fellow of Somerville College. Anscombe co-taught a course with her in Trinity term 1951, the term when LW died. The two women were close friends and Labowsky gave Anscombe some assistance in the translating of the *Philosophical Investigations*.

[98] Georg Christoph Lichtenberg (1742–1799), German physicist, satirist and Anglophile. G E Moore recorded Wittgenstein as having quoted 'with apparent approval' Lichtenberg's statement 'Instead of "I think" we ought to say "It thinks."' See G. E. Moore, 'Wittgenstein's Lectures in 1930–33', in his *Philosophical Papers* (London: Allen & Unwin, 1959), 309.

[99] Gap left here in the text.

148. The Rockefeller Foundation wanted to give him money in 1950 and a representative of theirs came to see him in Oxford.[100] He said it was out of the question then, because he was not well enough to do good work; but promised (what he knew was all nonsense) to let them know and ask for a grant if he got to doing serious work again. Not that his last work was not perfectly serious; but he didn't think his state and the amount he did made sense of a grant. [222]

149. I vaguely heard a story of his trying to return payments to the Moral Science Board because he considered his lectures to have been no good—much to their embarrassment. [223]

150. In Cambridge, walking as we rarely did toward Grantchester at one time, he said: 'It may be that what I have found out is like Longfellow's discovery of the Hiawatha metre. That must have seemed a colossal thing.' [168]

151. 'I never produce fire, but only superficiality and sham superficiality in people' Wittgenstein once said to me. When he gave up the chair Wisdom wrote to him 'You have changed philosophy'. He showed me the letter and said 'I wish I hadn't'. He liked the letter that Broad wrote to him— something about Broad's never having had the attitude that Wittgenstein had towards philosophy. [99]

152. He once said something about fearing to be in a hurry to publish. I said no one could think he was that if he published then. He corrected me: 'I didn't say anything about *seeming* to be in a hurry, but about being in a hurry.' [136]

153. When Ayer[101] published some stuff in *Encounter* which angered Wittgenstein some of his friends pooh-poohed it

---

[100] On 11 January 1951 Chadbourne Gilpatric met with Wittgenstein to offer him, on behalf of the Rockefeller Foundation, funding for any forthcoming publications.

[101] A. J. Ayer; see Appendix. Ayer's piece was in fact published in the *Listener*. (*Encounter* was only founded in 1953, after LW's death.) In it Ayer refers to 'the school of Ludwig Wittgenstein', but the views he then alludes to are those of that 'representative' of the school, John Wisdom. The incident, and LW's annoyance, are reported at

and thought he should take no notice. He was indignant. He said people's attitude was that he was 'Vogel frei'—i.e. anyone could take a shot at him with impunity, he was a sort of outlaw. [20]

154. Wittgenstein used to take people out to the gas works, or rather to where you could see the gas works from by the river on Midsummer Common. There was a rotating sieve to be seen in the distance, which offered a startling example of 'seeing as'.[102] He said he had asked the manager and found out that it really did always rotate in exactly the same way. It was his thoughts on seeing as that proved most destructive of the old idea of a sense datum. [95]

155. I once read a paper at the Moral Sciences Club[103] about saying things in one's head and said one couldn't do many things in one's head, e.g. not 'fall off a log in one's head' as opposed to imagining falling off a log; one couldn't do physical movements in one's head. Wittgenstein said 'You are wrong: if you hold your hand as if it had a pen in it you can write your name "in your head": you may make some slight movements in doing it, but you've no idea just what they are'. [109]

156. In the late nineteen forties—in 1947, I think, Wittgenstein came to Oxford for a meeting of the Philosophical or Jowett Society—probably the latter.[104] He wouldn't 'read the paper'. Oscar Wood read a paper on 'Cogito ergo Sum', of which Wittgenstein said 'He is educable'. Prichard[105] came but didn't hear anything, obviously. He asked Wittgenstein whether

---

somewhat greater length by Malcolm, who however doesn't reveal Ayer's identity; see Malcolm (1984, 56–57). Early in 1947 Ayer published a revised and extended version of his *Listener* article in *Polemic* (Issue no. 7) under the title 'The Claims of Philosophy'; this may be what Anscombe is referring to in sec. 167 as a 'reprint' of the earlier article.

[102] The concept of 'aspect-perception', famously discussed by LW in the *Philosophical Investigations* and elsewhere.

[103] Probably 'Talking to Oneself' (6 February 1947).

[104] Jowett Society meeting on 14 May 1947.

[105] H. A. Prichard (1871–1947), English philosopher. He was White's Professor of Moral Philosophy in Oxford and retired in 1937.

he believed the statement 'Cogito ergo sum' was right. Wittgenstein said he didn't know what it meant. Prichard said 'I don't believe you'. Wittgenstein said 'If someone were to say: "I think it'll rain today—therefore I exist", I wouldn't know what he meant'. But it shouldn't be taken like that, I think, only like: 'I am thinking, therefore I exist'. [121]

157. In Oxford in 1949 (I think it was) we talked a good deal about certainty. I remember sitting in Christ Church considering the example of a surgeon who finds a man's head full of sawdust. I can't remember how the discussion went— but Wittgenstein may have suggested in the end that the case would simply dry out of sight. —He said that certainty was a 'logical status' which we hadn't investigated.[106] [100]

Friends and Colleagues

158. Wittgenstein used to say that Kreisel was 'green'—to Kreisel, who told me. [12]

159. Kreisel's turning against Wittgenstein is an oddity of psychological history. He does as much harm as he can to Wittgenstein's reputation. He claims not to be able to have any feelings towards someone who is dead; but this seems belied by a certain malignancy on his part. [13]

160. Once I asked him why he wanted to dissuade [Kanti] Shah from philosophy as a profession. He said he feared it would not be nourishing for him. [56]

161. He liked the riddle: What is the difference between a hairdresser and a sculptor? —the first curls up and dyes, and the second makes faces and busts. The collapse of meaning, I mean the revolution in the transition from noun to verb.

---

[106] These themes get discussed in *On Certainty*, and the example of a man with sawdust in his head appears at *OC* sec. 281.

He got that from Ben Richards, on whose affection, with that of Con Drury,[107] he so much relied in the last years of his life. Ben was mostly rather silent but he enjoyed many of the same sorts of things as Wittgenstein and particularly the same sorts of jokes. Wittgenstein worried about Ben and used to nag him about his career and plans. The oddest thing I knew about Ben was that he read *Principia Ethica*[108] through with immense enjoyment, a thing which I am sure was always happening to people fifty years before—but it was surprising in the late nineteen forties. I said this to Wittgenstein and he replied, 'Oh, Ben is *extremely* old fashioned'. [80]

162. I heard that when Wittgenstein first went back to Cambridge he used to go to parties! —the idea certainly seems strange. I believe those were the days when he used to talk with Leavis.[109] Leavis later spoke hotly against Wittgenstein—called him a 'megalomaniac' and regarded him as a *sinister* influence for anyone to fall under. The only thing that Wittgenstein ever said to me about Leavis was that his idea of an 'elite' which had a culture, an educated 'elite', was *no good*. I think he meant that a culture was a deeper going thing than to be acquired as part of the education of an 'elite'. I don't think he thought of it as something you could *choose* to impart. [86]

163. When at the Moral Science Club Ewing[110] said: 'If someone said he thought he was dead, he'd be making a mistake', Wittgenstein turned on him and said 'Are you a

---

[107] Con Drury; see Appendix.

[108] G. E. Moore's famous work, beloved of the Bloomsbury Circle.

[109] F. R. Leavis (1895–1978), English literary critic. He was directors of studies in English at Downing College, Cambridge. Leavis left a short memoir of LW, to be found in Rhees, ed., *Ludwig Wittgenstein: Personal Recollections*.

[110] A. C. Ewing (1899–1973), English philosopher. Ewing was antipathetical to LW's philosophy and it was he who was responsible for the invitation of Karl Popper to the Moral Science Club in 1946; the nebulous 'poker incident' took place at that meeting.

human being?' Ewing had his grin on as he said 'I think so'. (I told this story to Austin Farrer[111] who said 'Good Heavens! is that how people behave to one another in Cambridge?') [94]

164. The first time he detained me after his lectures—in October 1944, he said: 'It's not lack of talent that mostly makes people into bum philosophers. Look at Ewing. Do you think his trouble is lack of talent?'[112] [34]

165. 'Moore has no *nose*' he more than once said. He told me how they would go to crushes in one another's rooms when he was an undergraduate, and once in Russell's rooms Russell said to Moore, who was sitting on the floor, 'You don't really like me, Moore, do you?' Moore thought a bit and said 'No'. Wittgenstein felt very shocked—how could Moore say that and go on coming to Russell's rooms?[113] [97]

166. There was a similar reaction about Ramsey getting psychoanalysed and lying on the couch thinking 'Filthy little Jew! Filthy little Jew!' all the time. —But Ramsey surely meant just that these thoughts went unbidden through his head. (Question about 'assertion'.) [98]

167. I remember when he was angry with A. J. Ayer for his silly essay in *Encounter* I persuaded him to write to him *more* gently than he had been going to. I spoke of 'giving him a chance', feeling that anyone must feel convicted of error and

---

[111] Austin Farrer (1904–1968), Anglican philosopher and theologian at Oxford.

[112] LW's view of Ewing was shared by others whether or not his diagnosis of Ewing's failings was. H. L. A. Hart, when considering whether to leave his job as a barrister to become an Oxford philosophy don, wrote to Isaiah Berlin in 1944: 'I am I fear a hack like Ewing and fear of revealing the deutero-Ewing in me might just absolutely stultify me at the disagreeable age of 41' (N. Lacey, *A Life of H. L. A. Hart: The Nightmare and the Noble Dream* [Oxford: Oxford University Press, 2006], 115).

[113] There is an interesting counterpoint to this story in LW's diary entry for 16 October 1930. Seven days earlier he had asked Moore whether he was glad when LW came to see him; the diary entry reads: 'Moore later answered my question to the effect that while he does not actually like me, my company nevertheless does him so much good that he thinks he should continue to keep it. That is a peculiar case' (Klagge and Nordmann, *Ludwig Wittgenstein*, 59).

bad behaviour if accused by Wittgenstein! He remarked that Ayer must be in his mid-forties and wasn't likely to be corrigible—nevertheless he did write a different letter from the one he outlined to me. Ayer wrote back a fulsome kind of apology; but I believe he later reprinted the article just as it stood, so he didn't mean anything by that.[114] [183]

168. J.B.[115] told me she once asked him about Peter Geach[116] and he simply said: 'He reads Somerset Maugham'. [102]

169. I remember Martha Kneale[117] coming and reading a paper on promising; at his class the next day Wittgenstein dismissed some rather derogatory remark that (I believe) Casimir [Lewy] made about the meeting, which had not in fact been a very interesting one— 'She was nice'. [110]

170. He was always jealous and upset at first when his friends got married. His family told me how he was terribly worried about Rudolf Koder getting married and wanted them to prevent it if they could. He told me that he had been worried, but when he saw a photo of Lisl Koder he'd said 'Oh well, that's all right'. He liked her very much; with other

---

[114] See also sec. 153. In his autobiography Ayer records how LW 'sent me a letter of rebuke, by registered post. It began with his saying that he had every reason to believe that I was not so ignorant of his recent work as I had pretended to be in my broadcast and in my article in *Polemic*, and ended by asking me whether, if I was ashamed to acknowledge that I had received many valuable ideas from him, would it not be more in accordance with elementary decency to refrain from mentioning him than to spread misleading insinuations about his teaching. I was upset by this letter, both because I was sorry to have offended Wittgenstein, and because I did not believe that I had done anything to deserve so sharp a rebuke. I wrote what I hoped was a dignified reply, explaining why I had thought it right in the circumstances to refer only to his published work and adding that so far from being anxious to conceal the debt that I owed to his *Tractatus*, I had frequently proclaimed it. He answered briefly, saying that be accepted my apology but that if one really wanted to be fair to a man one would avoid even the appearance of unfairness. Though my intention had been rather to justify myself that to apologise, I received this answer with relief' (A. J. Ayer, *Part of My Life* [Oxford: Oxford University Press, 1978], 305–306]).

[115] Joan Bevan.

[116] Peter Geach, Anscombe's husband; see Appendix.

[117] Martha Kneale, née Hurst (1909–2001), English philosopher. She was tutor and Fellow in philosophy at Lady Margaret Hall, Oxford and was one of Anscombe's tutors when Anscombe was an undergraduate at Somerville.

marriages he remained unhappy. I remember his telling me of someone who did afterwards marry a friend of his: 'She wants him'. And he obviously disliked her and hated the prospect; and he spoke to me with puzzlement of his friend's being 'radiant with happiness' after the marriage. I never met the wife so I don't know whether Wittgenstein's suspicion and dislike had any justice about them. [112]

171. I once commented on the practice of congratulating people on the birth of a child as if it were necessarily a cheerful fact— 'All births are illegitimate' he capped me with. [113]

172. I write down from time to time quite stray recollections of Wittgenstein as they come back to me, if I have the chance when they do; hence they are quite rambling and disorganised. But memory of what I do remember of him is most of it not at my beck and call. I wish that I had made notes or kept a diary of my conversations with him; I only once or twice made a short record of some set philosophical discussions.[118] In particular, I wish I had been able to note how funny he could be—but it is possible that the jokes which came often in his lectures or his talk were just for the moment. I remember Ben Richards, in commenting on Norman Malcolm's memoir, of which I said that it made too grim and cramped an impression, said 'Yes, you couldn't imagine that character speechless with laughter'. I told Norman that I found this 'grim and cramped' picture wrong and he wrote back to me that that was how it had been for him, that he couldn't speak of *enjoying* Wittgenstein's company, that it was always a great strain. He quoted Bouwsma[119] in support of his feeling, Bouwsma told Malcolm that he was always terrified of Wittgenstein,

---

[118] For example, the notes included in this volume of meetings with LW and Wasfi Hijab.

[119] O. K. Bouwsma (1898–1978), American philosopher. Malcolm studied under him at the University of Nebraska.

that being with him was like being in a cage with a young lion. Well, I understood that; it was something like Peter Geach's saying that he felt 'as if a young atom bomb were in the house' when Wittgenstein was there. But it is not quite the same as what I call being grim and cramped. [139]

173. There was that dreadful gloom and unhappiness too, which would occasionally emerge. Once he rang me up and said 'I am in an antechamber of hell'. When he said such things, I listened in silence; I had never anything to say. The man who did have something good to say, I believe, was Con Drury. [140]

174. Once we were for some reason speaking of Drury and of war; it was some time in the late nineteen forties when the fear was of war with Russia. Wittgenstein said something suggesting fear lest Drury have to return to the army. I said he surely wouldn't have to if he didn't care to—he was, after all, in Dublin. 'I am sure Con would do his duty' he said. I was very surprised. 'But why on earth should it be his duty, or should he think it was?' I asked. Wittgenstein said nothing. [141]

175. Smythies was a friend for whom Wittgenstein had a great esteem—he once described him to me as a 'pure white soul'. I told Smythies this and he laughed and said it was fantastically mistaken. But Wittgenstein was often irritated by his impracticality and indecision, and he didn't like his marrying and was offended at his hesitations over leaving Cambridge where he had some sort of job and could go to Wittgenstein's lectures; he was a hearer whom Wittgenstein valued. He never got on very well with Polly Smythies, but conceded 'She has sense', which Smythies had not. But he told me once he could not understand the friendship that existed between me and her. [161]

176. Smythies told me that Wittgenstein once said to him: 'If Miss Anscombe had 5 husbands I shouldn't

mind'—I gathered he was indicating *some* sort of indifference about his friends' actions from the point of view of morals—but when Smythies said 'If _ had been a Nazi, and had done the things Nazis do, wouldn't you care?' and he granted that he would. [51]

177. Hearing of Conrad Pepler[120] Wittgenstein asked me 'Is he obedient?' I had to reply that I didn't know; but this was partly because I did not understand the question, except vaguely. [16]

178. When he talked to Conrad Pepler—which he did several times in Oxford[121]—I had the feeling afterwards that he had enjoyed himself and was stimulated; but Pepler's steps as he went away sounded heavy and sad. (I never asked Pepler anything about this[122] and the impression may have been fanciful; but it was certainly strong.) [85]

179. Lately I did have occasion to tell Pepler about my impression that his footsteps sounded depressed when he left Wittgenstein. He said he hadn't been depressed; that he'd been rather alarmed at going to see Wittgenstein, but had been touched and disarmed by him; Wittgenstein had wanted to see him as a priest, and not to argue with him or persuade him of anything. So *that* impression of mine was fanciful. [132]

Wittgenstein and Anscombe

180. In the earlier years of our acquaintance he used to call me 'old man'. This ludicrous habit may have stemmed from his way of saying 'Gentlemen' at his lectures—once or twice

---

[120] Conrad Pepler; see Appendix.

[121] At Anscombe's house.

[122] As the next section shows, Anscombe must here mean 'never asked Pepler anything about this at the time'.

he'd say 'I include you because you wear trousers'. (I think at that point there weren't other women present.) In the last years he dropped this habit and used to say 'M'dear'. He did not ever call me, or I him, by Christian name. [182]

181. He once reproached me with my attitude to philosophical problems. I had said that I felt stuck by some problem or other. He said: 'You know, you strike me as like a person who is walking along a road and comes to a lamp post which is in his way (we were walking along St John Street in Oxford at the time and there was a lamp post we were coming to). And he says: There's a lamp post. I can't go on. It doesn't occur to you to walk round the lamp post. —I have a *prejudice*, which is that problems are soluble.' [166]

182. 'You have a trouble and a puzzle. Everyone has troubles. Kitty has troubles. . . .' He was upbraiding me, I think, for mixing up a trouble and a puzzle; and for not putting up with the trouble better. [17]

183. Very early on in my acquaintance with him we had some discussion, the rest of which I have forgotten, about people of different religions denying each what the other said—was there a real disagreement here? Wittgenstein's arguments will have tended to throw doubt on this, and I said 'I thought of the difference as *propositional*' and he said 'You are talking like a bloody scholastic'. (Cf. his remarks in the pre-Tractatus notebooks about his best work coming from his most strongly *scholastic* feeling.) [52]

184. It was on this occasion that at one point he said: 'If you ever—as you may, if you have much to do with me— become like a sparrow on the housetops. . . .' I forget the conclusion—maybe it was something I might *then* have the right to say. That has never happened to me up till now. His friendship became altogether milder and less minatory in character; or rather his friendship *was* so as it came about, for at that stage I think we had only just begun to know one

another. It was round about then that he told Smythies that he had had some good conversations with me, but would not see me anymore, because he did not just want to be a thinking shop; however he must later have changed his mind about my attitude towards him, which indeed wasn't that at all. [53]

185. He gave me Angelus Silesius.[123] Once when much later I said my beliefs were the same as those of Angelus Silesius he was irritated and said I could not begin to be in the slightest degree like Angelus Silesius in my thoughts—as different as chalk from cheese. [65]

186. He more than once ticked me off for being 'cock-sure'. He used to blow me up for any manifestation of this. —I remember once saying something like 'What people have had such a history as the Jews!' and he said at once, with irritation, 'What do you know of the histories of all the peoples there have been on the earth?' [66]

187. I remember once speaking to him of a woman who was supposed to be a serious Catholic and an active lesbian, marvelling how she could combine them. 'How can you be so bornée!'[124] he said with weary impatience. [174]

188. Of some work of mine that he saw, he said 'Bought for a farthing' and 'Shit on the floor'—though the way he put this latter to *me* was 'Not house-trained'. [19]

189. He had a special aversion to ties.[125] Once I went to see him and he brandished a tie in the air and said with great emphasis: 'Today I put on a *tie* for you and went to see the

---

[123] Angelus Silesius (c. 1624–1677), born Johann Scheffler and also known as Johann Angelus Silesius, was a German Catholic priest and physician, known as a mystic and religious poet. Born and raised a Lutheran, he adopted the name Angelus (Latin for 'angel' or 'heavenly messenger') and the epithet Silesius ('Silesian') on converting to Catholicism in 1653.

[124] Narrow-minded.

[125] Cp. sec. 14.

Principal of Newnham!'[126] He was abusive about her both for being stiff and for being ugly. I said she looked like a bull-dog and he said 'No! a bull dog is a noble animal—she looks like a pug-dog'. He wanted to persuade her to give me some teaching; I was an exception to the rule by which he usually wanted to dissuade people from doing philosophical teaching. When he first asked me if I wanted to I said 'Not much, except to earn money' and he replied 'I think you should do it, it is the right thing'. [33]

190. A reason why people were not natural with him was the bright light of close attention and hard thought which he was apt to scrutinize their sayings with. I remember a woman, Helen Smith, wanting to come to his lectures, and he felt he couldn't exclude her, though he was not pleased. He said to her: 'I hope you won't write an article about philosophy in Cambridge like Miss Stebbing!'[127] She replied that one never knew what might happen. I had the story of this from Smythies, who was there at the time. He asked me what I thought of her reply. I said 'What an ass she must have been to say that!' But he told me that Wittgenstein had been rather pleased by it. —Miss Smith later said to me that she found his lectures very boring, like listening to people who will tell their dreams. I was in my original state of besotted reverence for Wittgenstein and was extremely shocked. [186]

191. At that time, I'd be inclined to say that almost anything that Wittgenstein said sounded true and important to me, except for some things about religion. But it is not entirely true, since I argued with him a good deal in philosophy.

---

[126] This was Dame Myra Curtis DBE (1886–1971), editor, civil servant, and Principal of Newnham College from 1942 to 1954.

[127] Susan Stebbing (1885–1943), English philosopher. In 1932 Stebbing read a paper to the Aristotelian Society entitled 'The Method of Analysis in Metaphysics' in which she examined the kind of philosophical analysis which she took to be carried on by philosophers at Cambridge, especially Moore.

Sometimes I plain did not understand what he was saying, and then I more or less had to leave it alone; sometimes I understood his sentences but could not understand the reasons for them and that was where I had the most instructive arguments of my life. But once I understood I was inclined to be convinced. But to a great extent this was a matter of an overwhelming influence. And in philosophy that is not good. That is to say, influence which improves standards of argument and seriousness—which he certainly had on me—is good; but not influence which makes something seem convincing because it is part of X's teaching. *That* light of convincingness is bad; and I soon began to struggle against it. I told myself that I had no right to think something which impressed me in this way; I had got to be able to think whatever I could really claim to think in, so to speak, a dull way, and with reasons which I could give and which ought to be visible as having point and force to minds that had not suffered that great impression. [187]

192. I remember eating a meal with him in the restaurant above a cinema in Cambridge when it was determined that I was going back to Oxford; he remarked 'But you are Cambridge now!' That was the time when he was talking so bitterly about being 'Vogel-frei'.[128] On that occasion too we talked of bad writing in philosophy and he remarked: I had good luck; I was very well brought up. I believe he was referring, not to his philosophic training but to his home; certainly all his family had very exacting standards—e.g. in music. Wittgenstein spoke with admiration of Faraday's *Chemical History of a Candle*: 'Full of its subject'. Affectation, pretentiousness, shallowness, false notes (and a lot of stuff in one long false note) he was *very* sensitive to. [133]

193. He had an aversion to people being intellectual, but he had a quite particular meaning for this word; for he said that

[128] Cf. sec. 153.

I was *not* intellectual. This was when he was complaining of some woman for being so and I was puzzled as I would not have called her so. I think the particular meaning that he put on the word had to do with a lot of *chat* about matters of culture etc. [74]

194. We often walked on Midsummer Common. Once for some reason we spoke of catching a pony—how to hold him still. I said you would have him, if he were broken in, once you had him by the nose, one hand on his neck and one hand gripping his nose; a squeeze would restrain him. 'I wouldn't dream of doing such a thing!' Wittgenstein said, and seemed almost indignant. [96]

195. Long-lasting slow walks I remember mostly in Cambridge [as opposed to Oxford]; Wittgenstein would ring up and I would always go for a walk with him if I possibly could, though it was sometimes difficult to arrange. We talked mostly about philosophy, though often about other things; this was always more desultory and relaxed than when I went to see him at Trinity. *There* it was extremely strenuous. I would come in, he would be lying in a deck chair and merely look at me by way of greeting, or perhaps give a slight nod; he tended to look grim on those occasions; and then he would immediately start something; like (an occasion I put in what I wrote about the *Tractatus*[129]) 'Why do people say it was natural to say the sun went round the earth?' 'I suppose', I said, 'because it looks as if it does'. 'And how would it look as if it looked as if the earth rotated on its axis?' [216]

196. When we were letting lodgings in Cambridge he once nearly had his sister Mrs Stonborough come and stay with us; but the only room there was was on the second floor and she had a weak heart, so to my relief she didn't come there.

---

[129] See G. E. M. Anscombe, *An Introduction to Wittgenstein's Tractatus* (London: Hutchinson University Library, 1959), 151.

But it had been fixed up between him and Peter [Geach], and when I was told I said 'Oh dear, it isn't very grand'. 'I have seen it' he said with a pleasant smile. So we seemed to be in for it; but the next day I went to see him and said 'You know, I really think she'll be awfully uncomfortable and it will be bad for her', and he told me he had found a grand ground floor room at the University Arms. I was much relieved; she was not at all the sort of person to rough it, and it was a crazy idea of his to put her with us. [217]

197. Another time we were driven by being hard-up into occupying that small room ourselves; and once when Peter was lying naked in bed and I was sprawling on the hearth rug with my hair down, Wittgenstein appeared; he had brought a friend to see us; and someone downstairs had directed him up to come and find us. We were all rather embarrassed; it was I think the only time when he was not welcome [. . .] and he left quickly. I don't know who the friend was, he didn't get as far as our room. [218]

198. I remember that Wittgenstein was irritated by the fact that my husband would speak in Polish to a Polish cleaning woman that we had. 'Why do you speak to her in Polish? She understands English!' he said in an impatient voice; I suppose he perceived that Peter (who had learned Polish as an adult)[130] was making a special thing of it; all the same, it was not true that Mrs Pawlek understood English well enough for me to be sure she made anything of instructions given in English. [237]

199. In 1946 I decided to learn German, and started with Hugo.[131] I told Wittgenstein, and he said 'Oh, I am very

---

[130] A main part of Geach's motive for doing so was that his mother had been of Polish extraction; see Appendix.

[131] An elementary textbook for teaching yourself German, named after Charles Hugo (who founded the 'Hugo Languages Institute' in c. 1890).

glad. For if you learn German, then I can give you my book to read'. This had been my hope, and it spurred me on. We read the introduction to Frege's *Grundlagen* [*der Arithmetik*] together. He professed amazed admiration at my laying hold of the construction of the sentences. He said, what no doubt was true, that it must have been the fruit of a training in Latin. But I was struck by the incongruousness of his admiring the exercise of so elementary a skill, which I thought a very slight display of intelligence when one would get into fearful trouble in his lectures for not grasping something which I was sure it needed great powers and hard thought to grasp. We eventually read the early part of the *Investigations*; I remember he reacted with real pleasure when I told him I had read to §35 and had found it intoxicating; which was the case. As we read it we discussed translating it—he would explain the import of words, and I would suggest an English rendering, about which he would be very enthusiastic. (I don't know if I remembered any of these when I came to translate the book for its publication in 1953.) [229]

200. When Wittgenstein was in Dublin he stayed at a hotel called Ross' Hotel; he liked the woman who was manageress; it was comfortable and quiet. After having breakfast he would go (partly by public transport, I think—my recollections of Dublin are a bit vague) to the Botanical Gardens and there he would walk about in the semitropical houses with his pocket notebook in his hand, thinking and writing down his first draft 'Bemerkungen'.[132] He took me there once. I visited him in Dublin in 1948 in need of some help and advice because of a matter that was troubling me. He was at peak form working at the time, and

---

[132] Remarks.

reflection shewed me that this must be an interruption; but he responded to a request for help, booked a room at the hotel, and never shewed that I was disturbing him. This was the only time I made demands on him and he turned up trumps. I had certainly got into a queer state of mind, partly assisted by having employed a hypnotist to help me to give up smoking; this had been partly successful, as I had succeeded with efforts of will power but I was beset by a troublesome obsession and by insomnia. Wittgenstein got Con Drury to advise me, who first got me into good nights' sleeps, and reassured me by his good sense and friendliness. In the hothouses Wittgenstein sniffed the good smell of the soil and the things that were growing there and described how he walked and wrote all the morning and early afternoon—he would arrive there between ten and eleven. Then at about four o'clock to the town restaurant, an old fashioned place where he would eat a couple of fried eggs; then he returned to his hotel and looked at his large manuscript volumes, to which he transferred what was worthwhile of what he had got down in the small notebooks. He shewed me the marks he had set against the entries in the large books—an *S* meant 'bad'—schlecht—a *C* meant 'something in this' but not quite right, a *C* [enclosing a dot] a little better, an *I* meant 'passed'. Entries marked *L.L.* he had transferred to his loose leaf notebook, the fair copy that he made of what is *Philosophical Investigations Part II*. I remarked on the great compression he envisaged, of a large mass of typescript into some sixty pages, and he exclaimed 'I would like to write a book *that* thin', holding his fingers quarter of an inch apart. [204]

201. It was in that old fashioned town restaurant that he said to me, in the context of some discussion or other— 'If I have convinced myself, *for whatever reason*, of the existence of

a God ...' but I have lost the apodosis; the general impression came from the protasis. I remember also telling him of experiments in self hypnotism I had engaged in. None of the hypnotisms were quite successful. I tried hard to co-operate, but it was always as if there were a core within me saying 'Nothing is happening'. Once when the man who was hypnotising me tested to see whether I was under— 'you can't open your eyes, they are as heavy as lead, you won't be able to open them, etc' and then: 'Now try to open your eyes!' I was amazed to discover that they as it were stuck a little, that it really cost a little effort to open them, as if they had been lightly glued and were a bit stuck. He seemed a little chagrined that that was *all*. I used to try to hypnotise myself, lying on my bed in Somerville and telling myself I was on a bedding of many deep black quilts and sinking into this. (All this was in aid of telling myself I could give up smoking.) The time of greatest effect as far as my feelings went was when I had the idea that I was suspended by an elastic thread in a black well, and I went down into the well and then the elastic contracted and pulled me up again, and I had the idea that if only I could stretch out my hand and find a pair of small scissors and cut the thread when it was fully extended I would fall down into some-where quite different. I told Wittgenstein this story and he said 'Don't do it again'. Both he and Drury advised me to resume smoking. [205]

202. I was anxiously preparing the last version of an essay called 'The reality of the past'[133] and was in a bad state for concentrating on it. Wittgenstein said he was keen that

---

[133] 'The Reality of the Past', first published in Max Black, ed., *Philosophical Analysis* (Ithaca, NY: Cornell University Press, 1950), 36–56; reprinted *in Metaphysics and the Philosophy of Mind. The Collected Philosophical Papers of G. E. M. Anscombe*, Vol. II (Oxford: Basil Blackwell, 1980), 104–119.

I should finish it and get it out; I asked why and he said 'Because it will be good for your reputation'. But he added 'I am taking it for granted that it will be good'. This assumption seemed to me a very doubtful one and I did not take the risk of showing it to him; I was too cowardly. Smythies, I thought, had described it right when he said 'no daylight anywhere'. [206]

203. What one feared with Wittgenstein was unforeseeable condemnations, which would be wholly unanswerable when they came. It seemed clear that what one did must be pretty rotten and he would make one realise this and make one feel a wretch for not having been good enough not to do such stuff; but in advance one did not know what would be so disgusting. This was a painful condition to be in. The amazed pleasure when he liked what one wrote was very great. This happened to me twice, once when I read a paper to the Moral Sciences Club on 'Appearance and Reality', and once when I wrote something for him in one of our private meetings; he had told me to come with something written and I brought a bit of writing on irregularity, on not being able to find any regularity in a language that a strange people were speaking. The only other time he saw something of mine was when he had the stuff I sent in to Newnham; and that, I knew, was very bad, and I was horrified when I heard that it had come into his hands. — So I didn't show him the piece on the reality of the past, out of cowardice. [207]

204. Looking back, I can see that the disagreeable relation of fear and stupefaction was for the first four years or so of our friendship, and largely in connection with philosophy; about other things and in practical communications I had no difficulties of that kind. [220]

205. We went to the cinema in Dublin, I remember. In Cambridge he sought companions to go to the cinema

with; never me; he had certain requirements. I remember his scrutinizing my face when considering whether we should go to the cinema—my impression was to see whether I should be a companion he could put up with on such an expedition. I can't remember the film, it was something stupid, I think. What was really enjoyable was going to the Dublin Zoo, where he was a Fellow (a present from Drury). The keeper opened the cage where a huge crocodile was in a tank, and threw a great piece of meat in the air; the crocodile, eight foot long and apparently somnolent, leapt straight up, all of him almost out of the water, with a startling noise, half bark half roar, and very loud. All happened so quick and was so unexpected, I leapt two foot backwards where I stood;[134] I can still see Wittgenstein, who was standing solid with his stick under his two hands in front of him, looking back over his shoulder at my reaction. [208]

206. Sometimes when we were talking my mind would wander and become fixed on one of the troubling images that were disturbing me; he observed this and recalled me, saying 'I can see you are not in your usual state'. But after a few days of good sleep and reassuring friendliness and having resumed smoking, I was quite cheered up and returned to England. I did not manage to give up smoking after that until 1960,[135] and resolved never to try hypnotism again. [209]

207. I tell the story to shew how it was possible to regard Wittgenstein as a port of refuge, and he acted as one with both kindness and concern, in *spite* of the fact that there

---

[134] Cp. *Intention*, p. 15: 'Now among things known without observation must be included the causes of some movements. E.g. 'Why did you jump back suddenly like that?' 'The leap and loud bark of that crocodile made me jump.'

[135] Anscombe moved from cigarettes to cigars, in fact.

was that bad relation of fear of unforeseeable judgment. It was bad because it did not operate to make me simply attend seriously to the problems that interested me. When I did *that*, it was all right; but I didn't realise that; and so I was stupefied. Others may have been the same. [210]

208. Dummett[136] once said to me, à propos Wittgenstein (whom he did not know but had some impression of through stories): 'If you have the capacity to leave others without a word to say, I believe you should use it very sparingly'. [211]

209. Wittgenstein told me that he had tried going in for hypnotism at one time, before the first world war. He had the idea that he might be able to solve his problems if he could be hypnotised and then asked questions, which he gave the hypnotist first. As people have abnormal physical strength under hypnotism, so he thought he might attain immense concentration. It didn't work; he thought he was quite unaffected and on one of these occasions sat up, with the idea it was all over, and then fell back feeling deadly exhausted. [212]

210. In Vienna we would catch a train and go to the Prater and walk there. Once he took me to the Lusthaus for coffee. On the whole he didn't do that sort of thing, never kept drinks in his rooms for people, was not an offerer of casual refreshment. —Walking in Oxford and observing some party in progress he remarked how in his youth in Vienna there were of course always parties—but never 'drink-parties'; elegant jugs of chocolate would be served. [128]

211. In Vienna he took me to see his friend the sculptor Drobil,[137] a little man with white hair and very powerful forearms. He was working on a statue, I *think* of someone

---

[136] Michael Dummett (1925–2011), English philosopher. He was a close friend of Anscombe's and a fellow Catholic.
[137] Michael Drobil (1877–1958), Austrian sculptor.

like Osler,[138] which was to go, if I remember rightly, in front of the old hospital, or in the quadrangle. Drobil, I remember, warned me against wandering in the Prater alone on account of 'Gesindel'.[139] He had damaged his sculpture, cut a bit off that he hadn't intended to, and he told this to Wittgenstein, who received it with a sort of grim sympathy but made no comment. Wittgenstein made him look at me—a 'schöner Kopf, nicht [war?]'[140] and he agreed. That reminds me of a time when I was sitting for some sculptors I knew in Oxford and Wittgenstein came along to see; I think he was disappointed to find they were not especially talented. He fell into a dispute with them about the asymmetry of my face, which they assumed on the grounds that all faces were asymmetrical—I think he criticised one of the heads they were doing for this. He insisted that my face was not asymmetrical in the way that they—or one of them—thought, and calipers had to be brought out to settle the point. He was right. —When we left Drobil I remember Drobil took some rather serious farewell of Wittgenstein, since it was likely that when Wittgenstein next came to Vienna, 'ich nicht mehr da bin'.[141] He did not know that it was Wittgenstein who was then mortally ill; but I don't know which of them died first. [129]

212. On that other occasion in the sculptors' studio in Oxford I remember we fell into talk about a small boy whom we all knew slightly, a very closed-in child. Wittgenstein said 'He needs a she' (the boy was separated from his mother) 'but someone who can unlock him—not Miss Anscombe say!' and we all smiled. [130]

---

[138] Presumably the 'father of modern medicine', Sir William Osler (1849–1919).
[139] Lowlife, rabble.
[140] 'A beautiful head, don't you think?'
[141] 'I'm not there any more.'

213. Wittgenstein told me of his sister Hermine's conversion. She lived at Gmunden with her sister Salzer during the war; there was a very good priest there. She had long reflected on these things when finally, I think in the latter 1940s, she made a return to the Church formally, in the presence of all her household. —'That's oil in your lamp' he said drily to me. [83]

214. In this connection, I had a scruple when he asked me to tell a lie if anyone asked about his illness in Austria. I said I couldn't make that promise. He was a bit put out and later returned to the subject— 'You're saying you can't tell a lie'. 'Nothing is more likely than that I should tell a lie' I said, 'It's only that I can't make you that promise. I tell lies, I think, about twice a week. I mean quite straightforward ones.' 'Good!' he replied. 'I would find it difficult to be friends with someone who couldn't tell a lie.' He didn't ask me to explain the objection I felt; but he was very discerning, and probably guessed. How could I pray for him to God who hates lies and coolly undertake to tell lies for him? My prayers were feeble as it was. [84]

215. Once he found out I had no macintosh at a rainy time and no money to buy one. He exclaimed: 'But this is *poverty*! This is poverty!' I protested that you wouldn't say that to someone who preferred to waste her money on smoking. He went off with me to a shop and bought me a cheap white cape macintosh which would at least keep me dry. [181]

216. I found Wittgenstein a kind and considerate man. If he heard of someone in trouble, he would ask 'Can I help?' If one was in trouble oneself, it was possible to go to him and get help and advice, even though this was obviously interrupting him in work. He was not carelessly amiable or carelessly generous; there was a good deal of thought in what he did for people. [184]

217. When he was in Cambridge in the nineteen thirties he had lodgings above a grocer's shop. He helped these people at a time of difficulty for them by giving them a good deal of money in advance, which he took back in goods as he needed them. (Smythies told me of this.) They were very devoted to him; I remember his taking me to see them at one time. I was repelled by the desolately empty and unlived in appearance of their highly respectable sitting room.[142] [192]

218. He hated meanness. I heard a story, told by Ryle,[143] of how his [Ryle's] brother's family (I think it was) had evacuee boys staying with them, and sent them off to get them out of the way on some occasion. Wittgenstein said 'So that's how you treat the children of the proletariat!' This went around as a funny story, as if he had said it in either a comical or a pompous fashion, and I could not recognise him in the story and did not believe it; but I mentioned it to Ben Richards, who said it was true, and that Wittgenstein had been struck by the meanness and lack of concern—these boys had nothing to do and were merely put up with and not thought about. Then I understood the story: 'To you, these are the children of the proletariat, and so you don't look at them humanly'. [185]

219. Once when he was visiting Oxford he found I had no waste paper basket. (I was then living in very narrow lodgings, in a room that was later turned into the bathroom of the house and was appropriately small.) He said 'You are a *writer*, you have to have a waste paper basket,' and we went

---

[142] Anscombe is referring to the Barbrooke family, with whom LW had spent Christmas 1941 directly after Francis Skinner's death. It was Skinner who rented the flat above the grocer's, on East Road in Cambridge.

[143] Gilbert Ryle (1900–1976), English philosopher, much influenced by LW. Before World War II he was a fellow and tutor at Christ Church, Oxford, being appointed Waynflete Professor of Metaphysical Philosophy at Oxford after the war.

to buy one at the blind workers shop; he bought a large sturdy one designed to carry an acid container, with two handles. He examined anything he bought very appraisingly, and pronounced this basket to be all right. In 1950 he bought me 'two lousy chairs' of wood, as there was rather a shortage of them in the house in Oxford. One was of the pattern of kitchen chair that I rather admire, the other an ugly thing with a round seat and rails. Neither lasted more than a dozen years, but the waste paper basket has lasted very well and done a great deal of work. [190]

220. I remember his bringing Ben Richards round in 1945, with a toy for Barbara who was two years old; one of those sets of plastic rings on a stick which are very common now, but then had only just appeared in the shops. [219]

221. Wittgenstein was extremely keen on cleanliness. I remember his saying 'Wanted, a Pharisee' about having cups clean on the *outside*. I was puzzled at this as I had thought the thing about the Pharisees was that they only fussed about the outside and let the inside be dirty,[144] but Wittgenstein disagreed with me; except for the figurative character of the Pharisee, of course, which he ascribed to himself. I don't remember how he came to do so on the occasion I am thinking of, but it was an occasion when I was using his pantry in Trinity; I had come to see him and asked if I might wash my hands which had got dirty. 'Yes!' he exclaimed, 'do wash your hands! Here you are! Use lots of water.' He hated the use of too little water for washing dishes; a great deal of water was essential.[145] —This

---

[144] See Matthew 23:27, 'Woe unto you, scribes and Pharisees, hypocrites! for ye are like unto whited sepulchres, which indeed appear beautiful outward, but are within full of dead men's bones, and of all uncleanness.'

[145] In his *Memoir* Malcolm writes: 'When he [LW] came to supper he would sometimes insist on washing up the dishes. He had the idea that this could be done more efficiently in the bath tub, where a continuous stream of hot water was available from the geyser. More than once he washed the dishes there, not dissuaded by the severity of

particular strong feeling of his for great cleanliness made it rather surprising that he put up with me, because I have never been good at keeping clean and often find that my hands are rather grey and it does not bother me very much. He certainly noticed this, as his gladness that time I wanted to wash shewed, and I also remember Smythies telling me of his remarking on it. Smythies thought him obsessively clean; but his toleration of my own slovenliness went against that. But I remember his writing to me once that historians would say of that period that 'a wave of dirtiness swept over Britain'. [193]

222. He suffered from insomnia which he controlled with very small doses of sodium amytal, to which he was very sensitive; and he also used a fan to make a gentle noise. [106]

223. In December 1950, when he was living in my house in Oxford, he said one day: 'You'd better diet, eat Ryvita or something'. I asked him if I were looking fat in the face for example, and he said oh, everywhere; I told him I was pregnant and he seemed very startled and kept saying 'You poor thing!' [153]

224. At first when he came to my house he lived on the first floor, i.e. the middle floor; but he could hear the couple below— my family hadn't yet moved to Oxford—and 'she bickers soprano'. So he moved upstairs to the smallest room in the house. I remember when he left for the Bevans[146] at one point he seemed almost apologetic and said: I feel a bit as if I were in a grave in this room. His room at Joan Bevan's

---

the back-bending. Wittgenstein had rigorous standards of cleanliness. He was disturbed if he thought that we were washing up without an adequate supply of soap or clean, hot water. He presented my wife with a dish mop, as an improvement on a dish cloth' (Malcolm [1984, 45–46]).

[146] Edward and Joan Bevan; see Appendix.

was painted pink and much more cheerful. It is possible
that if I had not been pregnant I should have felt hurt at his
departure, but it seemed wholly reasonable as things were;
and in any case it was quite excellent for him to be at the
Bevans. [162]

225. He had told Dr Bevan how he feared the idea of dying in an
English hospital 'with a starchy English nurse'. (He particularly loathed being washed with a flannel—smeared with
a flannel, as he said, by a nurse when one couldn't wash
oneself in bed.) Dr Bevan gave him the kind invitation
to come and die in his house, which was very characteristic of him; he used to visit his patients in hospital. So on
February 8th 1951 we set off for Cambridge. Wittgenstein
was very frail then. We took a 1st class carriage so that he
could lie on the seat, and there was some complication
about paying extra for a ticket I already had. The inspector
came to alter the charge that had been made, and explained
that it was a matter of interpretation of rules. With rules,
he said, the thing was, there was always more than one way
you could take them. 'Yes, yes' Wittgenstein said and tried
to wave him away, but he laboured the point for all it was
worth. I was very much amused and Wittgenstein mildly
so; he muttered something about not escaping lectures in
philosophy. —We were reading *Der Prinz von Homburg*
on that journey.[147] I went to Cambridge as often as I could
while term was on and of course there was a vacation. Once
he had an attack of bad pain in my house then and I gave
him some brandy which did a great deal of good; he was
much impressed with it, but it did not serve so well another
time. [154]

---

[147] See sec. 68.

226. The von Wrights had given him a little red wine every day
when he was staying with them in Cambridge, and when
he was so ill in Oxford that he had to stay in bed I imitated
them. (This wasn't often; he was very keen on looking after
himself and even at his weakest he managed to take his
bath, but he stayed in bed and let me give him meals.) He
once remarked that he'd never gone in for wine much, as
some people did; Goethe for example drank a great deal of
wine. He wondered whether there was anything that went
with that. I said 'Well, you don't go in for women either'. He
said, 'I did once—for one woman. But she wouldn't have
me; and she was quite right'.[148] [155]

227. He praised the small attentions I gave him at that time—I
think because I rapidly observed his particular desires for
how things should be done and he did not have to mention any preference more than once—except on one occasion when I made a futile attempt to make a 'chaudeau'[149]
as they called it in Vienna, of which he had been fond. I did
not manage it well or on time and he, having taken some
medicine which he was supposed to take a certain time before eating, was much irritated. I felt rather ill-used. On another occasion he got violently angry with me for having
told Miss Deneke[150] he was too ill to see her—he feared it

---

[148] LW was probably referring to Marguerite Respinger, the young Swiss woman to
whom he had felt attracted in the 1920s, even considering marriage with her.

[149] A sort of eggnog.

[150] Margaret (Marga) Deneke (1882–1969) was a pianist, musicologist, and author,
friend of Paul Wittgenstein. She more than once attempted to effect a reconciliation between the brothers. In her *Memoirs* (unpublished typescript 1962–1964, 2 vols., Lady
Margaret Hall, Oxford) she writes of a visit to Anscombe's house in St John St when
she did manage to see LW. 'He was sitting in a dressing gown over a fire. His voice still
had its old musical huskiness but it sounded weak and suffering was written on his pale
face. After a minute he asked me to leave him. He said it made him shudder to recall old
memories and seeing me brought back thoughts of Vienna that were too much for him.'
See Waugh, *The House of Wittgenstein*, 295–296.

would get back to his family. 'It was bloody of you, it was absolutely bloody of you!' he kept on saying. I didn't feel particularly badly treated on that occasion, but when I saw him again he said, 'You've got an apology coming from me!' That was the apology. [156]

228. In Vienna at his sister's house he was served rather fine food, at least it seemed so to me whenever I had lunch with him. (He had his meals in his room; his sister[151] was dying—she died very soon after I came to Vienna; I saw her only once. He told me how she had said to Rudolf Koder: 'Play me death-music', and he, after a moment's reflection, played her the theme and variations from Haydn's Emperor quartet; and as she listened tears streamed down her cheeks. But she was too far gone when I saw her for me to do anything but see her.) [157]

229. But in England he hated any attempt at fineness in food, and no doubt in America too. When he was in Cambridge dictating Part II of *Philosophische Untersuchungen*[152] in the summer of 1948, he used to come to have lunch at my home every day, and got very plain and unpretentious food because I understood that he preferred that; I remember once his murmuring over a plate of rissoles of minced beef, with fried onions and spinach, which I had almost felt ashamed to give him: It's too good for me, too good for me. This remark wasn't addressed to me. If I had tried to give him something fine, I believe I should only have irritated him. [158]

230. When I saw him in London, in Mrs Rhees' flat, on his return from America in the summer of 1949,[153] I had the

---

[151] Hermine.

[152] *Philosophical Investigations*. In fact LW dictated Part II in 1949, between 20 June and 12 July; see R. Monk, *The Duty of Genius* (New York: Penguin, 1991), 544.

[153] LW returned to England in late October. He stayed at the Rhees flat in London till 9 November.

greatest impression of hopeless misery and suffering he
ever gave me. That was before his cancer was diagnosed;
the doctors in America hadn't succeeded in this. He went to
Cambridge then and Edward Bevan diagnosed it. He took
hormone treatment for about a year or more, and during
that time was less intellectually powerful than in the last
few months of his life, when he gave it up. I don't know if
there was any connection. [159]

231. He died on April 29th of 1951; he was writing two days
before, and took a chill from walking in the cold. I had
been in Cambridge and walked with him in the garden of
Peterhouse and noticed how very frail he was. Smythies
and I and Ben and Con Drury were sent for; and Smythies
and I asked Conrad Pepler to come. Wittgenstein knew
he was dying and asked Edward [Bevan] to ensure him
a good night in preparation for seeing his friends in the
morning. But he never came to properly. Once he opened
his large and fierce looking eyes, flung out his hands,
and shut them again. Edward told him we were there
and that Conrad Pepler was coming. Ben and I held his
hands; he groped to have his hand held if it was not. Con
Drury arrived from Ireland very near the end and took
my place. Pepler came, but was disinclined to come up as
Wittgenstein was not conscious; or hardly so; but Edward
said 'Do whatever might be good'. So Pepler came up and
gave a conditional absolution. After Wittgenstein was
dead we sat in the Bevans' drawing room and Con Drury
said he would like him to have Catholic burial. He asked
Ben who said he would like it, and Smythies, who was a
Catholic and said he would. I thought they would ask me
and was going to say I wouldn't do it myself but would not
oppose them; but I guess Dr Drury thought I would like it
anyway and he did not ask me. Conrad hesitated but said
alright, since he had been a Catholic originally and had

never made any formal renunciation of the Church, but had indeed put himself down as R.C. in Guy's Hospital, he would contact the parish priest. So Wittgenstein had Catholic burial at the hands of the parish priest the next day; Moore was there, and the von Wrights. I was struck by the severity of the service, which speaks so much of the nearly desperate state of the departed, and I wondered if anyone thought it was a specially nasty form for such people as Wittgenstein. [160]

232. Joan Bevan made a picture of him eleven years after his death from memory entirely, which is very good. The lower half of the face looks wrong; it is so pinched; but that is probably accurate, as she only knew him really in his last days. [163]

233. When I met Wittgenstein again after an interval I used to think soon: 'I had *forgotten* what he was like.' The impression of vitality, of mountain air, was so great; and also the impression of the extraordinary. [36]

234. I did not understand him. I think I told him so once, for I remember him saying in answer 'How should you understand me?' and something about his life being different. [37]

235. He once said 'I've lived like a madman' (I think he meant it as one might speak of someone running or eating like a madman). [38]

236. In his last days he spoke of his life as having been one of on the whole cheerful music—the grave and solemn and terrible notes had not been played through him. [39]

237. I used to try to argue (feebly) with him when he spoke of his desperate state; but he could always crush these attempts. I remember once he parted from me, or dropped the subject—I believe it was a parting—saying 'Only the Deity can help me' in a flat, clipped, final and matter of fact

sort of voice.[154] His friendship was one of the best things I ever had and was of great use to me and I do not know of any harm it ever did me; I wish that mine had been of use to him, but it could hardly be, I had too little understanding. [197]

[154] Cp. sec. 114.

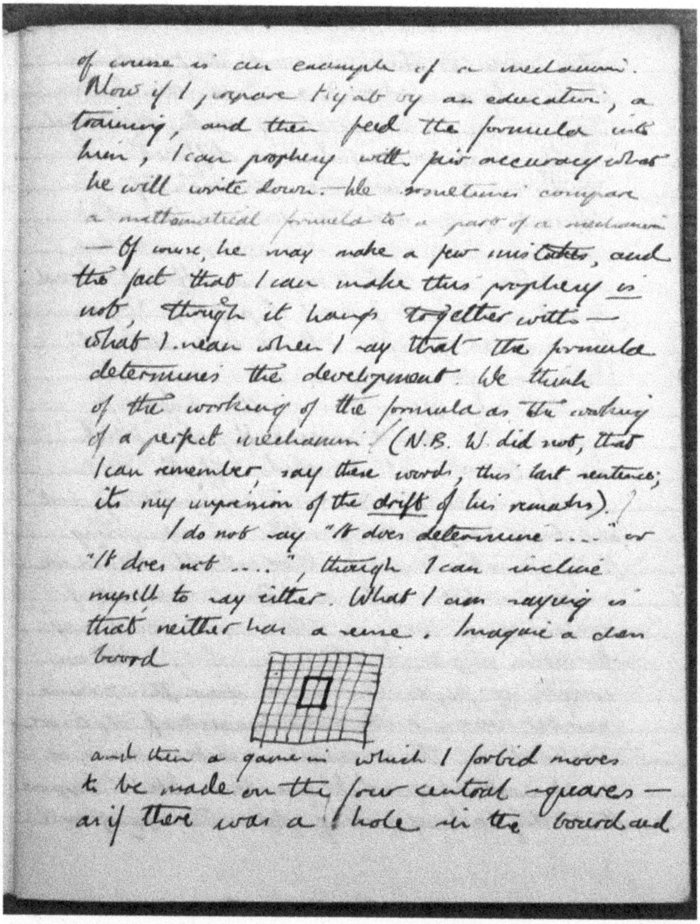

of course is an example of a mechanism. Now if I prepare him by an education, a training, and then feed the formula into him, I can prophesy with fair accuracy what he will write down. He sometimes compares a mathematical formula to a part of a mechanism — Of course, he may make a few mistakes, and the fact that I can make this prophecy _is_ not, though it hangs together with what I mean when I say that the formula determines the development. We think of the working of the formula as the working of a perfect mechanism. (N.B. W. did not, that I can remember, say these words, this last sentence; its my impression of the **drift** of his remarks.)

I do not say "It does determine ...." or "It does not ....", though I can incline myself to say either. What I am saying is that neither has a sense. Imagine a chess board

and then a game in which I forbid moves to be made on the four central squares — as if there was a hole in the board and

Fig 4.1 Page from Anscombe's handwritten record of her discussions with Wittgenstein in 1946–1947. *Photo by John Berkman, File 518, Box 12, Collegium Institute Anscombe Archive at the University of Pennsylvania, Kislak Center for Special Collections, Rare Books and Manuscripts, used by permission of the Collegium Institute*

4

Discussions between Wittgenstein, Anscombe, and Hijab, 1946–1947[*]

Elizabeth Anscombe

December 4th 1946

EA: About the cube and the other examples with which you made it seem plausible to imagine people calling red and green the same colour—you did make it seem plausible, by apparently reducing it to a case of "seeing as". But that makes it seem, not a divergent use of the concept, but a quite secondary one. —On the other hand the consideration of the yellow wall, which is "really" all sorts of different colours, seems to go against me. But I can't get rid of the idea that "this is green", when I understand it, is a paradigm such that I shall know for sure what is a continuation of the concept and what not.

W: It's important to remember that this is a fictitious case, purely. Let us consider the fact, which I have often pointed out, that colours are all *more or less* on the same footing. That has to do with the fact that e.g. we can mix paint of any colour we like. Still they are not all quite on a level. You know about black and white, how in some circumstances they are colours, and some not. What should we say of a tribe for which red and green occupied the position occupied among us by black and white?

* Editorial additions are in the form of italicized text within square brackets.

Elizabeth Anscombe, *Discussions between Wittgenstein, Anscombe, and Hijab, 1946–1947*
In: *Anscombe on Wittgenstein*. Edited by: John Berkman and Roger Teichmann,
Oxford University Press. © Oxford University Press 2025. DOI: 10.1093/9780197648988.003.0004

EA: But I feel you would only have to shew them the colour circle. — But what would you be trying to correct? How would you find out?

W: Precisely. How would you find out? Well, for one thing, we would never use black and white for a flag — if they did, and if you heard things like "She was gaily dressed in black and white", would this make you begin to think, "Their colour concepts are different from ours"?

That all our colours are not on exactly the same footing, is clear. Take brown, for example. It is impossible to imagine brown in a flag, it would be disgusting. It would make even less sense to call it gay than black and white. Black, grey, brown are on a different footing from other colours. This may seem just to be bringing in aesthetics, but aesthetics is unimportant here.

The case is not sufficiently described. We must realise what a different world these people must be imagined to inhabit. E.g., if green were a very rare colour, and only occurred when a red thing went bad, can't you imagine it being treated as a degenerate case of red?

You remember my idea of the dividing line, with red one side and green the other and they say "red" all the way along. We'll imagine that they know quite well how to translate for purposes of talking our language. Take 2 tribes, one that does as they do, the other says red and then green the other side. You will have no hesitation in saying which colour concept corresponds to ours? —unless, that is, you start considering the case of the yellow wall?

EA: Yes.

(He had talked already about "what is homologous?"—as in comparing different animals and their parts, and spoken of people who use sticks for money; that is quite simple, we say that's their money — But suppose they use coins just like ours, but then behave in a way that looks crazy, then we don't know whether to call it money.)

HIJAB: It might, where the saying "red" and "green" looks just like ours, really be like the case of the people whose coins are the same, but they acted quite differently all the same.

WITTGENSTEIN: This whole business, particularly the case of the yellow wall, connects with what people like Russell wanted to say, about a physical object and its different views, that you make up the object from the views; but the views are in the same position as the physical object—a child learns to call that a black door, and Russell says the blackness is in the visual impression, but I might say, what do you mean? You call it black, what about those white lines and shiny patches. But the child learns the language game "black door" in this context—perhaps you will say, just a little patch like a colour sample should be taken as the paradigm, but this doesn't happen, the child simply learns to say "black" as it learns to say "door". — There is of course a language game of impressions, and the language games touch at certain points.

When I say I could imagine a tribe saying "red" all the way through, what is your difficulty? Is it over my saying I could imagine it?

EA: No.

W: No. You know Frege in his *Groundwork of Arithmetic* wrote against the people who said that mathematics and logic were matters of psychology, for he said the laws of psychology (here) are laws of things appearing true to us whereas the laws of logic and mathematics are laws of their being true. He said that he could indeed imagine people who did not use the laws of logic, but he would simply say: "What strange madness." He said madness, but this would not necessarily be a case of madness. It might not be soft and wobbly and moronic [*sic*], like a stick which you handle and it bends and is soft and does not behave like a stick at all. Suppose Hijab said after seeing children taught to work out the decimal figures of π, said that it seemed to him a very queer thing that they should agree. You might say, well you see they are taught and beaten and made to do it, so no wonder they do it. And this would be an answer if what puzzled him was how they agreed up to 4 or 5 digits, which they were taught to work out. But not, if what puzzled him was, that they agreed further on, in what they had not already done.

EA: The only thing for you to do for him would be to teach him to do it himself?

W: You might say: "What? Don't you know?" — suppose he said he wondered how to go on counting after a thousand. Perhaps he has had a thousand as a limit. But mightn't it be a philosophical doubt? Is it any use saying to him: "Well, you just go on in the *same* way"?

EA: If he couldn't do it, wouldn't he be stupid?

W: It might not be a case of stupidity. I might say of him "I don't understand." This is very important. — I feel that somewhere I have committed a great blunder, but I do not where. You remember we were speaking last time of a concept determining what should be done?

EA: You mean, as if it already contained the future development?

W: Yes, but what is wrong with that? The explanation of what this meant would be by giving a mathematical example of working out a formula. And isn't it true? If you say, is it determined how counting or adding 2 or π will go on, isn't this a *mathematical* question? And the answer is yes. If you say, mightn't the application diverge, and this is a *mathematical* question, the answer is no. (It's not like the case of unsolved mathematical problems where forking is possible.) If it is a psychological question, are you asking for prophecy of human history? —but if the question is, if humans do diverge, can they both still be e.g. counting, this is still a mathematical question and the answer is no. And in the case of the colours, don't I already know what the application of red and green is? Yes.

If 2 tribes diverge, are we to say that they have different colour concepts?

EA: If the concept is described, by giving the use and the agreement is in the greatest part, the central part of the use, and the divergence on the fringes, we should not say so.

W: "central"?

EA: I mean, the divergence would be central if it cropped up all over the place.

W: Yes, cropped up all over the place — it is a question of its *role*. It appears to me that this question, whether the concept is the same or different, is *either* a straightforward question of definition, or it is a mathematical question. That sounds queer, but what I am thinking of is e.g. questions about what is the same direction, first on a plane then on a sphere.

December 10th 1946

H: I'd like to raise a point that you made earlier last time — that saying that the formula determines what comes later is a mathematical remark. One feels that one says it in another sense altogether.

W: Yes. But this is the point at which I ask, to whom and for what purpose do you say "It determines what comes later"—– or, to make the same point, "as opposed to what?" If the remark is a mathematical one, you can answer this. The idea here is that of a super-physical necessity. — We are familiar with causal necessity [;] take for example a piece of mechanism:

[*diagram*]

(a wheel and rod moving a piston.) We can [,] given this wheel and rod and piston, describe just how the point A will move, in what ellipse—kinetics, geometry and motion. We say "It will move like that if it is absolutely rigid." But what's rigidity? We know of course that steel isn't perfectly rigid, that you can bend it a little, compress it a little. We think of the formula as having an absolute rigidity. Causal necessity is one thing, it may break down, anything may happen, but logical necessity is absolutely unbreakable. I once wrote of "the hardness of the logical 'must'", using this example and also an analogy with what people might say about the law—a judge may be flexible, may be bribed, but the law is inflexible. Of course the law may be flexible, may make provision for extenuating circumstances, and whether it is or is not flexible in that way is like the *mathematical* question whether the future development is already determined by the formula. But in another sense, you say, the judge is flexible, the law inflexible.

EA: But that only means, that if the judge does otherwise than *this*, he is acting not according to the law. And in the case of the mechanism and the formula, to say that the formula is rigid, is only to say that if the mechanism does not behave so-and-so, it is not acting according to the formula. I'm objecting to what you put into our mouths in interpreting this remark. We don't say that the law is a super-inflexible judge.

W: We do say it: "The law condemns you, not I." But I'm not putting anything into your mouth, only into my own. I have these inclinations very strongly.

I hope that it is clear to you that when someone says "the formula determines the development", I'm not contradicting this? That I'm not saying "No it doesn't, it leaves it undetermined?"

EA: Yes, quite clear.

H: But the trouble is, one does not say the opposite at all, that it is undetermined.

LW: That is not true! That is exactly what the intuitionists said. The formalists said: "It is determined, we can't do as we like, it's not a matter of taste what is according to the rule" and the intuitionists said "But behind every rule there can be another rule for interpreting it, so at each step I have a fresh intuition." I know exactly what movement of thought to make in order to produce either inclination in full strength. I have *both* inclinations. And if you say "I am inclined to say . . ." I can answer you sincerely "So am I."

We need to talk about "mechanism", the enormous part played in our thought about this subject by the notion "mechanical". Does one do a calculation mechanically, or thinking about it? Or if mechanically, is the real thing all the same, the thought [?].

There are calculating machines, and this of course is an example of a mechanism. Now if I prepare Hijab by an education, a training, and then feed the formula into him, I can prophesy with fair accuracy what he will write down. —We sometimes compare a mathematical formula to a part of a mechanism. — Of course, he may make a few mistakes, and the fact that I can make this prophecy *is* not, though it hangs together with—what I mean when I say that the formula determines the development. We think of the working of the formula as the working of a perfect mechanism. (NB: W. did not, that I can remember, say these words, this last sentence; it's my impression of the *drift* of his remarks.)

I do not say "It does determine..." or "It does not...", though I can incline myself to say either. What I am saying is that neither has a sense. Imagine a chessboard

[*diagram of an eight-by-eight grid with a **bold** border around the central four squares*]

and then a game in which I forbid moves to be made on the four central squares—as if there was a hole in the board and they weren't there—but they are there, only I draw a line around them. This looks arbitrary and dictatorial. Really what you need is a different board, one in which the connectivity is different, if you had that you would not feel that there was a gap or an arbitrary prohibition, only that this is a different board. (He cut a hole out of a piece of paper.) To you this is a bit of paper with a hole cut out. But can't you imagine not seeing it like that but seeing this as the shape of the paper? You don't regard Hijab's head as a cube with bits knocked off it.

I want to try to describe something, but I don't know if the picture I'm going to try to make is a picture at all. Could we imagine a tribe with a different concept of regularity from ours, so that we should say: for these people, this is a regularity? Let us imagine a people who write down the prime number series or the development of π, as we write down the cardinal number series, or could write down odd numbers. We'll suppose that they do it by writing down the appropriate numbers of dashes.

1 2 3 5 7 11 13 17 19 [*under each number the appropriate number of dashes*]

and they go on like that without any calculation. We should be inclined to say, they have an intuition, it must be intuition. When do we talk of intuition? If you show me a large number, and I looked at it and said "yes, I feel that's a prime", we should say I had an intuition; like saying "I have a hunch", though that again is different. But you would not say so, if it was that I had been told before that that was a prime. And yet, someone might say, that memory is intuition. How is it that I can tell you what I was doing two hours ago? You might say, he can do it without any reason given, it's intuition. And if someone says, he worked back, how does that help? There is nothing to work back through. But, about these people who write down prime numbers: we feel inclined to say "they must have an intuition", but we don't say a man who counts as we do has an intuition. If we come upon savages who have primitive counting systems, we say that we will teach them arithmetic and give them the *real* thing; but we could not say that to these people. Of course, we could say that we would teach them what we did, but it might be that we could not learn what they did at all. Should we be able to say anything about what they did?

EA: If writing down the prime numbers or π was their first thing, but belonged to a system of arithmetic in which our counting came later as a result of calculation, and they did sums and so on, this might tie up with our system.

w: Perhaps. But I want to ask, what becomes of the rigidity of logic in my present thinking? At first sight it may look as if it all went to pieces. But there is still a rigidity of logic in my thinking: that would be a mistake. Can you see how it is?

EA: At *any* point you can make our concepts wobble or crumble, but when you do it at *some* point, that is supposing that the *rest* remains solid.

w: You are quite right. That is correct. But let us see how it is about regularity. If you want to shew someone "what's regularity?" how do you do it? You shew him simple regularities. Then is there any possibility of saying: "For these people, there is a different concept of regularity".

EA: Has this to do with what you said at the end of last time, that the question whether a concept is the same or different may be a straightforward question of definition, or may on the other hand be a mathematical question?

w: Yes it has.

The question is one of homologousness. You can compare me and Hijab because we are so alike. You compare nose with nose, you don't compare a nose and an ear. Now if it is a question of regularities, where is the homologousness? Could you give a description of a tribe with a different concept of regularity? Why call it regularity? Can you give it the role, the surroundings, that are possessed by regularities in our life? We point to examples and say: "These are regularities." Does it make sense to imagine that we might point to something quite different and say: "These are their regularities."

Other remarks during this discussion, but I don't remember where:

One has a desire to construct a logic like a crystal. This is what I tried to do in my first book: this was the point of it.

Some people have said that mathematics or logic is a game. When I hear that, I say why not say it as a dance—you might *do* it in dancing. Of course it is not a game or a dance.

January 21st 1947

We referred to a previous conversation between W. and E.A. —on the inclination to say "A game in whose rules there is a vagueness is no game", "A rule in whose interpretation there is a vagueness, is no rule" — "There can't be a really fuzzy edge."

w: Suppose that there is a ribbon painted in black down that wall, with clear edges. We know that this is a possibility; and also, that we could paint a black band on that wall, which gradually merged into its surroundings. If someone says of the one case that this is a definite edge, and of the other, that this is a case of blurredness, then I can understand him. But if someone says that there is no real blurredness in things, I want to know "as opposed to what?"

EA: The person who says that is arguing against someone who says that an indefinite description is true in such a way that, if a more definite description were substituted for it, this would be a correction—if the more definite description is right, the less definite is wrong.

w: No, the indefinite won't be wrong because a more definite description is substituted for it—he would not have to say that; but only, that it would be wrong if an *absolutely definite* description was substituted. But what is the first man saying?

EA: He can't give an example of indefiniteness existing in reality, because his whole point is that this is impossible.

w: But is he saying that the blurred band isn't blurred? I can show what is *meant* by a blurred band. No: he is saying something different, that blurredness is not indefinite.

EA: He claims that indefiniteness is in the description only.

w: What would that be like? Suppose I painted a picture of this book with a blurred edge, you might say: The book hasn't got a blurred edge really, its edge is perfectly clear-cut; it's only Wittgenstein's portrayal of it that is blurred, and this expresses the fact that he doesn't know what its exact position is. But saying "There can't be indefiniteness" isn't like that.

You know we measure in such a way as to say "300 ± __ inches" [*for*] some small fraction. Suppose the reading was the same every time—you are comparing a rod with a ruler, there is a black line on each, and the two lines make one dead straight line, which on the ruler is called 300 inches—you say, it's not 300 ± 1/1000—or whatever the fraction is, it's just 300. Suppose someone asks: "Then it's not 300 ± α inches" —when α is some *much* smaller fraction, are you to say "No, it's exactly 300?" — This has no sense.

Suppose I have to measure a rod, and I measure it like this:

[*diagram of long horizontal line with two small verticals attached at each end*]

the rod consists of swinging particles, and I measure the length by measuring from one swinging particle to another. — This would *not* be what we called having an indefinite length— this would not be a fluctuating rod—for here the length is *defined* as measured from one particle to another.

Suppose I claim to have a more accurate method of measurement (than exists). I can make the claim, but what makes you accept it *as* a more accurate method of measurement? Suppose that there is nothing that we do, to which it makes any difference; nothing whose happening we explain by reason of a difference such as I claim to be able to measure?

My method of measuring, say, consists in doing something with photography, and I say "You see, the light rays do such and such."

H: Someone might say: "This is not a new concept of length, it is the same concept as we always have; all that is new is our knowledge of the fact that light rays behave so-and-so."

W: No, you cannot say that; for the ideas about the light rays might be wrong; and still the method is a method of measuring.

This reminds me of similar problems about the duration of a note. Getting its duration accurate to an amount less than the time of a single vibration has no sense. And yet there might be a method devised which gave such a result. But that would not necessarily say anything about what happens in the case where these notes are produced by a siren.

Suppose that Hijab and I are weighing something. You know how I mean "weighing"—we look at the pointer on the balance, and write down the readings between which it swings. Now suppose Hijab and I each make 10 weighings, and it happens that he gets exactly the figures that I get, in the order that I get them. This would not interest anyone at all. You would merely say: "What a queer coincidence".

EA: Unless it kept on happening.

W: Yes, it would become a matter of interest.

I'm thinking at present of the possibility of talking about an indefinite number. Last week I said to Miss Anscombe that one could not speak of seeing a definite number of raindrops, only an indefinite number, and she said that that was true, but that one could only speak so of sense data, not of reality—it would have no sense to speak of the number of hairs on Hijab's head as indefinite—unless this meant, simply, that we didn't know how many there were.

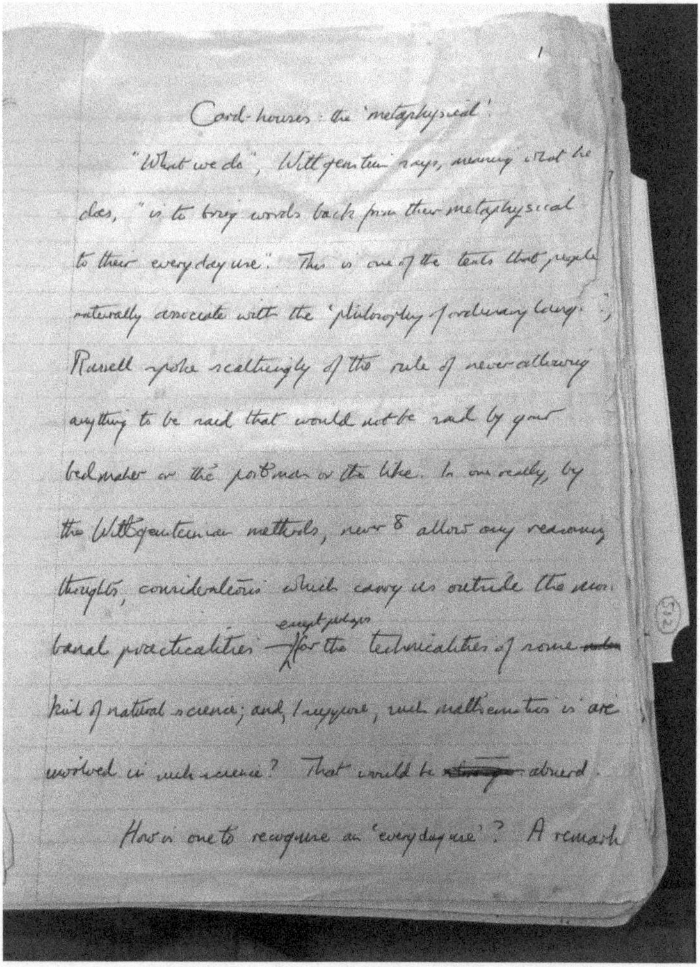

Fig 5.1 Opening page of Anscombe's unpublished essay 'Card-houses: The Metaphysical'. *Photo by John Berkman, File 502, Box 12, Collegium Institute Anscombe Archive at the University of Pennsylvania, Kislak Center for Special Collections, Rare Books and Manuscripts, used by permission of the Collegium Institute*

5

Cardhouses: The "Metaphysical"

Elizabeth Anscombe

"What we do", Wittgenstein says, meaning what he does, "is to bring words back from their metaphysical to their everyday use".[1] This is one of the texts that people naturally associate with the 'philosophy of ordinary language'. Russell spoke scathingly of the rule of never allowing anything to be said that would not be said by your bedmaker or the postman or the like. Is one really, by the Wittgensteinian methods, never to allow any reasoning, thoughts, considerations which carry us outside the most banal practicalities—except perhaps for the technicalities of some kind of natural science; and, I suppose, such mathematics as are involved in such science? That would be absurd.

How is one to recognise an 'everyday use'? A remark which no one could make except as the fruit of reflection, which perhaps it took the talent of some one man to make and was especially characteristic of him—would not be in violation of *this* conception of 'everyday use.' Here is an example from Wittgenstein himself.

"We use the expression 'the steps are determined by the formula . . .'. *How* is it used? We may perhaps be referring to the fact that people are brought by their education (training) so to use the formula $y = x^2$, that they all work out the same value for y when they substitute the same number for x. Or we may say: "These people are so trained that they all take the same step at the same point when they receive the order 'add 3.' We might express this by saying: for

---

[1] *Philosophical Investigations* sec. 116.

Elizabeth Anscombe, *Cardhouses: The "Metaphysical"* In: *Anscombe on Wittgenstein*. Edited by: John Berkman and Roger Teichmann, Oxford University Press. © Oxford University Press 2025. DOI: 10.1093/9780197648988.003.0005 these people the order 'add 3' completely determines every step from one number to the next. (In contrast with other people who do not know what they are to do on receiving this order, or who react to it with perfect certainty, but each one in a different way.)"[2]

This (which, by the way, is not Wittgenstein's sole interpretation of "The steps are determined by the formula. . . .", but of the others more later) is a thoroughly surprising construction to put upon that expression; an unusual thought, which it can be used to express in a supposed context of consideration. But it is nevertheless not a departure from 'an everyday use of language'.

We must ask: what is the basis of the proposed critique of the 'metaphysical', and what does Wittgenstein mean by that epithet?

The first question is best approached by answering the second. Kant also attacked metaphysics. But Wittgenstein did not at all mean what Kant meant. What Kant considered metaphysical were propositions about e.g. the world's having or not having a beginning or the existence of God. But Wittgenstein meant rather propositions like "Every rod has a length", "Any object is identical with itself", "Time has a direction", "Only I can know that I am in pain", "The formula *determines* the series" (as that is said in certain contexts of discussion), "What you know has to be the case"; the assertions "I exist", "I am here", "This is here", divorced from contexts which give them a harmless practical or everyday sort of meaning, i.e. give them a particular application.

Let us consider "This is here". Wittgenstein invites us to consider in what special circumstances this is 'actually' used; we should understand this as meaning: circumstances which give it an application, i.e. some special work to do. It is easy to think of such circumstances. One might be surprised at some particular object's presence and exclaim "*This* is *here*?!" But now we do not get an example of a proposition that 'has to be true'. The 'this' could be replaced by e.g. a definite description or name. Say "The Venus de

---

[2] *Philosophical Investigations* sec. 189.

Milo". Or again, I am looking at a list of books, and I say, pointing to something in the list "This is here, I saw it here a short time ago." Or I am noting which objects of some set are here (in my office) and which at home. "This is here, and this is here." Namely, my passport and my address book. Quite generally, the word "this" only 'has to have a bearer' in the sense of having to latch onto something that one can be attending to (it might even turn out to be a 'private object' like a patch in one's visual field which was after all only an afterimage). That means that if one said "This" without any object of attention, as in Strawson's case where I look into my cupped hands and say 'This is a fine big red one', but it turns out that I didn't mean to be referring to anything, one is merely *pretending* to communicate a thought that one has; but the hearers will understand something because they latch onto the cupped hands and me looking into them, and they suppose that *I* mean to refer to something and do at least latch onto something; indeed what I intend to refer to when I say 'this' may not be there at all, as when I say "These are all empty", pointing to a row of petrol pumps. I mean, of course, that the tanks they are connected with are empty; but perhaps there are no tanks. (Quine calls this sort of thing 'delayed ostension'.) So we may distinguish between the 'bearer' and the 'reference', which indeed often coincide but also often do not. Consider for example someone eating a pudding and saying "My mother used to make this".

Now how are we to evaluate 'bringing back to the everyday use'? Is there an argument running: such are the everyday uses, so only such makes sense? Hardly! Wittgenstein does 'bring words back' to such uses—but was it wrong to use the words in another way, just because it was unlike them? How could it be wrong? This is the protest against the appeal to 'ordinary use'.

But imagine this. You are expecting a consignment of objects and lamenting "*None* of them has arrived." I say "Well—*this* is here," and I point to something. You say: "No, that isn't one of them."

Suppose I now said "Well, at any rate *I said something true*, for all I said was 'This is here'." That might be a sort of irritating joke, like the pub sign "Credit tomorrow"—except that the latter has a point. ("Don't ask for credit.") This one is pointless. And yet, put forward 'seriously', it has the character of some typical Cambridge constructions characteristic of the time of Wittgenstein's youth. Moore might have said it 'seriously', as a proposition that 'has to be true'. This is the 'metaphysical' proposition, as Wittgenstein means "metaphysical": there is an assumption of a sense which one knows, which the statement can 'carry with it' into an utterance of it divorced from or taken as independent of the features of the context which give it its sense. Those features, indeed, meant that it could very well be a mistake.

'I said something true—for it had to be true!'. This, as we imagined it, was said in the actual situation. But from the standpoint of the question "What bearing did saying 'This is here' have on the situation?" what I said was false, might have been true, and if it had been true there would have been such-and-such consequences—alleviation of distress, perhaps, or increased anxiety because of separation of the items, etc.

With these things that 'have to be true', introduced into a conversation about what has happened, what to do, how things are going, etc. it is often the case that they are jokes; usually irritating ones because they aren't good enough. E.g. someone told me that NN was interviewed by some newspaper which wanted to know his weight, his birthday, and his favourite football team. I said "I believe he *has* a favourite football team." My interlocutor said: "He also has a weight and a birthday . . ."[3] In fact such jokes are often witty not when they assert what is 'necessary' but rather when they imply the correspondingly impossible. E.g. William James' sailor riding a horse whose hoof got caught in the stirrup, and the sailor said "If you are going to get on, I shall have to get off." But there is a 'positive' example in a Marx Brothers joke: "I've been told to look out for a man going round with a black moustache" — "Well,

---

[3] At this point in the MS Anscombe has written 'GOLDSMITH'. See n. 4.

you wouldn't expect a black moustache to be going round by itself, would you?"

Goldsmith has some lines.[4]

No doubt examples could be multiplied. But now let us reflect: we are inclined to philosophise: "Being a body, _ must have extension" or "Every rod has a length." Wittgenstein comments: "We are inclined to say 'Of course!' Why don't we say 'Nonsense!'?"[5] Of course there is a reason. The reason which he gives (in the latter case) is this: the proposition, which has the appearance of giving something generally true, about rods, does not in fact do that; it is a 'grammatical' proposition, i.e. a proposition of grammar, meaning something like: we call something "the length of a rod". —But don't we call something a man's favourite football team? And don't we call something a man's clothes? We would never express *that* fact by 'Every man has . . '.

Here, however, we may call 'must' and 'may' to our aid. "A man may be clothed (or moustached)"; "A rod must have a length". But for the difference between "may" and "must", these are similar and may be understood as the grammatical proposition: "clothed" is an adjective which yields good sense, unexceptionable sentences, when connected with "a man", or with the name of a man, and names of lengths, adjectival expressions "so-and-so long", make good sentences when connected with, say, "this rod". Fact these are points of grammar is clear enough. But what of that difference between "may" and "must"? Well, "This man has no moustache" (unlike, say "This table has no moustache") is an unexceptionable sentence, as unexceptionable as "He has a moustache". But that does not mean that men and moustaches are merely externally related to one another.

---

[4] In the MS this sentence stands alone; Anscombe may have intended to go back and supply the Goldsmith quotation at a later date.
[5] *Philosophical Investigations* sec. 251.

Indeed 'clothed', 'moustached', 'shod', 'lined', 'equipped with', 'with a cover', 'with knobs on', 'armed' are adjectives or adjectival phrases belonging to a special range which we might want to mark off as a definite part of speech. There is, so to speak, a principal party and a subsidiary one. The principal is the man or whatever it might be that was an appropriate subject in each case. If we have a noun for the subsidiary party, the principal is said to 'have' the object named by the noun—not in the sense of property! —and the noun is not used to name something independently of its connexion with a principal. (Hence 'You wouldn't expect a moustache to go round by itself' is a *grammatical* joke, i.e. a joke based on something in grammar.)

"This man has no moustache" is an unexceptionable sentence. But "This rod has no length" is one which would puzzle us if offered apparently as a piece of information. "How d'you mean—has no length?" Until some interpretation has been supplied for it we should not know how to take it. Is it to be construed parallel to the way one would construe "It has no strength", has "length" another meaning here, (say) "varnish", or is there some quite special application to be made of the sentence? —something to do with a special physical state; are we dealing with some scientific theory?

The noteworthy thing is that we feel as if we could discern *a* sense, but an impossible one, in the sentence. But this is not, as are the logical contradictions, a sentence with a special role in a system of reasoning, such as the role of contradiction in reductio ad absurdum proofs.

Here we have another instance of Wittgenstein's reversal. *Not*: because every rod has (must have) a length, we would not know straight off what to make of "This rod has no length", but rather: because we do have a use for "This rod is 2 foot long", etc., but do not off hand know what is being said with "This rod has no length" —because of this, we frame the proposition "Every rod has a length" and what it corresponds to in reality is the *grammatical* facts just mentioned. Or one might say: what it reflects. Certainly when we have a joke the joke is connected with the grammar—the joke, for example, of something which sounds like assimilating "going round with a black moustache" to, say, "going round with a black dog". For all I know, grammarians have a technical term for the sort of 'having' that is connected with, say, a moustache. (It is a reflection of the thick-headedness induced by some methods and teachings in modern philosophy, that one could imagine a practitioner of it saying solemnly "But it would be logically possible for a moustache to move about by itself.")

That *here* we have to do with grammar is sufficiently clear. But what about the case of the rod? Has Wittgenstein a right to call it 'grammar' when he says "We call something the length of a rod, and nothing, for example, the length of a sphere"? And also my addition: we have as yet no application for "This rod has no length"? Well, what are grammatical questions? Anyone will call it grammar if we are told "We use this construction for state, that for motion", and "Since this word means "towards" we use it in this construction". But can't someone 'sit towards the door'? Ah, well, then it means "near" or "facing", and both have an indirect connexion with motion. —These are indeed grammatical points. But suppose we wanted to combine 'towards' in its primary sense of a preposition of motion with a 'static' verb like "sitting" or "sleeping". What are we to say? You *can't* do it? or: we don't do it? Well, the latter is certainly true, but isn't the former also? But in what sense? Is it that the meanings won't combine to make sense? Someone might say that, and say it was a *logical* fact. The boundary between grammar and logic is not a quite sharp one, and grammarians may often appeal to logic. Isn't the distinction between defining and other relative clauses a grammatical and also a logical one? Logical, because they have different consequences. E.g. "Wives, who need the protection of the law, will . . ." and "Wives who need the protection of the law will. . . ." Grammatical, because grammarians make the distinction.

Let us go back to "You can't combine a preposition of motion with a static verb, without changing the meaning of one or the other." The verb becomes a verb of motion, as when people said a ship "stood towards ...", or the preposition becomes static in sense. Rest and motion are incompatible—at least, in the same respect. The grammatical facts are as they are *because* of the logical fact. The logical fact is what Wittgenstein is always trying to construe as a grammatical fact and hence as arbitrary.

Wittgenstein gets to consider this. Sec. 499, "To say 'This combination of words makes no sense' excludes it from the sphere of language and thereby bounds the domain of language. But.... if I draw a boundary line that is not yet to say what I am drawing it for.

"Sec. 500 When a sentence is called senseless, it is not as it were its sense that is senseless. But a combination of words is being excluded from the language, withdrawn from circulation."

And "'Even if one does conceive the proposition as a picture of a possible state of affairs and says it shows the possibility of a state of affairs, still, the most the proposition can do is what a painting or relief or film does, and so it can at any rate not set up what is not the case. So does it depend entirely on our grammar what is called (logically) possible, and what not—i.e. just what it allows?' —But surely that is arbitrary! —Is it arbitrary? —It is not every sentence-like formation that we know how to do something with, not every technique has an application in our life; and where we are tempted in philosophy to count some quite useless thing as a proposition, that is often because we have not considered its application sufficiently."[6]

Let us first dwell on the remark "it can at most do what a painting or relief or a film does, and so it can at any rate not set up what is not the case." I found this so difficult to understand that I failed to translate it right;[7] but the German word simply does mean "set up" or "put there". What is the thought? Well, it is surely in the first

---

[6] *Philosophical Investigations* sec. 520.
[7] I.e. in the first edition of Anscombe's translation of the *Philosophical Investigations*. The German word is 'hinstellen'.

place a rejection of the *Tractatus* idea that a significant proposition is a logical working model. That when we frame a proposition, we, as Wittgenstein actually said in the *Tractatus* "put a state of affairs together experimentally." That is the idea that you can see the possibility in the proposition, whether or not it is true. If it is false, still the state of affairs has been set up for you in the proposition itself. To this, the speaker (for the passage is in quotes) says: No, nothing like that happens. Of course, he might add, if you have the state of affairs (since the proposition is true), the possibility is guaranteed. But if you haven't the state of affairs, he says, does the mere fact that the proposition is one which our *grammar* permits, secure the possibility? —And to this he supposes the objection: *But surely that is arbitrary*. And then in his own person Wittgenstein calls that in question. It is *not* arbitrary, he suggests, because it is not a matter of mere choice for us. *We* are not able to 'do something with' just every sentence like formation.

And then he seems to go off at a tangent—talking about sentence like formations which we 'are tempted to count as propositions.'

One wants to say: "Wittgenstein, you are being evasive." Let us go back to my suggestion: "Suppose we wanted to combine 'towards' in its *primary* sense of a preposition of motion with a 'static' verb. What are we to say? Are we to say: we can't do it or rather: We don't do it?" You, Wittgenstein, certainly seem to be saying "We can't do it." But not for the reason that would usually be given, that it is *logically* impossible; that there *could* be no sense so formed—but just that it's not a formation we know how to do something with, that a technique of so constructing a sense has no application in our lives. What this means is: people with different lives might be able to do something with this, but *we* can't. You have taken "arbitrary" ("willkürlich") in its original sense of being merely chosen, a matter of will or even whim. And then you went off at a tangent, talking about the temptation to 'take some quite useless thing as a proposition.' But we understood "arbitrary" to mean, not "a matter of choice", but something else: a mere brute fact with no justification about it, as when we speak of the arbitrariness of fate. It's no answer to that complaint to say we aren't (as it happens) free to choose or modify our grammar, just as we aren't free to adopt just any style of painting. You, Wittgenstein, went off at a tangent, talking about the sort of proposition which philosophers want to call 'logically necessary' and which you call 'useless', like "A thing is identical with itself". But we were thinking about what 'our grammar' does not allow, and not of the trivial cases of this which we know are alterable (whether or not we could succeed [to] carry the alteration through culturally or even in our personal own practice), but the cases where we find a certain alteration quite impossible. An alteration in grammar would here have to be an alteration in what we were speaking of—we *could* not *be speaking of the same* and yet make certain suppositions. E.g. to change the example, we could not—now—be going to do something yesterday. And if you say that it's a matter of grammar, when we object "But that would be arbitrary!" we don't mean "But then it's up to us what is called logically possible, we can change it at will"; we mean that if it's a matter of grammar then a different grammar is possible and it's a mere brute fact that we have this one.

Let us first get one thing out of the way. That expression "some quite useless thing" which we are tempted to "count as a proposition" does make a reader's mind fly to the palmary example of a 'useless sentence': "a thing is identical with itself" which Wittgenstein gives at sec. 216 and hence to the whole class of propositions called "necessary", and also to the example "These deafmutes have learned only a gesture-language, but each of them talks to himself inwardly in a vocal language" (sec. 348) and so a whole class of propositions of which people would say "they are logically possible, although unverifiable and unfalsifiable". But there is nothing in the text to exclude the things we want to call 'impossible' from the description, 'some quite useless thing', 'a sentence-like structure with which we can do nothing'.

That the 'useless things' include the 'impossible' indeed comes out in the next remark.

"Sec. 521 Compare 'logically possible' with 'chemically possible'. One might perhaps call a combination chemically possible if a formula with the right valencies existed (e.g. H-O-O-O-H). Of course such a combination need not exist, but even the formula HO_2 cannot have less than no combination corresponding to it in reality."

HO_2, H-O-O, is 'chemically impossible'. So we should compare that to the logically impossible. But remember that we aren't talking about the negations of propositions of logic and mathematics but rather with such a proposition as: Here is transparent white; they travelled backwards in time; he remembered a time before he existed. To having the right valencies there corresponds 'a technique's having an application in our life', or 'our knowing how to do something with a (given) sentence-like formation.' What, then, is the meaning of "a technique"' as it is spoken of here? There is of course the technique of putting words together (as, of writing down the element symbols linearly with hyphens between, or with numerical subscripts). But that seems to be all, because if we imagine anything further, any intelligible application which does not exist in our lives, straightway we have an application to make of the words—namely to point out that we have *not* that application of language. And this could be expressed by using the considered form of words with some negation. Imagine, for example, a people who are quite unacquainted with dreaming. When they meet us, and hear us speak of dreams, they want an explanation and they think we are crazy. "What you are conscious of in sleep, i.e. in *un*consciousness—that's absurd!" But after a bit they get used to the idea, as we get used to the idea of curious experiences which others have and we do not. Then they can say 'We don't dream'.

Thus if 'technique' means anything much more than putting the words together it seems that the sentence-like formations do 'have application'. Only if we describe a further procedure in connexion with the words which we can make nothing of, which 'we couldn't imagine entering into'—if we tried, we'd make hopeless mistakes, act quite ineptly—only *then* could we speak of a technique which 'has no application' in our lives. People employ a number series like ours, for example, but we observe that at the new moon it goes haywire, certain numbers are left out in reciting the series, 'calculations' (what have the general appearance and some of the typical consequences of calculations) are counted right which we, and they at other times, would count wrong, and we cannot at all learn which ones will be right (though they all agree)—and so on. We cannot fathom what they do.

Wittgenstein says "When a sentence is called senseless it is not as it were its sense that is senseless. But a combination of words is being excluded from the language, withdrawn from circulation." Now this is not entirely accurate. Perhaps it is true of 'nonsense poems' containing words 'that don't exist'. Perhaps it is true of "Colourless green ideas sleep furiously". It is not true of "Here is a piece of transparent white glass", or "Here is black light." For something is sometimes *called* transparent white glass, namely plain glass; and something might be *called* black light. Only plain glass isn't white as transparent yellow glass is yellow. It is not the 'combination of words' but the *sense* that is being called "senseless" when we say it makes no sense to speak of transparent white. This throws light on Wittgenstein's: "We *call* something the length of a rod." Actually he says "We *call* something (or *this*) the length of a rod."

It would be better to say: Certain combinations of senses are excluded. And that leaves open the possibility of 'a technique with no application in our lives' in which those senses were combined. A technique which we cannot (i.e. just haven't the capacity to) envisage, and if we can envisage something, we cannot enter into it or go along with it.

This, then, is Wittgenstein's account of the 'logically impossible' (apart from logic and mathematics). The correspondingly 'logically necessary', together with some other constructions like 'I exist', 'This is here' (as we have discussed this latter) are alternatively characterised as making no sense, pure nonsense, *or* as expressing a 'grammatical proposition'—i.e. as being a formulation of some fact of grammar.

APPENDIX

Biographies of the Main Characters Referred To in Anscombe's *Reminiscences*

The Family

Karl Wittgenstein (1847–1913). LW's father, a German-born Austrian steel magnate. Karl Wittgenstein's grandfather was a Jewish estate manager, Moses Meyer, who adopted the name Wittgenstein after his birthplace of Siegen-Wittgenstein. As a wealthy young man Karl was fascinated with the United States and ran away there for a few years before returning and settling down, eventually taking over the family steel business. Already one of the wealthiest men in Austria, in the decade or so before World War I he moved most of the family's wealth into US stocks and securities. During World War I the Austrian economy was destroyed while the American economy flourished so that after the war Karl Wittgenstein's estate was enormous, one of the largest fortunes in all of Austria.

Leopoldine ('Poldy') Wittgenstein, née Kalmus (1850–1926). LW's mother. Her father was a Bohemian Jew and her mother an Austrian-Slovene Catholic.

Hermine Wittgenstein (1874–1950). LW's oldest sister, who never married, and who became the matriarchal figure in the family after the death of their mother. Hermine was the sibling who continued to reside in the family house in Vienna (on the Argentinierstrasse) and in the palatial summer home (the Hochreit) until her death. In a letter to Ludwig Hänsel (13 December 1920) Hermine wrote: 'It is not easy having a saint for a brother.' When Anscombe went to live in Vienna from January to June 1950, LW would have arranged for her to stay with Hermine at the family house, but Hermine was too ill and so Anscombe stayed with the Koders. Hermine returned to the Catholic Church late in life (see *Reminiscences* 213).

Johannes ('Hans') Wittgenstein (1877–1902). LW's oldest brother, who like his father ran away to try his luck in America. Unlike his father, Hans never returned. He drowned in mysterious circumstances in Chesapeake Bay in Maryland.

Konrad ('Kurt') Wittgenstein (1878–1918). LW's brother, an army officer and company director. Kurt shot himself on 27 October 1918 just before the end of World War I. There are different accounts of what actually led up to his action; see A. Waugh, *The House of Wittgenstein: A Family at War* (London: Bloomsbury, 2008), 126–128.

Helene Salzer, née Wittgenstein (1879–1956). LW's sister, the one with whom LW probably had the closest relationship. She married Maximilian Salzer (1868–1948). Their children were: Fritz (b. 1902), of whom little is known (it seems he died at an early age in a hunting accident), Felix, Marie (1900–1948), and Clara (b. 1913). Clara (q.v.) married Arvid Sjögren (q.v.).

Rudolf ('Rudi') Wittgenstein (1881–1904). LW's brother and the third oldest son. He was studying chemistry at the Berlin Academy when he killed himself in a Berlin bar aged twenty-two. (See *Reminiscences* sec. 28.) Having asked the pianist to play Thomas Koschat's *Verlassen, verlassen, verlassen bin ich* ('Forsaken, forsaken, forsaken am I'), he mixed himself a drink of milk and potassium cyanide which he then drank. He had left several suicide notes, one to his parents that said he was grieving over the death of a friend and another that referred to his 'perverted disposition'. His father Karl forbade the family ever to mention his name again; see A. Waugh, *The House of Wittgenstein: A Family at War* (London: Bloomsbury, 2008), 22–23.

Margarete ('Gretl') Stonborough, née Wittgenstein (1882–1958). LW's sister. She married Jerome Stonborough (1873–1938) and they had two sons, Thomas and Jerome. Margarete was painted by Gustav Klimt. LW, along with Paul Engelmann, designed Haus Wittgenstein in Vienna for her. (See *Reminiscences* sec. 17, 52, and fn. 13.)

Paul Wittgenstein (1887–1961). LW's older brother and a famed pianist who lost his right arm in World War I. He commissioned several works for left-handed pianist by composers such as Hindemith, Prokofiev, Schmidt, Strauss, Britten, and (most famously) Ravel, who wrote his Piano Concerto for the Left Hand for Wittgenstein. With the rise of Hitler Paul emigrated to the United States.

Under Nazi racial laws the Wittgensteins were considered Jewish on account of their maternal grandfather. Hermine and Helene stayed in Austria during the war where they were in considerable danger. They survived primarily because the Nazis wanted a cut of the Wittgenstein wealth, which was largely held in Switzerland. LW's sisters negotiated with the Nazis for their safety during the war, a negotiation which was opposed by Paul, who was by then living in New York and not personally threatened by the Nazis. Paul broke with his siblings over their plan to pay the Nazis in order to procure safety for Hermine and Helene; he was never fully reconciled with them (see *Reminiscences* sec. 20).

*

Ayer, A. J. (1910–1989). English philosopher. He read *Literae Humaniores* at Christ Church, Oxford, and after graduating spent a year in Vienna; his *Language, Truth and Logic* was published in 1936, a work heavily influenced by the logical positivism of the Vienna Circle. From 1946 till 1959 he taught philosophy at University College London. The story of LW's annoyance at what he took to be Ayer's misrepresentation of his ideas in an issue of the *Listener* (misremembered as *Encounter*) is told by Anscombe at *Reminiscences* sec. 153, 167. Ayer and Anscombe are reported to have had the following exchange. Anscombe to Ayer: 'If you did not speak so quickly, people would not think you so clever.' Ayer to Anscombe: 'If you did not speak so slowly, people would not think you so profound.'

Bevan, Edward Vaughan (1907–1988). Sportsman and doctor. Bevan was an undergraduate at Trinity College, Cambridge, and at the age of twenty he represented Great Britain in rowing at the 1928 Summer Olympics in Amsterdam, winning an Olympic gold medal. As a doctor in Cambridge he shared a practice with Rex Woods, the Olympic shot putter. It was Bevan who diagnosed LW's prostate cancer, treating him with hormones. Near the end of LW's life Bevan invited LW to stay at his house in Storey's Way, Cambridge, where Bevan and his wife Joan cared for LW until his death on 29 April 1951. (See *Reminiscences* sec. 224–225, 230–232.)

Drury, Maurice O'Connor ('Con') (1907–1976). Psychiatrist. Drury went up to Trinity College, Cambridge, in 1926 to read Moral Sciences (i.e. philosophy) with the plan to enter a seminary after graduation. His tutors included G. E. Moore, C. D. Broad and the logician W. E. Johnson. In January 1929, during Drury's third year at Trinity, LW returned to Cambridge, and soon met Drury at meetings of the Moral Sciences Club. The two men quickly became friends. Following his graduation, Drury enrolled at Westcott house in Cambridge to study theology in preparation for ordination in the Church of England but he abandoned his theology degree at the end of 1931. LW's influence can probably be felt in Drury's decision to give up his plans for ordination.

In 1932, at the height of the Depression, Drury worked for various social services in Wales. He applied for a position as a psychiatric nurse but was told that with his qualifications he should instead study medicine. Drury was short of the necessary funds but when he informed LW of his plan the latter raised the money from various wealthy friends. So it was that in 1933 John Maynard Keynes funded Drury's first year of medical studies at Trinity College, Dublin, to the tune of £150. Upon graduating in 1939, Drury worked for a short period in the Rhondda Valley and then served in the RAMC in England, North Africa, France, and Germany. In 1947 he moved to St. Patrick's Hospital, Dublin, where he spent the rest of his working life, first as a resident psychiatrist (1947–1969) and then as a consulting psychiatrist (1969–1976). He died on Christmas Day 1976.

Anscombe had met Drury at least by December 1948, when she went to Dublin to meet with LW and Drury in connection with some psychological troubles that she was then having (see *Reminiscences* sec. 200, 201). Anscombe and Drury were among the handful who were with LW when he was on his deathbed, along with Yorick Smythies, Ben Richards, and Fr. Conrad Pepler. (See *Reminiscences* sec. 231.)

Geach, Peter Thomas (1916–2013). English philosopher and husband of Elizabeth Anscombe, only son of George Hender Geach and Eleonora Frederyka Adolfina, née Sgonina. Eleonora, a poet, was of Polish extraction. Geach's father was employed in the Indian Educational Service and would go on to work as a professor of philosophy in Lahore. Geach went up to Balliol College, Oxford, to read *Literae Humaniores* in 1937. He met Anscombe in May 1938 and they were engaged by the end of that year. They married on 26 December 1941.

During the war Geach was a conscientious objector and worked in forestry. His record as a conscientious objector may possibly have led to the difficulties he encountered securing a post in philosophy after the war; he didn't obtain a post until the autumn of 1951. Despite being unemployed he gave lectures in Cambridge and engaged in a variety of other academic projects there. During the years 1946–1951, when Anscombe was teaching at Somerville College, Oxford, Geach was raising their two oldest children Barbara and John in Cambridge, with Elizabeth returning occasionally during termtime and living in Cambridge outside of term. LW was giving lectures in Cambridge at this time which either Anscombe or Geach would attend, the other staying at home to look after Barbara and John. Geach's lecture notes would later be published in Wittgenstein's *Lectures on Philosophical Psychology, 1946–47* (ed. Geach), along with those of K. J. Shah and A. C. Jackson.

From 1966 until 1981 Geach was Professor of Logic at the University of Leeds.

Hänsel, Ludwig (1886–1959). Hänsel was a teacher in Vienna and a prominent figure in the field of education in Austria, writing works on educational theory, psychology, religion, literature, and philosophy. He met LW in early 1919 when they were fellow prisoners of war at Cassino, Italy. His influence seems to have been decisive for LW's vocation as primary school teacher. The two men had many discussions on questions of philosophy, ethics and religion and remained close friends until LW's death. (The last letter from LW to Hänsel is dated 1 February 1951). He was in the habit of sending his work to Wittgenstein for comment and correction. An example is Hänsel's essay *Wertgefühl und Wert* ('Sense of Value and Value'); the copy of this with LW's annotations survives on the cover of which LW has written: 'Auch ein Museum braucht einen Kurator, der weiß, <u>was wohin</u> zu stellen ist, und nicht Dreck + Wertvolles durcheinander in alle Schränke stellt' ('Even a museum needs a curator who knows *what* to put *where*, and who doesn't jumble together rubbish and valuable stuff in all the cupboards').[1] It's clear from the *Reminiscences* that

---

[1] The MS now belongs to the Moscow Center for Consciousness; see https://hard problem.ru/en/posts/Books/ludwig-wittgenstein-s-autograph/#1.

LW didn't think Hänsel an intelligent man; his affection for him came from his being 'a wonderfully good and lovable man' (*Reminiscences* sec. 22).

Hijab, Wasfi (1919–2004). Palestinian philosopher. After graduating in mathematics from the American University of Beirut, he taught science and philosophy in Jerusalem during the war. In 1945 he went to Trinity College, Cambridge, where he studied with LW from 1945 to 1948. Hijab was secretary of the Cambridge Moral Sciences Club 1946–1947, the year after Anscombe. He and Anscombe attended LW's classes during 1946–1947; see Anscombe's discussion notes in the present volume. Hijab returned to the Middle East in 1948 amidst great upheaval in his homeland. He taught in Syria for five years, then in 1953 went to the University of Florida where he obtained a PhD in mathematics in 1956. He then joined the faculty of the American University of Beirut. In the last years of his life he worked on a philosophical autobiography that focused on the impact of LW in his life.

Koder, Rudolf (1902–1977). Austrian pianist and teacher. Koder taught at the school in Puchberg where LW was also teaching in the early 1920s; on hearing Puchberg playing the 'Moonlight' Sonata LW walked into the music room and introduced himself, after which they would meet regularly to play music together, LW on the clarinet. In November 1923 when LW was suffering from a painful colonic ulcer his brother Paul wrote to Koder asking him to exert some pressure on LW to eat plenty of gruel and barley soup, without telling him the advice came from Paul. (Their relations were strained.)[2] Paul even offered to send the appropriate ingredients. Koder became friends with both brothers and they both corresponded with him over the years.

Kreisel, Georg (1923–2015). Austrian-born mathematical logician. In the 1940s he studied in Cambridge where he met LW, attending his lectures. At first LW thought extremely highly of him. Despite Kreisel's efforts he failed to obtain a post in Cambridge, taught for a few years at Reading, and then moved to the United States where he taught at a number of academic institutions. After LW's death Kreisel seems to have turned against LW and he was the source of a number of negative stories about him, but his reliability was often questioned. (See *Reminiscences* sec. 159, 71.) When Anscombe was editing the *Philosophical Investigations*, she at various points relied on Kreisel for assistance with her translation.

Malcolm, Norman (1911–1990). American philosopher and a close friend of LW up until his death. He studied philosophy with O. K. Bouwsma at the University of Nebraska, then in 1933 enrolled as a graduate student at Harvard University. Coming to Cambridge, Malcolm attended LW's lectures on the philosophy of mathematics throughout 1939. He served in the United States Navy from 1942 to 1945 during which time he corresponded with LW,

---

[2] See Waugh, *The House of Wittgenstein*, 155.

sometimes visiting him when on leave. He returned to Cambridge for the academic year 1946–1947, LW's last year of teaching in Cambridge. For the last decade of LW's life Malcolm and Wittgenstein were in regular correspondence. Malcolm regularly sent LW care packages, often including American detective fiction of the sort LW particularly enjoyed. In 1947 he joined the faculty of Cornell University and eventually persuaded LW to visit him there. LW would spend almost three months in the United States, leaving England on 21 July 1949 and arriving back in England on 27 October. Malcolm's *Ludwig Wittgenstein: A Memoir* was published in 1958. Anscombe refers to it (*Reminiscences* 172) where she describes the picture it paints of LW as 'grim and cramped'.

Moore, G. E. (1873–1958). English philosopher. He became a Fellow of Trinity College, Cambridge (where he had been an undergraduate) in 1898 and was later made Professor of Mental Philosophy and Logic, holding the chair from 1925 to 1939. His *Principia Ethica* (1903) was influential, notably on members of the Bloomsbury Group. (See *Reminiscences* sec. 161 for a reference to Ben Richards's having read it right through.) Moore made LW's acquaintance in 1912 shortly after LW's arrival in Cambridge to study with Russell. Moore quickly realized the genius of the younger man. The two would meet at least twice a week, often for several hours, not only for philosophical conversations, but also to discuss music and poetry. When LW returned to Cambridge in 1929 he was short of funds and Moore and Ramsey approached Trinity College on his behalf; funding would depend upon LW's obtaining a doctorate. On 18 June, Wittgenstein was awarded a PhD for the already-published *Tractatus Logico-Philosophicus*, the title of which had originally been Moore's suggestion. Moore and Russell acted as Wittgenstein's examiners and in his report Moore described the thesis as a 'work of genius'. Moore went on to attend LW's lectures in the early 1930s; see G. E. Moore, 'Wittgenstein's Lectures in 1930–33', in his *Philosophical Papers* (London: Allen & Unwin, 1959); and D. G. Stern et al., eds., *Wittgenstein: Lectures, Cambridge, 1930–1933, from the Notes of G. E. Moore* (Cambridge: Cambridge University Press, 2016). LW and Moore continued to meet regularly despite Moore's apparent ambivalence (see *Reminiscences* fn. 113).

Pepler, Conrad, O.P. (1908–1993). English Dominican priest, scholar, and editor. Pepler wrote particularly on the history of English spirituality. He was Anscombe's favourite Dominican priest in Oxford and so it was Pepler that Anscombe arranged to see LW when he asked to have a Catholic priest visit him in 1950. Pepler was called to LW's bedside when LW was dying and gave him conditional absolution (see *Reminiscences* sec. 231). In the early 1950s Pepler was commissioned to found a retreat centre; this was Spode House. Columba Ryan, a young Dominican, began a 'Philosophical Enquiry' group at Spode House in 1954 which met every September for over a decade; Anscombe and Geach attended its meetings in the 1950s along with other

Catholic philosophers such as Michael Dummett, J. M. Cameron, Herbert McCabe, Anthony Kenny, and Charles Taylor.

Ramsey, Frank Plumpton (1903–1930). Philosopher, mathematician, and economist, and close friend of LW. When still an undergraduate he translated Wittgenstein's *Tractatus Logico-Philosophicus* into English. Ramsey married Lettice Baker in 1925 and they had two daughters; for Lettice's collaboration with Helen Muspratt, see *Reminiscences* fn. 35. Ramsey's early death, consequent on an abdominal operation, was a great blow to LW.

Rhees, Rush (1905–1989). American-born philosopher who spent his adult life in the UK. Rhees went to the University of Edinburgh (1924–1928) where he studied with Norman Kemp Smith. After teaching for a few years, he began a PhD under G. E. Moore but never finished it. While at Cambridge Rhees got to know LW and from the late 1930s onwards became one of his most regular conversational partners. He had great difficulty getting an academic post but in 1940 obtained a temporary one at the University of Swansea which eventually became permanent. During the war LW would often go and stay in Swansea when he wanted to go somewhere to work. In the early 1940s LW asked Rhees to translate some of the *Philosophical Investigations*, but the effort was not a success. LW named Rhees one of his three literary executors along with Anscombe and G. H. von Wright. Rhees was known as 'Bob' to his friends.

Richards, Ben (1924–1995). English doctor, born into a family of doctors. His mother Noel (née Olivier) was from her youth closely associated with the Bloomsbury Group and the Cambridge Apostles. In late 1945, while an undergraduate at Cambridge, Richards began attending LW's lectures and by June 1946 LW had become very attached to him. Over the next five years LW and Richards exchanged some 350 (extant) letters; these were published in 2023 for the first time in a German translation. Through LW Anscombe also became a friend of Richards, and Richards would continue to be a close friend of the Geach family for at least the next twenty years. Under the influence of the eldest son, John, he took up the viola da gamba, playing consort music with John and his siblings (and on one occasion with Roger Teichmann, who had followed the same musical route).

Russell, Bertrand (1872–1970). English philosopher, mathematician, and public figure. He read for the Mathematical Tripos at Trinity College, Cambridge, graduating as seventh Wrangler in 1893 and becoming a Fellow at Trinity in 1895. During his student days he had become acquainted with G. E. Moore. With A. N. Whitehead Russell wrote the seminal *Principia Mathematica*, the first edition of which appeared in 1910. At Frege's suggestion, LW went to see Russell in 1911 in the hope of studying with him at Cambridge; Russell quickly realized his visitor was a genius. During World War I, when LW was fighting in the Austrian army, Russell spent some time in gaol for certain of his anti-war writings. That was in 1918; he had already been fined in 1916 under the Defence of the Realm Act 1914 and lost his job at Trinity College, though he was later reinstated. In 1929 Russell, with Moore, examined LW for a PhD on the basis of the *Tractatus Logico-Philosophicus*, to the English translation of which Russell had already written a Preface. In later years LW and Russell drifted apart philosophically, Russell regarding LW's later work as trivial and LW regarding Russell as having gone off the boil since his early days—though people attending the Cambridge Moral Sciences Club noticed how LW always behaved towards the older man with a special respect.

Shah, Kantilal ('Kanti') (1920–2007). Born in Gujarat, India. Obtained a BA from the School of Economics and Sociology at the University of Bombay. In 1945 Shah was admitted to Trinity College, Cambridge, to do a two-year course for a second BA in Moral Sciences. After obtaining his degree, Shah remained in residence at Trinity College for the 1947–1948 academic year. He had many conversations with LW. In one of these, LW warned him against being dismissive of his own Jain religion, a remark which Shah subsequently indicated was of profound importance to him. He also during this time became good friends with Anscombe and Geach. Shah went on to become Professor of Philosophy at Savitribai Phule Pune University, India, and then Professor of Philosophy at Karnataka University. Shah's notes from Wittgenstein's lectures, along with those of Peter Geach and A. C. Jackson, would be published as *Wittgenstein's Lectures on Philosophical Psychology 1946–47*.

Smythies, Yorick (1917–1980) and Polly (1916–2003), née Diana Pollard. In 1935 Yorick Smythies went up to King's College, Cambridge, to read Moral Sciences, graduating with a First in 1939. While an undergraduate he attended LW's lectures and after graduating he stayed on in Cambridge for an extra year and continued to attend them. During these years he got to know LW well and LW clearly had enormous respect for him. (See *Reminiscences* sec. 175.) Smythies applied to be a conscientious objector in early 1940. LW wrote a letter on his behalf and Smythies received a complete exemption from service. In 1942 Smythies took on a job with the Nuffield College Social Reconstruction Survey, working as a field officer evaluating various regions' future economic prospects in light of the war. The survey was terminated in 1943 at which point Smythies got a job at the Barnett House Library in Oxford, a post he obtained with the help of a testimonial from LW. Anscombe and Smythies will have met during 1942. By 1944 Smythies had made enough of an impression in Oxford philosophical circles that he was invited to teach part time, giving tutorials on Berkeley.

In the spring of 1944 Smythies converted to Catholicism. He wrote to LW telling him of this; LW wrote back:[3]

---

[3] B. F. McGuinness, ed., *Wittgenstein in Cambridge: Letters and Documents 1911–1951* (Oxford: Blackwell, 2008), 363.

The news of your joining the Roman Catholic Church was indeed un-expected. But whether it's good, or bad news—how should I know? The following seems clear to me. Deciding to become a Christian is like de-ciding to give up walking on the ground & do tight-rope walking instead, where nothing is more easy than to slip & every slip can be fatal. Now if a friend of mine were to take up tight-rope walking & told me that in order to do it he thinks he has to wear a particular kind of garment I should say to him: If you're serious about that tight-rope walking I'm certainly not the man to tell you what outfit to wear, or not to wear, as I've never tried to walk anywhere else than on the ground. Further: your decision to wear that kind of garment is, in a way, terrible, however I look at it. For if it means that you're serious about the thing it's terrible, even though it may be the best & greatest thing you can do. And if you're dressing up & then don't do the tight-rope act it's terrible in a different way. There's one thing, however, I want to warn you against. There are certain devices (weights attached in a particular way to the body) which steady you on the rope & make your act easy, & in fact no more dangerous than walking on the ground. This sort of device should not be part of your outfit. — All this comes to saying: I cannot applaud your decision to go in for rope walking, because, having always stayed on the ground myself, I have no right to encourage another man in such an enterprise. If, how-ever, I am asked whether I'ld rather you went in for rope walking, or for sham[m]ing, I'll certainly say: rather anything than the latter. — I *hope* you'll never despair, & I also hope that you'll always remain capable of despairing. [. . .]

I'm really interested in what sort of a *man* you are & will be. *This* will, for me, be the eating of the pudding. So long! Good wishes!

Affectionately

Ludwig Wittgenstein

A couple of months after his conversion Smythies married Diana 'Polly' Pollard and the couple moved into a house at 22 Banbury Rd in Oxford. In 1945 the Smythies moved to Cambridge where Smythies had a job as a librarian for the Cambridge Philosophical Society. In the autumn term of 1945 Smythies and Anscombe both attended LW's lectures. LW left Cambridge in 1947 at which point Yorick and Polly moved back to Oxford. Anscombe's house at 27 St John Street became something of a second home for the Smythies and Yorick be-came one of Anscombe's closest philosophical friends. It was Smythies to whom Anscombe turned in January 1948 when she was drafting her response to C. S. Lewis, and she rewrote it in the light of his criticisms.

In 1950, LW moved to Oxford, his health failing. When Anscombe had not yet returned from Vienna Polly Smythies did LW's grocery shopping for him. Later, when LW was dying in the Bevans' house in Cambridge, Yorick Smythies was one of those called to be by his bedside (see *Reminiscences* sec. 231).

Wright, G. H. von (1916–2003). Finnish philosopher, of both Finnish and seventeenth-century Scottish ancestry. He attended the University of Helsinki and after his graduation hoped to visit Vienna, home of logical positivism, but the Anschluss in 1938 put paid to that idea and instead he went to Cambridge to do graduate work under the supervision of C. D. Broad. Broad, though unsympathetic to LW's philosophy, allowed him to attend the latter's lectures, which is how von Wright and LW got to know each other. The correspondence between the two men includes forty published letters and postcards from 1939 to 1950, most of them from LW to von Wright. Anscombe first got to know von Wright when he was a visiting lecturer in Cambridge in Trinity Term 1947, the last term LW lectured before resigning his position. Von Wright succeeded him in the chair in 1948. He was to be one of LW's literary executors, along with Anscombe and Rush Rhees.

References

Anscombe, G. E. M. *Ethics, Religion and Politics. The Collected Philosophical Papers of G. E. M. Anscombe*. Vol. III. Oxford: Basil Blackwell, 1981.

Anscombe, G. E. M. *Intention*. 2nd ed. Oxford: Blackwell, 1963.

Anscombe, G. E. M. *An Introduction to Wittgenstein's Tractatus*. London: Hutchinson University Library, 1959.

Ayer, A. J. *Part of My Life*. Oxford: Oxford University Press, 1978.

Baker, G., ed. *The Voices of Wittgenstein: Ludwig Wittgenstein and Friedrich Waismann*. London: Routledge, 2003.

Berlin, I. *Personal Impressions*. Edited by H. Hardy. 3rd ed. London: Pimlico, 2018.

Citron, G. 'Wittgenstein's Philosophical Conversations with Rush Rhees (1939-1950): From the Notes of Rush Rhees'. *Mind* 124, no. 493: 1–71 (January 2015).

Drury, M. "Some Notes on Conversations with Wittgenstein." In *Ludwig Wittgenstein, Personal Recollections*, edited by R. Rhees. Oxford: Blackwell, 1981.

Geach, M., and L. Gormally, eds. *From Plato to Wittgenstein: Essays by G. E. M. Anscombe*. Exeter: Imprint Academic, 2011.

Geach, P. T., K. J. Shah, and A. C. Jackson, eds. *Wittgenstein's Lectures on Philosophical Psychology 1946-47*. Chicago: University of Chicago Press, 1988.

Gibson, A., and N. O'Mahony, eds. *Dictating Philosophy*. London: Routledge, 2022.

Klagge, J, and A. Nordmann, eds. *Ludwig Wittgenstein: Public and Private Occasions*. Lanham, MD: Rowman & Littlefield, 2003.

Lacey, N. *A Life of H. L. A. Hart: The Nightmare and the Noble Dream*. Oxford: Oxford University Press, 2006.

Malcolm, N. *Ludwig Wittgenstein: A Memoir*. Oxford: Oxford University Press, 1984.

Margalit, E., and A. Margalit, eds. *Isaiah Berlin: A Celebration*. London: Hogarth Press, 1991.

McGuinness, B. F., trans. and ed. *Ludwig Wittgenstein and the Vienna Circle*. Lanham, MD: Rowman & Littlefield, 1979.

McGuinness, B. F., ed. *Wittgenstein in Cambridge: Letters and Documents 1911-1951*. Oxford: Blackwell, 2008.

Monk, R. *The Duty of Genius*. New York: Penguin, 1991.

Moore, G. E. 'Wittgenstein's Lectures in 1930–33'. In his *Philosophical Papers*, 252–324. London: Allen & Unwin, 1959.

Rhees, R., ed. *Recollections of Wittgenstein*. Oxford: Oxford Paperbacks, 1984.

Russell, B. *The Autobiography of Bertrand Russell*. Single vol. paperback ed. London: Unwin Paperbacks, 1975.

Stern, D. G., B. Rogers, and G. Citron, eds. *Wittgenstein: Lectures, Cambridge 1930–1933, from the Notes of G. E. Moore*. Cambridge: Cambridge University Press, 2016.

Warnock, M. *A Memoir: People and Places*. London: Duckworth, 2000.

Waugh, A. *The House of Wittgenstein: A Family at War*. London: Bloomsbury, 2008.

Wittgenstein, L. *Culture and Value*. Translated by P. Winch. Edited by G. H. von Wright with Heikki Nyman. Oxford: Basil Blackwell, 1980.

Wittgenstein, L. *Philosophical Investigations*. Translated by G. E. M. Anscombe. Edited by G. E. M. Anscombe and R. Rhees. 2nd ed. Oxford: Basil Blackwell, 1958.

Wittgenstein, L. *Tractatus Logico-Philosophicus*. Translated by D. Pears and B. McGuiness. London: Routledge & Kegan Paul, 1961.

Wittgenstein, L. *Zettel*. Translated by G. E. M. Anscombe. Edited by G. E. M. Anscombe and G. H. von Wright. 2nd ed. Oxford: Basil Blackwell, 1981.

Index